ISSUES IN EDUCA
COMPARATIVE AN

ISSUES IN EDUCATION: A COMPARATIVE ANALYSIS

E. J. NICHOLAS

Harper & Row, Publishers
London

Cambridge
Hagerstown
Philadelphia
New York

San Francisco
Mexico City
Sao Paulo
Sydney

Harper & Row Ltd
28 Tavistock Street
London WC2E 7PN

Nicholas, E.J.
  Issues in education.
  1. Education
  I. Title
  370   LB17

ISBN 0-06-318250-5

Typeset by Burns & Smith, Derby
Printed and bound by Butler & Tanner Ltd, Frome

THE AUTHOR

E. J. Nicholas is Head of the Postgraduate Secondary Education Department
at Goldsmiths' College, the University of London.

To my father, W. E. Nicholas (1906–1981)
and
for my mother, Sarah Nicholas.

CONTENTS

Foreword

It is possible to describe, characterize, understand or criticize contemporary British education in many ways. For example, educational provision could, with truth, be described as a large business, and given this starting metaphor such a description would then proceed to identify and quantify matters of finance, personnel, clientele; structures, functions, malfunctions. Again, educational practice, say, could, with similar validity, be seen as a series of negotiations between those with prescribed authority (teachers) and others deemed potential initiates (children) about knowledge. Ensuing concerns would then include the nature of the institutions they inhabit, the quality of their interactions and perhaps the incongruities between the recipients' views of the knowledge and those of the dispensers.

These different, even incompatible perspectives suggest that all spectators of a landscape are dependent on the ground upon which they stand and the conceptual, categorizing spectacles which they decide to look through. This is not to say that what they say they see is wrong. Ideally perhaps, an authentic map of the ground would entail the varying though complementary foci of panoramic, close-up and peripheral vision from a variety of vantage points. But such complexity is rarely feasible. So it is essential to clarify what features of the English educational scene this book focuses upon.

The most outstanding feature of the scene is that over the last two decades education has become increasingly busy with argument, debate and controversy. The range of issues deemed volatile has become more extensive and the numbers and types of people who feel prepared to contribute to the discussions are greater. Most of this increased activity is to be welcomed as a healthy sign of vitality and interested concern; light as well as heat has been generated; spurious cases or the partial pleadings of vested interest have been less likely to go unchallenged. All this could well be because an increasingly successful, mass-orientated system of schooling has produced more people who are concerned and informed, not only about what was done to them and is now done to their children in various educational institutions, but also why. There are several easily identifiable groups of people involved in these discussions. First, the various agencies and agents of the central government — ministers, ministries, politicians and their advisers — who have to formulate, execute and justify policies, based on matters of principle or priority and fermented by political philosophies. Here the DES is obviously the most important single institution. Second, regional and local government bodies, notably the Local Education Authorities. Next, the clients of the system, including parents, employers, trades unions, community groups, as well as school children and students. Many of these have developed organizations to express their views — for example CASE, PTAs, the NUSS, and residents' or community associations. Again the media — national and local newspapers, radio and television — report on, and campaign about, educational items. Finally, there are the employees of the system — the teachers and other workers within it. The teaching force cannot be described as unified — witness the variety of teachers' associations and unions. Diversity of approach and interest is partly the product of the varying purposes of the institutions which teachers work in, from infant classes for five year olds through to universities serving students in their early twenties and beyond.

The interactions between these groups are very complicated and sometimes selected problems and preferred solutions are highlighted, offered and canvassed, through the use of the lobbying techniques of pressure group politics. Motives vary from the ulterior to the altruistic. But it is worth picking out some of the more obvious features of what goes on.

It has become increasingly inappropriate to describe the groups identified above in terms of experts and inexperts. Such imputations of inferiority and superiority have become blurred, not least because some participants have refused to accept such labels. Again the arguments, claims and counter claims have become far more public and publicized, making it necessary for previously cocooned professionals and policy-makers to justify what they do and to be vigilant about accountability. Teachers have become particularly susceptible to these developments, which have been encouraged by some of the recent policies of the DES. The 1980 Education Act is particularly important in this respect, for one of its central principles is that parents should have the right to choose which schools their children attend. To help them make informed decisions, detailed published evidence about the facilities, curricula, even examination results of local schools has to be made available. Another noticeable development is that debates about education have extended from the merely technical to take in philosophical and political concerns. So, starting from different viewpoints about the nature of humanity, of society and of knowledge, widely differing profiles and definitions of education, its purposes and functions have been constructed. Quite inevitably, they are infused with complex theories, variously grounded. Some of the ideas are new, internally consistent and coherent, but because they are radical in form and content, they constitute a threat to the traditional and challenge the existing distribution of power in society. But the debates thus formulated are not conducted in a vacuum, for they lead to decisions being taken — by policy makers, by teachers — which have direct practical effects on the lives of children and what happens to them in schools.

I have elaborated upon the claim that continuing debate is the central feature of the contemporary educational scene, because this starting point explains the main purpose of this book, namely that it should contribute to the public processes of problem recognition, analysis and solution currently being undertaken in England, not least by teachers and intending teachers. To this end, the stance taken and the analytical framework used are those of the comparative perspective. Chapter 1 explains in detail what is involved in the comparative study of education, and the unique contribution which such an approach can make. By describing some of the salient features of the current public discourse, I intend to make explicit the essentially interactive relationship between theory and practice and to discredit a simplistic horse-and-cart version of how they are connected. Chapters 3 to 7 are all concerned to amplify and illustrate this basic premise.

A few further notes of clarification have to be made:

1. In addition to the sources listed in the bibliography, some of my ideas are derived from information gathered and impressions formed from visiting each of the foreign countries discussed. I have also found continuing correspondence with researchers at the Academy of Pedagogical Sciences in Moscow, and ex-colleagues at Georgia State University, Atlanta, invaluable.

2. A glossary of all the abbreviations and technical terms which appear in the text is provided, p.227 ff. This device is used to avoid irritating those readers who might be familiar with all or some of them. Schools, and other educational institutions throughout the world, have a variety of names which are specific to a particular country. These are explained in the text as they occur. The words 'primary', 'secondary' and 'tertiary' are used throughout the book

as internationally valid terms for denoting the *level* of a particular institution.

3. Because schooling is organized differently in Scotland and Northern Ireland, the word England (to include Wales) is used throughout. What is said applies only to these parts of the British Isles, though even here, because of the many subtle differences of approach to education in Wales as compared to England, any of the conclusions drawn should be applied with caution to the former country.

4. The specific issues relating to the education of girls are not considered in this book, though occasional passing references are made to them. Through protracted conversations over several years with colleagues (particularly Ms Pat Mahony), I have learned to respect feminist arguments, have been introduced to some of its literature and come to recognize that I am not competent to cope with the problems involved adequately. There is, however, an urgent need for a comparative study of education and gender.

I am very grateful to Dr Jean Lawrence, David Steed and Dr Pamela Young for providing me with access to their as yet unpublished research data on disruptive behaviour in various countries in Europe, which I have used in Chapter 3. My sincere thanks are due to Professor Edgar B. Gumbert and Joe Buttle for reading and commenting upon early drafts of Chapters 1 and 4, and additionally to the latter for helping me to proof-read the entire book. I am also indebted to the anonymous readers of my first draft whose constructive critical comments helped me greatly in preparing this final version. I would also like to thank Bobbie Arnold, Shirley Chapman, Sue Hellier and Penny Spiers who helped with the typing of the manuscripts, but especially Ann Longrigg who, with enormous patience and skill, did the bulk of this task. Finally, over many years I have learned a great deal from countless hours of conversation with my colleagues and students in the Postgraduate Secondary Education Department at Goldsmiths' College, and many of the ideas contained in what follows reflect this. A public acknowledgement of my debt to all of them, but in particular to Ian Hextall, is by no means an adequate expression of my real gratitude.

E.J. Nicholas

PART ONE

EDUCATIONAL PRACTICES

CHAPTER 1

INTRODUCTION

1. The comparative study of education

No attempt is made in this section to provide an exhaustive discussion of methodological issues in comparative education. Such a task has already been accomplished by Jones (1971), though the most lucid and authoritative account is that provided by Holmes (1981). However, some characteristics of the comparative approach relevant to the orientation of this book do need discussion.

It is seldom appreciated that the comparative study of education has an ancient lineage, and emerged very early once systematic attempts were made to study education. For example, Hans (1949, chap. 1), Jones (1971, chap. 2) and Holmes (1981, chap. 1) have all drawn attention to a range of influential comparative studies published throughout the nineteenth century in several countries, i.e. Jullian de Paris and Victor Cousin in France; John Griscom, Horace Mann, and Henry Barnard in the USA; Matthew Arnold and Michael Sadler in England; K.D. Ushinsky in Russia.

Government agencies were also funded for this purpose, such as the US Office of Education, the Department of Comparative Education in the Soviet Union's Academy of Pedagogical Sciences (which still undertakes comparative studies), and the Office of Special Reports on Educational Subjects 1898-1911 at the Board of Education for England and Wales. The latter was initially staffed by Sadler and his assistant, Morant, and despite the bitter personal feud which developed between the two, particularly after Morant's promotion to Secretary to the Board, the ideas, arguments and evidences garnered by the reports were of great significance to the way the Board adopted and implemented policies. This was especially true for secondary education as developed through and after the 1902 and 1918 Education Acts (Gordon and White 1979, pp. 142-4). With the closure of the Office, the tradition of comparisons was not lost, for it has been continued by the inclusion of comparative data in one form or another in most official Reports on education commissioned by various governments since — for example, Hadow (1926, appendix IV); Spens (1938, appendices III and VI); Crowther (1959, appendix III); Plowden (1967, annexe C). The best example is the famous Appendix V in the Robbins Report (1963), which, among other things, formed the empirical ground for the report's central challenge, namely to doubt traditional English notions about the volume of the pool of talent among English youngsters. Other major controversies have invariably contained a comparative dimension. Sometimes this is overtly stated, like the use made by Pedley (1956) of Swedish and American experiences in his support of the comprehensive school idea. However, it is more usual for it to be used more covertly, particularly by the media, smuggled in either naively or perniciously to lubricate axe-grinding (e.g. *Black Paper Two*, Cox 1969).

Next it is important to recognize that comparative education has become well established in university departments of education worldwide, and several British centres have an international reputation. Professional associations and specialist learned journals of the subject have also been founded. Recognizable authorities have emerged, having produced a series of standard works, beginning perhaps with Kandel (1933, 1954) and continuing with Hans (1949), Lauwerys (1948 annually to 1970), Mallinson (1957), King (1958, 1962), Grant (1964), Holmes (1965), Armytage (1967, 1968, 1969a and b), and Price (1977). Some have had direct influences upon national, even international bodies — Kandel on the Spens Report; Lauwerys with UNESCO. The writings of English authors have been augmented heavily by contributors from abroad, like Bereday (1964), Eckstein and Noah (1969), Ulich (1967), and Husén (1967, 1979). Not unnaturally, these authorities have not always agreed amongst themselves, which is hardly remarkable, for a variety of approaches, schisms, even cries of heresy have often characterized academic work in most disciplines. Disagreements have been less vociferous about certain technical matters — for example, the usefulness of statistical techniques, or the merits of taxonomies to marshal data, the importance of field work, or the insights derivable from imaginative literature — than on certain other aspects of methodology. In this respect, the authenticity of the historicist explanatory theory of Kandel has been questioned; the validity of the conceptual frameworks used by Hans and Mallinson and Bereday have been challenged; the appropriateness to a social or humanistic mode of enquiry of the differing physical science based paradigms sponsored by Holmes on the one hand, and Eckstein and Noah on the other, have been attacked; the 'travel agency' flavour of other works has been highlighted. None the less, a voluminous literature has been produced, and the highly selective list of names above merely indicates a minute part of it. These, and other specialists, have undoubtedly generated a battery of techniques to facilitate the rigorous pursuit of comparative data; they have exercised great ingenuity in inventing tools of analysis; they have published sensitive and empathetic studies of varying cultures and sub-cultures. It is not therefore surprising that they have been unanimously critical of the comparative exploits of nonspecialists, and rightly aghast at the unrefined, even crude methodological procedures used in some quarters.

One example must suffice. A massive body of American writings on all aspects of education is reproduced in this country and the arguments, ideas and findings are blithely assumed by most readers to apply to England. It is as if such writings, merely because they are written in English, have transatlantic validity. Educational thinking, however labelled, can never be so culture proof.

A similar insensitivity to the singularity and specificity of the local, characterizes many of the comparative studies made by international agencies like UNESCO and OECD. In particular, Third World countries were persuaded to implement most unfortunate educational policies, which proved quite disfunctional, because they were thus naively and falsely premised (e.g. see Nyerere in Cameron and Dodd 1970, chap. 15).

However, it must be admitted that far too many of these kinds of strictures have taken the form of private grumblings. Comparativists, in fear perhaps of risking academic respectability, have remained too esoteric and, with the possible exception of Bell and Grant (1974), have failed to make their ideas public. Some unfortunate consequences have resulted. Again, one instance must suffice. Shortly after the publication of the Plowden Report (1967), an invaluable publication *Perspectives on Plowden* (Peters 1969) emerged, in which Peters and Dearden, Foss, and Bernstein and Davies showed in turn where the Report was philosophically, psychologically and sociologically inadequate. This was an important aid to subsequent public discussion of primary education. Yet the undoubtedly silly and unhelpful comparative sections of the Report went unchallenged. So comparativists in England have generally been singularly silent about their own society. Few have attempted to show, quite explicitly, what detailed implications their work and approach has for the conduct of English education. Others can thus be excused for thinking that, because comparativists have said nothing, they have nothing worth saying; or worse still, nothing to say.

Given this brief appraisal of the comparative education scene, it is now necessary to consider how the comparative perspective is understood, interpreted and used in the chapters that follow. At risk of over-simplification, certain features are picked out below in stark, propositional terms, thus:

1. The term 'comparative' requires the identification and detailed explication of both the similarities and differences between things — in this case certain features of education in selected countries or regions. The term also suggests the need to show that like is being compared with like. Thus some justification is required for the selection of particular countries or regions for comparison. Both of these issues are treated seriously in the next section of this chapter.

2. The question of *how* to proceed with a comparative analysis requires attention; something which the standard literature of comparative education has rightly considered exhaustively. In what follows here, every attempt is made to follow the traditional rules of empiricism; my organizing schema for the understanding of data, called Varying Epistemological Styles, is explicitly described and then used. But the major procedural guideline is the very broad and general principle, derived from history and anthropology, namely sensitivity to specificity when studying different cultures. Thus, prior to comparisons a reliable and authentic version of the alien culture must be made, but in terms of that culture itself. Versions using the cognitive or affective or judgemental ground rules of another culture lack integrity and validity. Historians have always been very conscious of this point. Anthropologists argue that the successful negotiation of this first stage is when the alien spectator can participate in the activities of the hosts, as an insider, as a member, not recognized as a visitor or an outsider.

3. There remains the *why* question — 'Why a comparative perspective?' Any reply must begin with a consideration of the thorny matter of cultural borrowing; what Holmes (1981, p. 19) calls 'Misconceived Comparative Education'. We have already seen

that when this is done either naively, or with premeditated malevolence, pernicious results can accrue. This is not to argue that such results are inevitable. It is more truthful to suggest that cultural borrowing, in some form or other, is the inevitable outcome and justification of a comparative approach. Thus, in the end, the point of the exercise is to augment our understandings of our own cultural context by comparing it with others. This is the unique contribution which the comparative study of education can make. In the process of refining understandings through comparisons, a beginning is made with analysis, logic and other elements of rationality. But further refinement emerges through words like insight, feeling, intuition, again the product of making comparisons.

Given these general points about the comparative study of education, it is now necessary to explain fully my own approach to the comparative analysis of education.

2. Varying Epistemological Styles

The organizing schema which governs the treatment of the issues discussed in succeeding chapters was originally stated in my article 'A Comparative View of Curriculum Development' (in Kelly 1980). There it was used to add depth of understanding to curricular matters. But it is a useful general framework for the analysis of other concerns, and must therefore be restated here. Further, it is important to explain the grounds upon which the various countries have been selected for treatment.

Succeeding chapters focus on four foreign countries; the USSR, the USA, France and the GFR. This selection is not arbitrary. Obviously these countries represent very different political, social and cultural systems. But they are also the sources and epitomes of three different, significant and influential Epistemological Styles. Of course there may well be other such styles in other parts of the world (e.g. Japan or South America) but the concern here is only with three. The USSR we can call Marxist-Leninist; the USA Liberal-Pragmatic; France, the GFR and the UK taken together are manifestations of a classical European tradition. Each of these styles has characteristic, idiosyncratic, and thus differing approaches to questions concerning the nature of society, humanity and knowledge, which we have already seen are currently the critical elements in the analysis of education and its development. It is the differences here which will decide local variations.

These variations contain three distinct and crucial facets as follows: (a) whether a problem is recognized as such in the first place: a problem in one culture may be deemed an unremarkable phenomenon in another; (b) problem analysis: the way in which the problem, once recognized, is then varyingly shaped, delineated, formulated; (c) problem solving: again, given (a) and (b), the varying ways that the problem can, by various policies or expedients, be eased, ameliorated, or solved.

Put diagramatically the above proposition looks like this:

Varying Epistemological Styles

1. Marxist-Leninist
2. Pragmatic
3. Classical European

Common ground between these styles and the countries which operate them is indicated by the area where the three circles overlap. Other degrees of similarity are where two circles cross each other. But it is now necessary to provide an outline profile of the areas of real difference.

(a) Marxist-Leninism — the USSR

Arithmetically speaking, most of the children in the world who attend school do so in countries which are organized on Marxist principles. The Soviet Union is discussed here because it is the oldest socialist system, and has undoubtedly been a most influential model, not only for Eastern European countries, but for nations elsewhere. Space precludes a survey of the shifts of emphasis and reinterpretations of Marx for society, and thus education, since 1917. Anyway the central general ideas concerning the role of schools and what they must teach has remained pretty constant among Soviet educators. Currently they can be paraphrased through the following theoretical propositions:

— Education is first and last a political matter.

— The political purpose of all educational institutions is to act as the main agent in the production of the new Communist Society of tomorrow.

— This requires them to meet the needs of Society, current and future, and must therefore involve them in inculcating into future citizens the skills, knowledge, attitudes and behaviour which are and will be needed.

— The processes of teaching and the quality of learning are critical for they have to be such as to guarantee the thinking, understanding, self-disciplined Marxist person. Thus, for example, processes which generate mere blind, rule-following behaviour, characteristic of indoctrination, should not, in theory, be permitted.

— In these terms, the aims of schools are extremely broadly defined, including not only the acquisition by students of subjects and knowledge, but also, for example, proper ethical and moral actions by pupils. Within this broad spectrum, the content of the curriculum in schools is selected for impartation on grounds of the needs of society.

— It follows, too, that all pupils need to acquire these abilities — not merely for equality reasons, but for the New Society to be born. In addition it is thought that with very few exceptions (i.e. those who are measurably physically impaired) they are all capable of doing so.

— The Communist Party is invested, as the vanguard cadre, with the duty of leading the process to Communism. As such it has the right to retain absolute control over all educational matters.

Educational issues in the USSR, then, are bounded by these propositional parameters, and educational discussion is conducted in terms of the ground rules of this Epistemological Style.

(b) Liberal-Pragmatism — the USA

The American pragmatic epistemological tradition appears initially less easy to describe than Marxist-Leninism, for, as might be expected in a more pluralistic society, it is rather less coherent and explicit. Also it does not derive from one authoritative writer and his interpreters, though undoubtedly John Dewey was a seminal influence. It is an historical amalgam of nineteenth-century Liberalism and twentieth-century Pragmatism. However, propositionally its elements look like this:

— The constitution charges that educational provision shall be the responsibility of the states, except in instances where there might be problems of national defence. Thus, federal agencies have only very rarely been granted powers to affect institutionalized education. So, for example, opponents of the civil rights movement organized their defences on claims of the unconstitutionality of the interference by the federal government. This legal situation was initially the product of, and subsequently reinforced, American notions of localism and individualism.

— Schools in twentieth-century America were encouraged to play the central role of homogenizing the children of vast numbers of diverse immigrants into being Americans. In this process they served necessary national needs in inculcating into children the common, agreed values, ideas, and information for liberal, American democracy.

— However, quite the most important feature of being an American was to be free — *from* poverty, persecution, etc., and *to* pursue individual happiness. This American Dream, as Myrdal (1944) put it, was that any citizen had maximum opportunities to achieve anything. The path from log cabin to White House, or its equivalent, was readily negotiable, given hard work, ingenuity and perhaps a little luck.

— Any wealth or power élites established were based on individual merit and thus just. Entry to them was open to anyone.

— Failures have themselves to blame.

— The schools, and what they taught, had to be seen as servicing to the full the needs of the individual, in his or her pursuance of freedom and social mobility. The pragmatic answer to 'What knowledge is most worthwhile?' was 'That which is most *use* — to the individual's perceived purposes'. Apart from basic national defence and cohesion reasons, socially determined needs were not to override those of individuals, who, after all, collectively formed society.

— In this tradition *knowing how* is taken more seriously than *knowing that*. Thus, traditional European academic disciplines, strong on propositional knowledge, were not necessarily placed at the top of a hierarchy of respectable subjects. Many new subjects were granted full status, both in schools and higher education. Similarly, boundaries between subjects were less firm, permitting integration, based on an eclectic selection of knowledge, depending upon the goals of a particular course, and the wants of those following it.

— Control over all educational institutions, and what they taught, in this context, could not but be localized, certainly at the state level, better still at the local level; certainly not at the federal government level.

The recent wave of radical critics of American education (notably Gumbert and Spring 1974) confirm this outline. Whilst they argue that what has been described above is, to some extent, a set of fraudulent and manipulative arguments developed by corporate capitalism to legitimize the *status quo*, their strictures evidence its existence, and resilience. Many of the new ideas promulgated by this radical literature are often restatements, in novel forms, of classical liberal and traditional ideas. They seek to return to individuals and families the freedom and liberty over education and its content temporarily threatened, even lost, by the activities of large companies and government agencies.

(c) European classicism

Many of the assumptions regarding what education should be, and thus what constitutes worthwhile knowledge in the European tradition, are derived from the Renaissance, and can be traced through the eighteenth-century Age of Reason, and to nineteenth-century notions of the liberally educated gentleman. A summary of the propositions underpinning this tradition might go as follows:

- Objective knowledge exists which should be pursued for its own sake; the search for wisdom, truth and beauty is the highest form of human activity.

- Some forms of knowledge are much more worth while to pursue than others, because they form the necessary foundations for eventual enlightenment. Such knowledge is essentially propositional (knowing that), often rational, and invariably referred to in terms of the mental discipline of a subject.

- Over time, certain shifts and extensions have taken place in the definitions and parcelling of this kind of knowledge. The original list (closely resembling, even derived from, classical Greek thinkers) of, say, classics, philosophy, mathematics, the fine arts, was augmented by the inclusion of history, the sciences, modern foreign languages, and the social sciences. This list of subjects constitutes the respectable, high-status knowledge of the European tradition and is what is meant by the term *Bildung* in German and *culture générale* in France.

- It follows that the Educated Man (for women were invariably excluded) in this tradition attempted not to become sullied or tainted by the practical world — hence the model of the ivory-tower university intellectual, or the lonely, garret-living painter of genius. So, knowing how (the knowledge of the economy, the workshop, etc.) is disparaged and situated low down in a hierarchy of subject areas.

— Only some people were capable of being initiated into this esoteric world. At first it was assumed that the few would be the children of upper-class families, but in this century the need for a meritocratic basis as a substitute for birth has been admitted.

— The German *Gymnasium*, the French *lycée*, and the English grammar school are the institutional manifestations of these assumptions. In addition, the *Abitur*, the *baccalauréat*, and the English university matriculation requirements are exact statements of what this prestigious knowledge looks like in school knowledge terms.

The following augmentary comments seem appropriate. First, the parallels between the ideas in this tradition and those of classical Greek thinkers, notably Plato and Aristotle, are very close. Indeed, the Renaissances of the twelfth and fifteenth centuries are both characterized by being the rediscovery, reformulation, and reapplication of Greek thought to later times. Similarly, through Aquinas the medieval Church accommodated itself to the classical formulation of central philosophical propositions or problems and their solutions, enabling philosophy to become the hand-maiden of theology. But again, the ultimately unworldly nature of theological knowledge, by definition the most important of all ways of knowing, reinforced many of the central features of this tradition. This stand not only kept worldly knowledge at bay for as long as possible, it also reinforced, as had the Greeks, its second-rateness.

There is irony, or casuistry, at play in our second comment. It was assumed that the few who could demonstrate that they were successful initiates into this world of mental esoteric knowledge should also be those recruited to élite occupations, be they commercial, political, administrative or professional. Just as theology was the qualification for entry to the medieval Church, and its clergy, in turn, played a major role, at all levels, in the affairs of the State, so the metaphor became applied to lay initiates into esoteric knowledge. It may be that in origin medieval European universities should be seen as vocational foundations for the study of theology, medicine or law. Undoubtedly, however, they developed this new rationale of dispassionate esotericism. But it was deemed proper that the pursuit of highly theoretical knowledge, for its own sake, was nevertheless properly translatable into, and cashable for, vocational, economic, status, and power rewards.

Finally, the university in Europe was and is a key institution in that its existence and purpose was explained in the above terms. As such it was the major agent of generating and replicating the kinds of knowledge above. Further, through its examining role its influence upon the school system below it was and is enormous.

Succeeding chapters will use this device, called Epistemological Styles, to aid analysis and understanding. Some justification of its validity therefore seems appropriate. There are proper empirical questions about these Epistemological Styles which could be asked, notably: 'Where did they come from?' 'When were they established?' 'How do they work?' 'How resilient are they?' The author is in process of researching answers to these and similar questions, at least for England, by looking in detail at the period 1902-1922.

However the device is more readily defensible at the following levels, listed in descending order of significance:-

1. It ensures that in seeking commonalities and similarities, differences are not glossed over.

2. It highlights the need to appreciate the variety of local modes of thought, types of understanding and methods of justifying that exist.

3. It takes seriously, but provides a way of negotiating, the potentially fatal judgemental trap in comparative studies, identified succinctly by Grant (1979, p. 176) as follows: 'There is little point in condemning a chisel for not being a screwdriver.'

4. It doubts the propriety, even feasibility of culture-proof analyses, laws, findings and prescriptions.

3. Summary

This book does not attempt to survey foreign countries with the intention of gathering an assortment of interesting ideas or worthy practices, ripe for importation to the UK. Nor does it seek to illustrate an argument, or press for a particular pattern of necessary change because of foreign developments. Again, it makes no suggestion that one country or another is superior or inferior with regard to education — that one country 'succeeds' more through its policies than others and should thus be seen as an exemplar. Further, it is not concerned to apply a physical science paradigm to the analysis of education by using the comparative method to test a hypothesis. The aim here is to highlight our domestic scene and help to understand it better, by providing an international setting. This can be achieved by seeing the extent to which we in England are typical, when compared with some other countries, in our practices; in respect of the reforms we are proposing; in the way we implement them; but most important, in the way we conduct our debates. A comparative dimension may make some things previously deemed routine more problematical and thus perhaps in need of either reexamination and rejustification on the one hand, or reform on the other. James Thurber, when once asked by a newspaper man, 'How's your wife?' replied, 'Compared to what?' We need to take the epistemological stance implicit in his question seriously.

Note

1. Hans (1949, pp. 1-2) mentions Marc-Antoine Jullien de Paris *L'Esquisse et Vues Préliminaries d'un Ouvrage sur l'Education Comparée* 1817; John Griscom *A Year in Europe* 1819; Victor Cousin *Report on the State of Public Instruction in Prussia* 1831; and Henry Barnard's inclusion of detailed information about foreign systems of education in the 31 volumes of *The American Journal of Education,* which he edited between 1856 and 1881. Jones (1971, pp. 36-45) elaborates on the work of Jullien, Cousin, and Barnard, and draws attention to the comparative data published by Horace Mann after 1837 while he was secretary to the State of Massachusetts Board of Education, in particular his *Seventh Report* of 1843. He also discusses Matthew Arnold's *Schools and Universities on the Continent* (1868), a report to the Schools Inquiry Commission 1865-67 and his essays, *Popular Education in France* and *A French Eton.* Arnold's *Higher Schools and Universities in Germany* was published in 1874, London: Macmillan. Holmes (1981, pp. 23 and 43) draws attention to the fact that Cousin's work was published in America in 1836 and to Barnard's *National Education, Systems, Institutions and Statistics of Public Instruction in Different Countries* 1872, New York: Steiger. Gordon and White (1979, p. 143) identify 14 articles written by Sadler on education in foreign countries in the volumes published by the Office of Special Reports of the Board of Education during his time there. In their bibliography (op. cit., p. 303) they list other publications and public addresses on comparative topics that he was responsible for. Higginson (1961) discusses these and other aspects of Sadler's life and work. Jones (1971, pp. 47-48) and Holmes (op. cit., pp. 25-26) discuss the work of Ushinsky.

CHAPTER 2

THE GENERAL FEATURES
OF EDUCATIONAL PROVISION

The purpose of this chapter is to provide a general, descriptive account of how our five countries organize their educational provision. The section on England and Wales then identifies the ways in which, comparatively speaking, we in this country are idiosyncratic. In this way, an agenda of issues is produced, the most crucial of which are taken up and discussed in detail in succeeding chapters. However, there are a number of educational characteristics and themes which are shared by all five nations, and these must be mentioned first.

1. Common characteristics in the provision of education

A noticeable feature of the history of each of our countries in the twentieth century is that in all of them the State has increasingly taken responsibility for financing and regulating educational institutions. In each case it has taken over from other educative agencies. Some of these were religious foundations, with missionary or charitable intentions, though most were the product of self-help by parents and families. In each country legislation has been introduced to make school attendance during the years of childhood and youth compulsory. On the face of things, education is generally very popular. Millions of parents go to great lengths to arrange pre-school activities for their children as preparation for their enrolment at the primary level. Given the chance, students press in increasing numbers to continue on a full-time basis after the completion of the secondary stage. Almost certainly the most important single explanation for this popularity is that people recognize the close correlation between the quantity of successfully completed schooling and placement in a given niche in the socio-economic, prestige, and status hierarchies of five societies which are all highly stratified. Schools are popular because, in this respect at least, they are seen as crucially important.

So far as schools themselves are concerned, they all share certain general endemic characteristics. Inevitably, time must be ordered. For example, the school year has to be divided — by quarter or semester (USA), or term (Europe); weekly and daily timetables have to be constructed indicating what activities are to be conducted when and by whom. Similarly, space has to be populated in that children have to be organized into groups and assigned places or locations. Rules have to be established to govern behaviour and mechanisms devised for dealing with misbehaviours and transgressions. Most time is taken up in teaching-learning groups, and whether the location is a workshop, a studio, a gymnasium, a laboratory or, more typically, a classroom, such groups are socially curious. This is because they comprise one teacher and anything between 15 and 35 children. Social psychologists, beginning as long ago as Waller (1932, Part 3) have drawn attention to the uniqueness, even artificiality of these groups. Certain modifications can be wrought by systems like team teaching and, say, open-plan areas. Nevertheless, what can be done is ultimately limited by the fact that there is a pupil-teacher ratio.

It is also worth stressing what is involved in being a pupil, and being a teacher, in all the schools in our various countries. So far as children are concerned, because they are required to be at school, they are conscripts not informed volunteers. Further, so far as schools are concerned, they are juveniles, not only by law, but by chronological and developmental age — in terms of what they know, understand and have experienced — hence, by their status. Of course there is a shading, or an element of degree in this juvenility, because, in terms of each of the above criteria, there are considerable differences between 5 and 17 year olds, and points between. Also, all children bring with them personal experiences and understandings. They are not totally empty or passive receptacles to be filled and schools recognize, in varying degrees, the validity of that which their pupils already know. Yet despite these partial exceptions, schools in all our five countries do define children as juvenile and thus, inevitably, in some sense as inferior.

It follows that schools, equally inevitably, confer certain things upon teachers. Anyone who agrees to be hired to teach in a school has, necessarily, at least two roles consigned upon them — that of being *in* authority; and that of being *an* authority (Peters 1966). It is true, of course, that children in some schools do not necessarily recognize or admit, or even tolerate the validity of this process; and by their uncooperative, even defiant behaviours reject the teachers' right to authority and the rites by which they seek to exercise it. This is a perfectly plausible way of explaining misbehaving or disruptive pupils. But it in no way diminishes the validity or the logic of these characteristics of teaching in institutionalized schooling.

Schools also manifest some of the features of closed institutions, and as with other institutions of this type (e.g. prisons, the armed forces, or hospitals) there is a tendency for habitual rituals to develop with members preoccupied with private local games. The uninitiated outsider often finds many of these both mysterious and pointless, because it is not always clear how they bear upon avowed goals or purposes.

Some of these points may appear obvious, but in identifying broad comparative generalities, by taking nothing for granted, and through seeing everything as anthropologically strange, several serious issues do emerge. For example, there is the question of what motives lie behind the process of State intervention in education and what purposes and functions schools were, and are, designed to further. The statutory requirement of school attendance raises issues of freedom, power, control and equality. These vital themes are discussed in Chapters 5, 6 and 7. Again, the argument that the imperatives of the schooling situation produce certain inevitable consequences could be developed to show that schools are evil, pernicious places, which ought to be abolished because schooling is antithetical to education. This was the conclusion that Illich (1971) came to, at least about America, and his analysis has subsequently been applied to each of our other countries (e.g. see Lister 1974, p. 1).

Adequate rebuttals of such claims rest on two premises. The first is that deschoolers hold to a deterministic, iron law of institutions, irrespective of time and place. They fail to distinguish between what is and what must be. The second is that what is, in one context, may not be indiscriminately applied to other contexts. Schools do not have to be coercive or repressive, and in some countries, or certain schools within them, they are agents of enlightenment. The descriptions which follow in this chapter, and the discussion of schools and classrooms in Chapter 3, are illustrations of these debates.

2. The USSR

Due to the uniformity consequent upon centralism, it is easy to construct a diagrammatical representation of the Soviet system (see Figure 1).

A commentary upon this diagram, proceeding vertically from bottom to top, needs to include the following points of clarification. Pre-school facilities are usually generous and plush, though opportunities for attendance vary from urban (common) to rural (uncommon) areas. Parents are charged fees, though on a sliding scale according to income and with a low upper limit. Often the crèche and kindergarten are combined in one building provided and financed

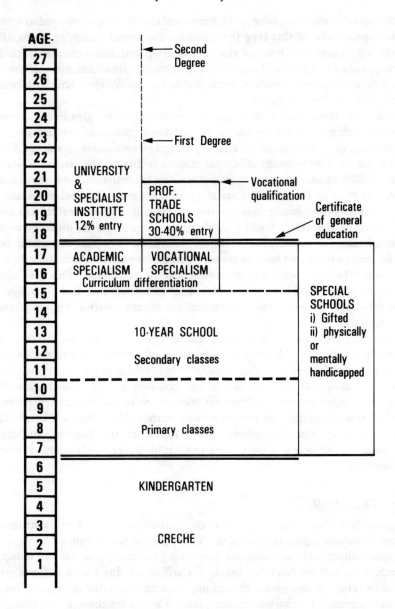

Figure 1   The education system: USSR

by a local productive enterprise for the benefit of the children of its employees. However, the education authorities specify exactly the nature of the regime, which always has two dimensions. First, considerable care is taken to provide medical supervision. The full-time medical staff, augmented by visiting specialists, supervise meticulously the nutritional levels in the food provided and the programme of physical education, while careful and regular checks for physical defects, however minor, are undertaken by detailed medical screening. All this ensures that those well-known physical inhibitors to adequate cognitive growth are identified and remedied. Second, a thorough programme of educationally approved activities is provided for each unit by the appropriate local education authority, which in turn implements the requirements specified by the all-Soviet Ministry of Education.

At age 7, children must begin their attendance at their local school, which, as this implies, recruits on a neighbourhood principle. Attendance is required for ten years, beginning with three years of primary classes, taught for all subjects by one teacher. Secondary specialist teachers take over thereafter. All schools are coeducational, with children of all ages, 7-17, on the same site. Teaching groups or classes are formed at age 7 on a random and therefore, in Western terms, a mixed-ability basis, and the children normally stay together for all subjects and for almost all their school careers. Details of the Soviet curriculum are discussed in Chapters 3 and 4, but at this stage it is important to stress that, with only some regional variations, reflecting and taking account of local language or cultural differences, what is taught is entirely identical for all children, at least up to the age of 15. For the last two years three broad and differing curriculum tracks exist which can be given 'academic', 'vocational' or 'general' labels. The career destinies of children following one or other of these tracks is obvious. The first leads towards higher education; the second to professional trade training and skilled employment; the third leads to unskilled jobs. However, the curriculum does not differentiate heavily between the three. It is rather that the academic and vocational courses have specialisms added to the broad list of subjects which constitutes a general education, so that two thirds of the work remains common.

Much attention is paid by the authorities to the quality of the general school atmosphere, with a premium being placed on cleanliness, orderliness, and providing an aesthetically pleasing environment. A certain view of moral, even ideological rectitude pervades all subjects taught and unambiguous models of proper ethical values are constantly provided — by teachers; by the example of past heroes; by drawing attention to exemplary children — in the quest for morally proper behaviour. There is no better illustration of this than the list of 20 school rules, common to all schools throughout the USSR, which lays down quite exactly what is expected of children. Interpersonal relations are undoubtedly formal and coded; but nevertheless friendly and polite. Most foreign visitors comment upon the real sense of purpose and the mutual respect between all members of the school's community, which undoubtedly exists.

Several groupings amongst the school's populations can readily be identified. In addition to being members of a class, children tend to be members of the Pioneer Youth movement — not because they have to, but because of the advantages which can be derived. Dozens of after-school activities can be enjoyed in the afternoons (for schools operate from 8 a.m. to 1 or 2 p.m.) at the Pioneer Palaces, where excellent facilities are provided and literally hundreds of clubs are available. Many are of a sporting or recreational or cultural kind, whilst in others the eager and probably those with singular aptitudes, or abilities, can pursue the serious study at an advanced level of one or more of the school's subjects, for example, astronomy, biology, languages, art. There are periods for Pioneer meetings also time-tabled during the school week, in which one form of grouping called the Link is utilized. This unit is made up of four youngsters, and it is used when necessary for disciplinary purposes in ordinary classrooms, as will be demonstrated in Chapter 3.

The teachers in schools are ranked by seniority. The most junior staff carry the label of primary generalist, or specialist teacher of a secondary subject, the latter grouped into discrete departments, each with its own chairperson. At the next level, there are usually two deputy directors and finally a school director, whose role is to ensure the exact implementation of those policies and practices laid down by government regulations, which cover all aspects of school life. In this sense he or she, (usually a he) has little autonomy, but will be expected to be, after suitable and specific training, an efficient administrator and, more important, a really expert teacher, capable of tutoring staff and delivering model demonstration lessons. All teachers are members of the USSR Trade Union of Workers in Education, Higher Schools and Research Establishments which provides, as other trade unions do, many necessary services including pensions, sick leave payments, holidays, and sometimes housing. As such, the teachers are often involved in union activities. Similarly, some teachers are members of the Communist Party and will be involved in its work. In percentage terms teachers are more in evidence in the Party than most other occupational groups. All schools also have a Parents' Committee, made up of one elected representative per class, which is very active in aiding, abetting and reinforcing the work and purposes of the school.

Special schools are provided for those children who are recognized as special cases. Separate institutions with extremely advantageous staff-student ratios and above-average accommodation and facilities are provided for the handicapped. So, as in most countries, special schools for the blind and partially sighted, the deaf or partially hearing, for delicate children, or those with congenital chromosomatic deficiencies leading to Down's syndrome or cretinism — and so on — are provided. A very large Department or Institute at the Academy of Pedagogical Services, with a worldwide reputation, conducts continuous research on behalf of such children. It is significant that all such children are expected to follow, as far as is possible, the ordinary curriculum of the 10-year school, though they have more time to master it because compulsory attendance at special schools is for 12 years. Soviet psychology does not recognize some Western categories of handicap, not so much in the area of clinical psychiatry (for example, schizophrenia is described and recognized in exactly the same way as elsewhere in the world), but in more nebulous areas like maladjustment or emotional instability. In general then, children with special needs are those with some identifiable, measurable physical or physiological deficiency.

The other category of special cases is in the area of giftedness. Special provision is made for a tiny percentage (about 2%) of children who are discovered by tests and attainments to be precocious in such spheres as music, ballet, the theatre, physical education (especially gymnastics) and circus arts. In addition, there are the schools which select their intake on the basis of all-Soviet competitive olympiads which discover youngsters who are brilliantly able at mathematics and physics. These schools are sited on university campuses and the pupils are taught by university teachers. They are the remnants of the incompleted initiatives of Kruschev, whose original plan was to augment them by opening similar schools specializing in chemistry, biology, geography, languages, and so on. The plan proved unacceptable to his successors, who saw them as palpably selective, potentially élitist, and as such, politically suspicious.

Much of both these forms of special education is provided in boarding schools, though in large urban areas the provision for the gifted is often on a day basis and, indeed, on occasions by part-time instruction. It is here also that some 10-year schools have been established with a special foreign languages orientation — usually English, French or Spanish. Here the foreign language is introduced very early and is even used as the medium of instruction for many subjects for older classes. These schools recruit about 20% of their students from outside the immediate catchment area.

Post-school institutions fall either side of a binary divide in that some are limited to running vocational courses leading to certification in a specific skilled trade, whilst others, like the universities and specialist institutes, teach students to first degree level and beyond. The former recruit 30-40% of a given age cohort; the latter are very selective, limiting themselves to accepting at most about 12% of youngsters. However, even here, various government ministries in control of the economy and of planning specify exact departmental entry figures, and the work of these departments is expected to have direct relevance to the needs of society. One final feature of Soviet education at this level is worth highlighting, namely the generous provision made for adult education, so that an avenue exists for second chancers. Courses, even at degree level, are available on a part-time correspondence basis, and students are guaranteed free time, in addition to normal vacations, from their work to pursue these courses. Anyone under the age of 35 has the right of access to these facilities.

It will be difficult, even in such a summary manner, to specify and particularize features of schools and educational structures in the other countries. This is because the USSR is unique in the way it makes so many things explicit and specific. This is partly because its system is heavily centralized, but mainly because it specifies exact tasks for its schools in the interests of achieving a clear (if in Western eyes a highly controversial) socio-political goal, namely the birth of a communist society. To this end, principles, policies and practices are laid down and explicated in exact detail, and usually with an internally consistent logic.

3. The USA

The American constitution delegates powers over educational provision to the separate States of the Union. Those federal and thus national agencies which were established were meant to protect the defence or general welfare of the nation. It follows that there is some degree of local variation in America, for schools were initially founded to meet the needs of local communities. So, for example, it is dangerous to generalize about pre-school facilities, except to say that they have a self-help, fee paying quality. Despite the lingering remnants of the compensatory education movement, including 'head start' opportunities for the children of 'deprived' families, opportunities are greatest in rich neighbourhoods. Similarly there is some variety of patterns of compulsory schooling. However, the thrust of the description that follows is to illustrate the argument that localism and thus variety have been exaggerated and that, over time, American education has acquired so many common features that it must be understood as a national system (see Figure 2).

Schools carry everywhere the common labels, according to level, of elementary, junior high, senior high. The features which distinguish a college, whether junior, or senior, from a university are universally recognized. A child's school career is usually six years at the elementary level, three years at the junior high school, and three years at senior high, though a six:two:four pattern is not uncommon and in some areas four-year middle schools act as intermediaries between four years of elementary classes and four years at high school. State law may allow school leaving at, say, 16, implying that only ten years of attendance is necessary. *De facto*, however, the overwhelming number of youngsters complete twelve years at school, with the intention of achieving a high school graduation certificate. Grave concern is always expressed if the percentage of drop-outs (those who leave prior to graduation age) in a district or at a school, runs into double figures. The annual calendar of all schools runs from the fall to late spring, punctuated by only short vacations. There are always two semesters, which in turn are divided in half, hence the term 'quarter'. The length of courses are always timed by such units so that measures of quality and degrees of difficulty are nationally understood by such designations as, say, American history: 30 quarter hours; social studies: 60 semester hours.

To achieve high-school graduation, students must complete those courses, specified by length and difficulty, as laid down in the graduation requirements. The power of any American school to grant certificates is the consequence of their having been accredited as worthy to do so by the local or regional educational authority. Many measures of worth are applied by visitational agents, such as the quality of the teaching staff, the range of courses on offer and the facilities available on the campus. Once accredited in this way, the schools are free to develop their own course specifications and assessment procedures, perhaps taking account of local conditions, needs and the particular opinions of their clientele, including parents, who can bring considerable pressure on a school through their PTA. These local factors, and the delegation of powers, do not, however, necessarily produce wide local discrepancies of practice. Over time, partly through mutual imitation and partly through the arguments and activities of national pressure groups, broad consensual practices have emerged.

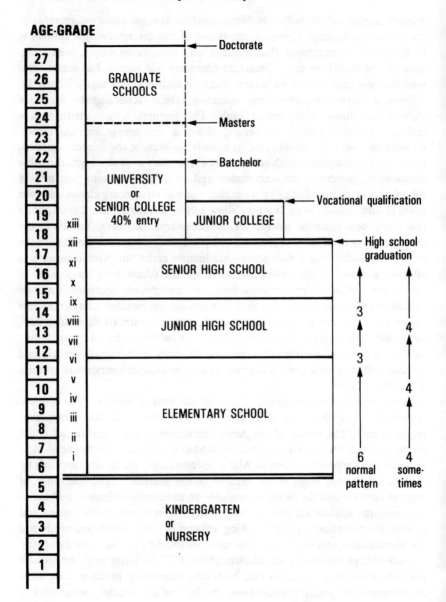

Figure 2   The education system: USA

So the general pattern of graduation requirements is remarkably similar in all high schools. Thus, all certification rubrics require that credits be earned in certain subjects: English, mathematics, social studies and increasingly a science, even a foreign language. State laws invariably require that American and State history be taught to all children. In addition, the elective program, from which students can choose augmentary courses, always has limits placed upon it. Invariably there are three somewhat different and parallel packages of electives offered, called tracks, which differ because the passing of more, less, or a basic minimum of more academically demanding subjects is involved. Each separate track leads to certification, but some are prerequisites for entry to certain levels of higher education and others have a more lowly, vocational cachet. It is significant, however, that in recent years track requirements have become increasingly similar all over America.

A novel and uniquely American mechanism in the above procedure is the credit system whereby, having satisfactorily completed a given course, students earn credit which is recorded to them, and these accumulate annually over the years of their high school career to the point when they can claim certification. The credit system was invented to facilitate flexibility and to permit individual choice, reflecting current interests. However, in addition to the limiting guidelines already alluded to, it is also important to emphasize that there is always a maximum number of credits a student can earn in a year. On the positive side, schools always provide students with very ample advisory facilities, to try to ensure that informed choices are made. But the corollary is that the responsibility for options made, and progress achieved, rests firmly with the individual.

With respect to the rich variety of courses on offer, not all of them merit a full unit of credit, so that a degree of subject hierarchization exists. The quality of courses is always governed by hours of classroom attendance and specified tests or evaluation procedures. But the most important index is that of the grade system. Here nationally recognized standards of achievement are involved in studying a subject at a certain level satisfactorily, and nationally standardized tests are commonly used to assess students. Thus a high degree of uniformity exists over the content of the work covered in a course of a specified grade. Everyone knows what is involved and what is meant by a student who is following, say, math or French at grade 9. This similarity of content and degree of difficulty has been greatly facilitated by the nationwide popularity of certain textbooks, which are sold by large publishing houses to School Districts via the Superintendent's office, and which thus become required reading in all that district's schools.

Teachers in America qualify to teach at a specific school level, either elementary or high school. In the latter they are certified as proficient to teach a particular subject, and to a certain grade. The academic faculty of a high school therefore is divided, first by subject departments and second by seniority of certification. But there is always another parallel staff providing a wide variety of counselling services, most of whom will have no teaching duties. This service includes advising students about personal or career problems, helping them to understand course and certification requirements and administering any psychological, diagnostic, aptitude or attainment tests thought necessary. The teacher population can be divided into two distinct groups: the academic faculty, with clear instructional and examining roles; the counselling staff, who supply a rich variety of complementary and support services which may encompass matters of student discipline.

Two principles, those of coeducation and neighbourhood, have always been and still are used in America as the basis for recruiting children to given schools. Thus, schools reflect the demographic features of their catchment areas, whether in terms of ethnicity or social class. In urban areas they tend to be rather homogeneous in these respects due to the existence of housing zoned by cost. Attempts at 'bussing' children across recruitment boundaries in the interest of greater heterogeneity, and thus equality, failed because affluent parents used the strategy which they had always employed, namely house-moving to more expensive areas.[1] Irrespective of their social or racial composition, however, American schools remain very large, at least by European and Soviet standards; their enrolment is always measured in thousands rather than in hundreds. It is clear that through decades of experience such large units have been made to work, though in most this requires somewhat rigid bureaucratic structures. It follows that the major role of the principal is that of administrator, who has to receive (though not always passively) and implement the instructions of his superiors at the Superintendent's office, and in turn supervise the complex workings of a very large, multi-faceted, big-budget institution.

We have concentrated on the American high school because, comparatively speaking, it is unique. It is also entirely original in that it was developed with the express purpose of providing secondary education for the masses, and, in historical terms, many decades earlier than such attempts in Europe. But its importance for America lies elsewhere, namely that it became the forcing house in respect of higher education. At this level there were universities, modelled on European principles, which pre-dated the high school movement. But the more typical modern state systems of higher education were developed to receive the products of high schools. These graduates had and have, as tax-payers, the right of entry to the state college or university, and despite the absence of grants, 40-50% of an age cohort do so, with most working their way through the system by part-time employment. So higher education in America must also be seen as serving mass needs, and therefore it developed in ways designed to accommodate a broad spectrum of students, most of whom achieve a bachelor's degree, involving four years of full-time study or its equivalent. Europeans who disparage their achievement do so at their peril, for first degree courses are designed for general and broad, as compared to specialist and élitist, education purposes. Real selectivity begins only at the graduate school entry point, initially in the recruitment to masters' courses and with increasing rigour at the doctoral and post-doctoral stages. The meritocratic élite thus emerge at age 22 or so, and those not selected or sponsored have at least had the benefit of a very protracted schooling. Similarly, professional training in orthodox fields such as medicine, law, and veterinary science comes after a general bachelor's degree, and at an appropriate graduate school, though the list of subjects which can be studied as major components of an undergraduate program is extremely extensive and includes many which sound vocational. Finally, it is worth pointing out that state universities in America have always had problems over academic freedom. Financed by tax-payers, and teaching the majority, professors at this level have rarely been granted, unchallenged, the right to pursue self-determined ivory-tower research, and have sometimes had to fend off unreasonable charges of political insubordination. On the other hand, many have become enmeshed in the strings attached to consultancies or contracts with large corporations or local vested-interest groups, seeking what might be regarded as unethical military or commercial ends.

4. France

In one respect France is similar to the USSR, in that it has a high degree of centralization in the organization of its educational system. This feature of French education makes it possible to generalize with some confidence and accuracy. In what follows, two themes particularly are highlighted. First the logic, coherence, even elegance of the institutional provision. Second, the endemic sorting and sifting quality of educational practice. Figure 3 is a diagrammatic summary of French structures.

The French Ministry of Education, through its 25 regional and 95 local administrative agencies, is responsible for providing and supervising this

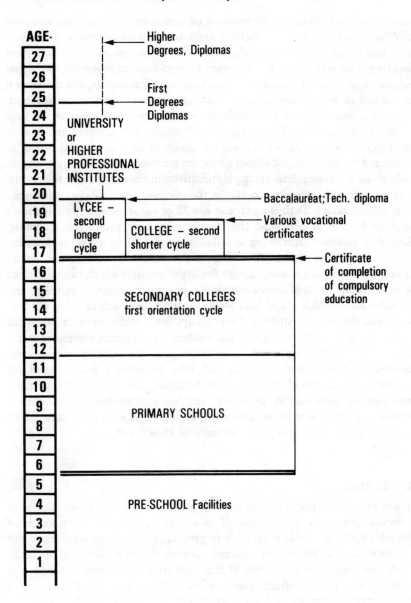

Figure 3 The education system: France

broad structure throughout France. Most features of the system are the consequence of national legislation, and the current situation is very largely the result of the 1975-1977 Haby reforms. The Ministry establishes national indices with respect to facilities, finance, staff-student ratios, teachers' salaries; and lays down very detailed specifications regarding teacher certification, school curricula, subject syllabuses, textbooks, school terms and holidays, and daily timetables.

Coherence is easily recognizable in the cycle principle which can be used to describe the broad limits of the structure with crystal clarity. There is the two-year pre-school preparatory cycle, which 95% of children attend at years 4-6 (King 1979), the vast majority having previously attended nursery classes from age 2, a right guaranteed in the 1975 legislation. The primary school cycle is four years long and the law suggests that the 'activity' principle should govern the teaching and learning atmosphere at this stage. After 1977, teachers were encouraged by ministerial circulars to adapt their pedagogy to take account of the concrete life experience of the children and to facilitate flexibility with respect to pace, space and progress. The requirement that children repeat a year if their attainment level is unsatisfactory has been legally abandoned, and undoubtedly the traditional, liberal, even leftist orientation of elementary teachers (*instituteurs*) has in recent years wrought changes in the atmosphere of French elementary classrooms. They have been pleased to augment their instructional roles by getting involved in holiday activities and leisure pursuits, so getting to know children as individuals and getting themselves known as people. Nevertheless, nationwide standards, even tests, of attainment in respect of the content of primary work are used, and bookishness has not been entirely abandoned.

Following this cycle, all children proceed to the first orientation secondary cycle, of four years, at their local secondary colleges. Here, again through Haby, the curriculum is supposed to be entirely common for all children throughout the country, with everyone being expected to achieve a general school leaving certificate, *brevet de collège*, awarded on the basis of school performance plus a simple, locally administered examination, by age 16. There follows the second secondary cycle, either long (three to four years) or short (two years). Courses here are clearly diversified and heavily hierarchized, and lead to very specific types of certification. Thus the long courses, conducted at *lycées*, lead to one of several *baccalauréat* awards, all, it is true, with a common core of subjects (e.g. French, mathematics), but some of an orthodox academic character and others with a technical or commercial orientation, carrying vocational labels. All shorter courses lead to some form of vocational certification, so that holders of one of the 60 or so *brevets de technicien* or one of the 300 *certificats d'aptitude professionelle* are qualified to enter one of several hundred skilled or semi-skilled occupations.

It could be claimed, then, that primary and first cycle secondary education provides everyone with an equal start, and equips them with a broad general education, mutually advantageous to individuals and to society at large. It then divides youngsters, on equitable principles based on merit and achievement and their personal preferences, into many discrete channels, all with clear vocational ends. Yet the system does have an overwhelmingly selective character to it. Indeed meritocratic élitism, a Napoleonic inheritance, has not been abandoned. Rather, the claim would be that recent legislation has introduced fairness, justice, and equity into the business of selecting. Further new criteria, involving the practical, the affective and the artistic human dimensions, have been injected to augment the traditional and exclusive preoccupations with things abstract, rational and intellectual. Finally, a pedagogy based on humaneness and taking account of the all-round sensitivities and experiences of children has been encouraged. There is some logic to the reverse side of this coin also. During the orientation cycle, children are constantly invited to consider what academic or vocational future they envisage for themselves and are meanwhile monitored and tested by teachers who attempt to check on their aptitudes and test their attainments. However, parents can see in precise detail what the system is and what it entails for their children. Those critics who make charges against the edifice by drawing attention to the undeniable fact that certain types of children (i.e. those from working class backgrounds), and children from certain geographical areas (i.e. rural *départements*) continue to underachieve, do so in terms of the internal logic of the system itself.

Selection, however it is justified, must carry with it connotations of worth and hierarchies of status. These terms certainly apply to the teachers who staff the different levels of schools in France, as indicated by the length and rigour of their training, their salaries, their conditions of employment and ultimately their rank. In this sense, then, teachers at secondary *collèges* holding a *licence* or *CAPES* qualification outrank *instituteurs*, but in turn have to defer to those *lycée* teachers who are *professeurs agrégés*. What is more, the continuation of the essentially instructional and assessing roles of all secondary level teachers is reinforced by the existence of a separate disciplinary staff in such schools, to whom the teachers refer all miscreants. Thus, older scholastic traditions involving intellectual achievement still infuse and flavour school life. Another index of this is that there has never been any evidence at any time that French teachers, even through their professional associations, have denied the right of the Ministry of Education to specify what they teach. They have often disagreed with what Paris has suggested, even conducted rear-guard campaigns over implementing policies; but they have not denied Paris's right to control. This is not explainable solely by the fact that all teachers are civil servants. Rather it must be that in their own interests and defence, given that they subscribe to status hierarchies, they cannot, properly, challenge those who are, in turn, their superiors.

Passage from school involves, for most children, entry into some form of further education. So, even semi-skilled employment involves further courses, albeit perhaps part-time, while certificates qualifying holders to skilled trades and occupations require full-time study at a third-level institution. All *baccalauréat* holders have a legal right of entry to a university, but this is not to say that higher education is not heavily stratified, for the competition for entry to the most prestigious institutions (e.g. the *écoles normales supérieures*, the *Ecole Polytechnique*, the *Ecole Nationale d'Administration*) is fierce, and for the *grandes écoles* quite ferocious. It is from the graduates of these places that France recruits its real élite — the very top of the pyramid, who occupy the most senior posts in the professions and the civil service, and who thus exercise enormous power.

The Debré Law of 1959 and its subsequent application does seem to have found an acceptable compromise to end the Church versus State struggle in and over education — a recurring theme, precipitating constant crises, during France's history in the nineteenth and twentieth centuries. The successful formula enabled the State to find a way of allowing the Roman Catholic Church to educate its own young parishioners, and even with the aid of State subsidy, because the Church in turn conceded that it had to incorporate the needs of the State within its schools, and agreed to eschew those ultramontane connotations which had previously been inherent in the form of separatism that it had wanted. So Catholic schools are financed by the State, and are as well equipped, furnished, housed, and so on, as State schools. In return for which, they follow Ministry regulations regarding such things as courses and syllabuses, thus bringing a greater uniformity of purpose and practice between the schools of the State and those of the Church. It is important to stress that these are virtually the only non-State or in some sense alternative or parallel educational institutions in France.[2]

5.   The German Federal Republic

After the Second World War, the occupying powers were responsible for the establishment of West Germany's new constitution. In the hope of guaranteeing democracy, the American federal principle, with its many checks and balances, was invoked and instituted. It was thought particularly important that education should not again be under the control of the central government, because the pre-war Fascist regime had used it as a powerful tool of totalitarianism. Consequently, as in the USA, responsibility for, and power over, education was delegated to the various *Länder*, each with its own Ministry of Education. Federal educational agencies were given advisory roles and their powers were limited to those of surveillance in matters that might have national significance or serve national needs. Decisions of the Federal Council of *Länder* Ministers of Education had to be arrived at by unanimous vote. This power of veto has meant that very few nationally binding policies have emerged.

On the face of it, then, regionalized control over education should have produced much regional diversity. In fact, however, all areas reverted to traditional policies and practices founded on a commonly held pre-1933 model of education. This drift was not challenged by the French or British during the occupation, for they were familiar with it; indeed in many respects the policies were similar to their own. So, for example, the majority of *Länder* stayed with the principle of tripartite secondary schooling. Subsequently some exceptions and changes have emerged. In those *Länder* where the SPD achieved power for a significant period of time, common schools for secondary age children have been established. Yet even here, they are invariably organized on a multilateral basis, with children assigned on entry to discrete sections, each with a separate pattern of curriculum. Where novel courses have been developed (e.g. in Hamburg), their potential as inspirational models, inviting imitation and change elsewhere, has never materialized because the certificates awarded at their conclusion were not recognized as valid by other *Länder*. Figure 4 is therefore a reasonably accurate summary of educational structures throughout the GFR.

The term *Kindergarten* has been internationally adopted, and shows that the education of very young children is a well established tradition in Germany. Pre-schooling is not compulsory or free, but the majority of parents arrange for the attendance of their children at such classes. Entry to the first primary class, notionally at the chronological age of 6, is governed by the result of a test taken by all children. This test was originally designed for diagnostic purposes with the humane intention of establishing whether particular children were, in developmental terms, ready for school. However, connotations of 'failure' have grown around this procedure; hence, perhaps,

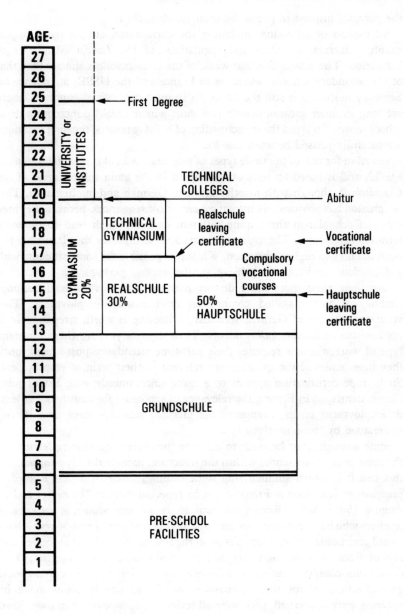

AGE-

| 27 |
| 26 |
| 25 | ← First Degree
| 24 |
| 23 | UNIVERSITY or INSTITUTES
| 22 |
| 21 | TECHNICAL COLLEGES
| 20 |
Abitur

| 19 | TECHNICAL GYMNASIUM   Realschule leaving certificate
| 18 | Vocational certificate
| 17 | GYMNASIUM 20%
| 16 | REALSCHULE 30%   Compulsory vocational courses
| 15 | Hauptschule leaving certificate
| 14 | 50% HAUPTSCHULE
| 13 |

| 12 |
| 11 |
| 10 |
| 9 | GRUNDSCHULE
| 8 |
| 7 |
| 6 |

| 5 |
| 4 |
| 3 | PRE-SCHOOL FACILITIES
| 2 |
| 1 |

Figure 4   The education system: German Federal Republic

the parental interest in preparing their children for it.

All aspects of schooling, including the curriculum, are governed by the statutes, decrees, circulars and regulations of the *Länder* Ministries of Education. The school day, and week, of the *Grundschule* is shorter than that of the secondary schools, where, as in France and the USSR, attendance on Saturday mornings is still the norm. As in most continental countries, there are long summer vacations, with two short winter breaks punctuating three school terms. To avoid the overcrowding of holiday resorts, the long vacations are carefully phased between *Länder.*

Selection for one of the three types of secondary school is now delayed until age 12, and is based on tests of attainment in the main subject areas of the *Grundschule,* though with priority given to German and mathematics. This assignation has obvious and important career consequences, because the three types of school run three quite different courses which lead to differing terminal certificates. The *Gymnasium* student who passes the *Abitur* has the right of entry to higher education. While it is possible for some students with a *Realschule* certificate to achieve similar access, perhaps via a technical *Gymnasium,* their more likely destiny is some form of vocational training, leading to highly skilled commercial or industrial employment. This vocational feature of German secondary schooling is worth stressing, for it applies also to *Hauptschule* students. Their courses prepare them for some type of work; the law requires their part-time attendance post-school, until they have achieved the qualification relevant to their form of employment. Such trade certification applies to a quite uncommonly long list of jobs. Consequently, as in France, the relevance of schooling for adulthood, at least in employment terms, permeates the German school system, and is well understood by those involved in it.

Some attempt must be made to describe the current qualitative features of the most prestigious school within the structure, namely the *Gymnasium.* To this end it is worth summarizing some findings made by Horst Rumpf, a professor of education at Frankfurt, as he reported them in *Die Zeit* (7 and 14 August 1981). What Rumpf did was to invite any students, parents or teachers who had delivered speeches that year at traditional end-of-year *Abitur* award ceremonies to send him a copy of the text of their talk. He received 250 replies from all over Germany and he argues that, taken together, these documents comprise authentic evidence from which to draw certain valid generalizations about the *Gymnasium.* So far as the speeches made by students were concerned, they were all serious and responsible in tone. Most did not suffer from over-idealism. Many admitted that they were the lucky ones in having had the chance of a *Gymnasium* education. Hardly any were hostile or aggressive. There was, however, much resentment expressed at the constant minor irritations which had to be endured (like homework loads), though most were attributed to the thoughtlessness, rudeness and insensitivity of authoritarian teachers, some of whose regimes bordered on tyranny. Many seemed sadly resigned to the loss of time which had been involved in their secondary school careers, because what had been required of them had been mostly hard work and the gathering of sterile information, which they did without much enthusiasm, for it lacked interest. There was much mention, too, of the pre-packaged nature of school work, where the main need had been to learn how the bureaucracy works, so as to achieve good grades. Rumpf's general conclusion from his review of this unique picture of schools (i.e. as seen from the students' point of view) is one of optimism. The speeches showed students to be very well informed and fully aware of what was happening to them. They were important because they demonstrated the students' refusal to accept that schools need be as they had experienced them. Neither were they prepared to tolerate a conservative version of things: that, as the élite, they should be thankful for the excellent mercies which had been bestowed upon them.

The teachers' speeches contained many grumbles, not least complaints about lazy children and falling standards. Yet most centred upon their position as agents of the system, their servitude to the bureaucracy, which debarred them from discussion of real educational issues. Many recognized the existence of hidden cruelties, even inhumanities, but blamed these, again, upon 'the system'. Rumpf found that parental speeches concentrated on two things. First, they saw themselves as people who had not questioned schooling as a thorough preparation for the rat-race of getting a job. Secondly, they maintained that for their own children this was not enough, which they explained by crediting them with a far higher degree of 'social intelligence'.

Although there is value in the public exchange of ideas permitted by these annual occasions, it is unlikely that any real change will accrue from them, as media coverage is at best sporadic and the attendance of senior administrators and politicians who are responsible for the things under criticism is extremely uncommon.

6.   England and Wales

What, then, do the general features of English education look like when compared with these four countries? An interesting beginning can be made by attempting to construct a table of English educational institutions, as has been provided for the other countries (see Figure 5).

The broad outlines of pre-school, compulsory schooling (years 5-16) and the general shape of higher and further education can be constructed. But *comparatively* speaking it is startling that it is not easy to say how compulsory schooling is structured in England and Wales. Some Local Authorities have two to three-year infant schools, followed by four-year junior schools, and then 11-18 all-through secondary comprehensives. Others have six (or seven) years of primary education followed by 11-14 junior high and 14-18 senior high schools. Again the 11-16 secondary school followed by 16-19 tertiary colleges is not uncommon. (One Authority, Croydon, has both these systems operating simultaneously.) Yet even the use of age 11 to demarcate the primary from the secondary levels does not hold nationally, because the Plowden Report's notion of the middle school has been put into operation in some areas, producing either an 8-12, 12-16, 16-19 pattern; or perhaps 9-13, 13-18 divisions. To complicate matters further, it must be remembered that comprehensive or common schools during the years of compulsory schooling do not exist everywhere, for some Authorities still retain selective grammar schools; while in other areas, though 11-16 common schools do exist, some pupils are moved at age 13 to 13-18 selective institutions.

The most likely explanation of this situation is that the various DES circulars of 1966 and 1967, which required Local Authorities to produce and implement plans for the reorganization of their secondary schools on the comprehensive principle, contained six suggested guidelines for their structuring. Given this invitation, based on a belief in the need to encourage flexibility so as to facilitate meeting local needs and the wish to promote local initiatives, the Authorities proceeded in their diverse directions. There are, however, several ways of interpreting this confusion, and these are discussed in Chapter 7. Meanwhile, at the very least, one important consequence must be alluded to, namely the serious limitations put upon the geographical mobility of parents with children of school age.

English schooling is idiosyncratic in several other respects. Contrary to popular opinion, schools here tend to be smaller in size — even at secondary level — than abroad. In the Soviet Union, a few schools of about 1,800-2,000 pupils have been opened on an experimental basis, but until it is proven that they can be run effectively, all other 10-year schools cater for around 1,000 to 1,200 children. This figure, or perhaps one marginally lower, is also the norm in France and Germany. American schools tend by these standards, to be immense, with high school campuses which accommodate 5,000-10,000

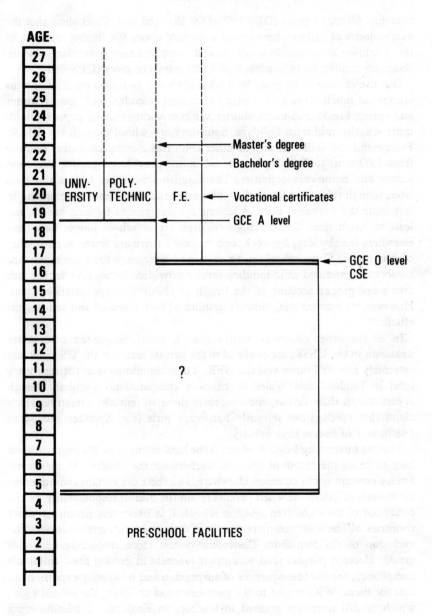

Figure 5 The education system: England and Wales

students. Official figures (DES 1979a) for England and Wales show that the vast majority of children here attend schools of under 500 in size, and that, of the 3 million or so children who attend comprehensive secondary schools, about 1.8 million do so in schools of 1,000 pupils or more (DES ibid.).

Our use of time — by year, by week and by day — is also peculiar. Terms are spread much more evenly over the annual calendar, with longer winter and spring breaks and much shorter summer vacations, but peppered with quite lengthy mid-term holidays. Saturdays are school days in the USSR, France and the GFR. In all our other countries a compacted day, running from 8.00 a.m. to 1 or 2 p.m., is the norm, providing time for afternoon leisure and homework activities. The English school day begins and ends later, though this is not to say that children spend more time being taught, in fact quite the opposite, because lessons are punctuated by long breaks, not least at lunch time. So, although children are at school longer here than elsewhere (i.e. by day, by week, and by year), there are fewer pupil-teacher contact hours. There are, of course, certain advantages to these arrangements, notably the extended child-minding service provided. It may also be that they take more proper account of the length of children's concentration spans. However, they do raise legitimate questions of both financial and pedagogical efficiency.

In all the other countries, coeducation is usual. Single-sex schools are unknown in the USSR, are confined to the private sector in the USA, and are extremely rare in France and the GFR. Their commonness at the secondary level in England and Wales is therefore comparatively peculiar, though arguments in their favour, most recently those in feminist literature which claim that coeducation seriously handicaps girls (e.g. Spender and Sarah 1980), may of course have validity.[3]

Another interesting English oddity is the legal status of *in loco parentis*, used here to cover the responsibilities of teachers for the children in their care. Such a concept is not common elsewhere, and there are certain consequences for matters of discipline when parents retain the overall responsibility for the behaviour of their children when at school. It is likely that parents in other countries will be informed more rapidly of their children's misbehaviours; the exclusion of children from classrooms occurs more frequently and with greater alacrity; parents tend to support teachers in getting their children's compliance, for the consequences of suspension and ultimately expulsion are dire for them. With regard to the punishment of children, the official right, which is still normally granted to teachers in England, of administering corporal punishment, exists nowhere else. Indeed its unofficial use is also very rare abroad, particularly in the USSR. Foreign educators remain bemused by the fact that English law permits an action by a teacher on a child which, if perpetrated on another adult, would constitute a criminal act — certainly that of assault, and conceivably that of grievous bodily harm.

They also find our habit of requiring school uniforms quaint, for although all Soviet children are required to dress identically at school (grey suits with white shirts for the boys, brown dresses or skirts with white blouses for girls), in other countries uniforms are not thought necessary. Of course limits are put on what is tolerable — for example clothes which are palpably offensive or provocative to others are not permitted. Functional clothing for some school activities, like sport, and for protection in workshops or studios, may be required, but otherwise it is left to the good sense of parents to dress their children as they see fit. It is not good enough to reply that parents have no such sense. So certain questions, genuine rather than rhetorical, appear pertinent. Are our uniforms particularly serviceable and sensible for school work? Do they really succeed in masking social class or wealth differences? Do they, on their own, promote a sense of loyalty to, or identity with, the school? What construction can be put upon the common phenomenon of children who constantly explore the very limits of what they can get away with in terms of conformity to dress codes? Does the constant campaign for conformity waged by teachers in many of our schools become an unnecessary irritant, directed at things which are essentially irrelevant?

Attention must now be given to the arrangements made for the religious component of education. This involves two separate elements. First, the teaching of religion in State schools; second, State support or otherwise of schools run on religious and denominational lines. The legal requirements made by the 1944 Education Act on English maintained schools — namely that they begin their day with a corporate act of worship, and that religious instruction be a compulsory subject on the curriculum save, in each case, for those who exercise its conscience clause—is most anomalous. While religion is timetabled in the secondary schools of the GFR, and is invariably defined as Christian studies, Soviet atheism debars the teaching of any form of religion, and for reasons to do with disestablishmentarianism, the same applies in France and the USA. The USSR does not tolerate, let alone subsidize, schools of any religious foundation. In the USA they are permissible, but despite a long series of legal cases in which denominational or parochial interests sought the right of taxation revenue subsidy for their schools, in every case the Supreme Court ruled that such payments would be unconstitutional. In France, sectarian schools, almost all of which are Roman Catholic, do receive State moneys, but they are required to teach the Ministry of Education's curriculum, and its subject syllabuses, and only after this may they provide augmentary dogmatic lessons. In this sense, then, there is one parallel to English practice, though it is not a close one. We apply the principle that some groups, namely Anglicans, Roman Catholics, Methodists, Jews, should not only be free to organize separate schools, but, to ensure freedom of religious conscience, they should also be almost totally financially sustained. This means that, notionally, they are free to interpret the whole curriculum and teach all subjects from a particular theological position. It must be noted also that this list of religious groups who currently qualify for State aid does appear somewhat arbitrary. No such aid is provided for other adherents, for example, Moslems, Hindus, Sikhs, or Seventh Day Adventists, all of whom have by now become numerically significant, which suggests a rather partial version of tolerant religious pluralism. Claims which might be forthcoming from such communities for equal assistance cannot logically be rejected, for the central principle of State-sustained religious toleration has, in justice, to be applied impartially. (The only other construction which such believers could put on a rejection of their plea would be that they are suspected of social or cultural subversion.)

Points germane to the specific levels of schooling can now be made. Far less provision is made by the State in England for the pre-school age group than anywhere else (apart, perhaps, from America). Currently only about 12% are catered for by way of nursery classes or nursery schools. Consequently, many parents in need of help resort to unofficial and largely unregulated child-minding facilities. In recent years another form of self-help, namely play groups, have proliferated in affluent neighbourhoods. Criticisms of the inadequacy of provision at this level are usually fended off by suggestions that because compulsory education here begins at age 5, and therefore earlier than elsewhere, pre-schooling is not necessary. As has been shown, such an argument has little if any comparative validity. There is no doubt whatsoever that primary schooling in England has gone much further towards adopting what are called 'progressive' aims, principles, approaches, methods and practices than elsewhere. Discussion of the merits and implications of this situation are deferred until Chapter 3, Section 3.

Our State-maintained secondary schools, whatever their structure, are similar to those abroad in certain respects — for example, they claim to be common rather than selective, and to be run according to the 'comprehensive' principle. Notionally a common school is one which enrolls students irrespective of such criteria as ability or attainment, race, religion or creed, gender, wealth or social class. One strand in the comprehensive principle is that, by daily association, children of all kinds come to understand and respect each other. In practice this very rarely happens because, understandably, the notion is that these schools should recruit, as they do in all other countries, on a neighbourhood basis, and most of our neighbourhoods, as in the USA, are not demographically heterogeneous. Thus, many of our urban schools tend to be homogeneous, at least in terms of social class and ethnicity. Another strand is that equality of educational opportunity is promoted not only by deferred selection, but also by providing children with an education tailored specifically to their individual needs, interests, aptitudes and potentialities. One expression of this principle is that parents should have the right to choose which school they send their children to. However, it is not possible to operate parental choice and the neighbourhood principle simultaneously — a conundrum which remains unresolved, but which causes severe difficulties in many urban and suburban areas.

This problem is exacerbated by another quirkish feature of our secondary comprehensives. We have seen that, apart from the GFR, all the other countries have developed a common curriculum for their common schools. This is justified on two counts: that any nation has the right to demand that all its citizens know certain things; in turn that all citizens have the right of access to this knowledge. Clearly this is an alternative version of the equality principle. Both versions will be discussed more extensively in Chapter 6. Meanwhile it is worth noting that, due to the absence of such a common curriculum in England, the tendency for parents to want to exercise choice is increased.

There is a further important extension to this state of affairs in England. Apart from the statutory requirements for the provision of religious education already mentioned, no requirements are made or firm guidelines provided for the curriculum. All matters of what is taught, how, when, and to whom, are left to the individual schools to decide. Those similarities in curricular arrangements which happen to exist are matters either of chance or, more significantly, the result of tradition. Agencies with powers equivalent to those of the Soviet or French Ministries of Education, the German *Länder* Ministries, the State legislature or the School District Superintendent's office in America, all of which lay down very specific requirements about the curriculum, do not exist in England and Wales. This form of localism, not only of structure but of the actual work of schools, is another quite startling feature of our secondary schools, comparatively speaking. Yet despite localism, two generalizations with respect to practice can be made. First, very different from elsewhere, *overt* vocational preparation is almost totally absent from our secondary school provision. This is not to say that we do not select or differentiate children. Streaming is still used in some schools; banding and setting are very common practices; options and choices are always offered, usually at the end of the second or third years — but with no clear, consistent rationale. Second — and this point applies to all levels of school — it follows that our teachers have a quite remarkable degree of autonomy because no formal requirements are made regarding any aspects of their work. They can even select which form or mode and examining authority their pupils' work (and therefore by implication their own) is assessed by. Those limits or inhibitors to their room for manoeuvre which do exist are informal pressures such as their own codes of professional practice or the influences of public, community, parental, and media opinion. Yet their degree of autonomy is quite unparalleled when compared with that of teachers in other countries. This situation requires further explanation, comment, and analysis, and this is provided in Chapters 3, 4, 5 and 7. Thus one preliminary example must suffice. The qualification granted to teachers in our other countries is quite specific, by level and by subject. A teacher is only certified to teach at a specified level: primary or secondary. In the latter case the subject or subjects are listed. In England and Wales, by comparison, entry on to the DES registry of those with Qualified Teacher status is a general licence to teach. Who is appointed to what post is left to the discretion of headteachers or LEAs.

Discussion so far has been restricted to the State system, but it is essential that it be extended to those schools outside its purview, which involve no more than 10% of all school age children. Despite its independent status, private schooling does have a common structure which can be summarized thus: ages 0-8: pre-preparatory arrangements; ages 8-13: preparatory schools; ages 13-18: 'secondary' establishments. Transfer at 13 is usually, though not always, dependent on passing the Common Entrance examination; 'common' because it is the yardstick used by most schools catering for the oldest age range to select their entrants. The examination tests attainment in a wide range of subjects, some of which, like French, are not normally taught in State primary schools. Hardly any independent schools are coeducational; further, schools for boys heavily outnumber those for girls. Irrespective of level, fee-paying is involved and scholarships to cover such costs are very rare indeed, despite the 'assisted places' provision.

The DES no longer compiles a register of independent schools it has deemed, after inspection by HMI, 'efficient'; which makes it difficult to be sure about the general quality of their facilities and teachers. The likelihood is, however, that many compare unfavourably with State schools in these respects. But some (i.e. those who are members of the HMC) have excellent facilities with well qualified and exceptionally well paid staffs. Most of these have the benefit of foundation endowments made rich by decades of careful husbandry, and a charitable legal status. Those few which are, consequently, outstandingly prestigious and called 'public' schools are extremely selective, adding many nebulous criteria to the two obvious ones: the intellectual calibre of the candidate and the fee-paying capacity of his parents. In these schools termly boarding is normal, though there are some, situated in large cities, which are day schools. It is important to remember that most public schools have very recent histories, having been established in the mid-nineteenth century to meet the needs of the *nouveaux riches* searching for social respectability for their sons. Some existing grammar schools became famous by the chance appointment of a vigorous headmaster and others, in secluded rural areas, were greatly aided by the ease of access provided by the growth of railways. Prior to such invigoration, those few schools with a more ancient lineage were in a moribund, even decrepit state and it is necessary to point out that most were originally established by benefactors (sometimes noble, even royal) to provide an education for the poor scholars of a particular parish.

Some clarification of the terms 'private', 'independent' and 'public' can now be achieved. They are 'private' because they can be exclusive of entry, according to any self-selected criteria, though fee-paying is always one of them. They are 'independent' — of the State. That is, they are not in receipt of its revenues or bound by its regulations, and they are closed to its surveillance and inspection. They are 'public' because a few were originally just that — set up on behalf of the lowest classes of society.

In the USSR no such schools are allowed, but no official bar exists in any of the other countries, though it is only in the USA that they exist in any significant numbers and even here, as in France and the GFR, some limits are placed on their independence. In comparative terms, then, perhaps the most unorthodox feature of our system is the existence of this parallel, separate sector of education. There is no question of the popularity of independent schools. More than enough parents choose to send their children to them. Many more wish they could afford to do so. No government has made serious moves to dismantle them. All of this suggests that they are deemed superior to State schools. It is certainly the case that they are conducted along lines with very different educational principles from those of the State system, though Gordonstoun (Hahn), Michael Hall School (Steiner), and maybe Summerhill (Neale) apart, none are based on the precepts of any single well-known educational philosophy. They are stoutly defended as providing healthy competition and novel, experimentally proven ideas for State schools, and on the grounds that parents must not be denied their freedom to choose which school they send their children to, or how they opt to spend their money. Critics who have replied that such a choice is only open to the few, and that it is the products of public schools who overwhelmingly populate all the élite groups of English society, have gone unheeded. They have failed to persuade the majority that such schools are the crucial mechanisms in the process of the self-replication of those tiny few who have great wealth and exercise real power.

As in the other countries under discussion, there is a binary divide between higher and further education in England and Wales, though the subsidiary fissures within these two categories — that is, between universities, polytechnics, colleges of higher education, colleges of further education, and centres for adult and continuing education — are wider and deeper than elsewhere. Our 44 universities are more generously funded than the other institutions, and due to the University Grants Committee system they retain autonomy over expenditure, which reinforces their capacity for self-determination of function. In the post-Second World War period there has been marked acceleration in the drift to separate 'gown' from 'town'. It must be recalled that the second, post-Oxbridge/London/Durham wave of universities (e.g. Manchester, Liverpool, Birmingham, Leeds and the University of Wales) were all locally funded initially, and intended to serve local needs. Most students were daily commuters. This was also true of later centres like Leicester and Hull. The process of separation is typified by the newest, post-Robbins Report universities, established in quite small, rather remote, and often cathedral towns, whose campuses were specifically planned on sites of large acreage on their very periphery. Students had to be resident. Further, the existence of mandatory grants facilitated the general trend for students to be nationally mobile, opting to apply and enrol at centres distant from rather than close to their homes. The separation is more than geographical, however. It is fundamentally intellectual, even cultural, and rests on such ideas as the need to maintain academic freedom and to pursue frontier theoretical research for its own sake in self-selected fields of study.

Our universities are not noticeably more selective than those elsewhere. The products of universities in most countries (i.e. those achieving a bachelor's degree or its equivalent) represent about 12% of a given age cohort. However, we tend to achieve this figure on entry by selective recruitment at 18. (As has been indicated already America is an exception, though there it is the Master's or the doctoral degree which could more properly be seen as the terminal qualification and thus the main selective device). So, different from France, the GFR and the USA, no taxpayer's right of entry for those holding minimum university entrance requirements exists, though apart from the USSR (where students can earn grant increments above the basic, according to how well they do in their examinations), the nature and amount of grant aid is extremely generous in comparison with these other countries. American students work their way through college, while in France and the GFR loans or other forms of self-finance have to be arranged.

Undergraduate courses in England are far narrower and more specialist in content than anywhere else, rarely requiring those following them to continue with a spread of subjects aimed at continuing their general education. The implication is that our first degree courses are essentially a preparation for pure research, during which the tiny few who will be allowed to conduct it are selected. Polytechnics were founded with the express purpose of compensating for, or complementing, the work of universities in that they were to develop work of an applied and technical nature, though of a superior standard to that of colleges of further education. It does appear, however, that their recent history is one of drift to academia, which is an indication that what counts as high-status knowledge is still determined by what goes on at universities. The universities' influence on education in England, not least upon schools, continues to be very considerable.

There has recently been international recognition that the model of full-time compulsory education prior to adulthood, and little thereafter, has several disadvantages. This has led to pressures for the provision not only of adult education but continuing education, known elsewhere as 'permanent', 'life-long', or 'recurring' education. Two main reasons are given. First, to ensure that the knowledge acquired at school, which after a time becomes redundant, can be updated. This redundancy can take various forms, requiring, for example, the updating of professional or trade knowledge and skills for whole groups of workers, or the reinforcement of an individual's newly acquired political or cultural interests. Second, to provide another chance for those whose ability and motivation develops late. Under the chairmanship of Richard Hoggart, the Central Advisory Council for Adult and Continuing Education has been most active. Its publications (all 1982) have claimed that England is an under-educated nation and what is more, that continuing education should be available as a right.[4] One report by Tight (1982) drew attention to the particularly poor contribution of universities in that their provision of part-time undergraduate courses was almost nonexistent. More interesting, from the perspective of this volume, is the point that England is comparatively backward in the general area of continuing education. The USSR's facilities have been noted above. In France, employers are required by law to provide paid educational leave for those who ask for it, and, at the moment, no restriction is put upon what might be meant by 'education' in this context. In the USA higher education can better accommodate the demand for continuing education because it is singularly flexible and porous. But in addition, community colleges have been widely established to meet such needs, with some, like City College New York, having aroused international interest due to their successes.

7. Summary and conclusions

In this chapter I have discussed both the common and the unique broad features of educational provision in five countries. I have argued that, *comparatively* speaking, England is idiosyncratic in the following respects:

1. The absence of a consistent national structure of schooling.

2. The use made by schools of time — by year, week and day.

3. The existence of a substantial number of single-sex schools.

4. That many schools require their pupils to wear a uniform.

5. That teachers are placed *in loco parentis* to their pupils.

6. The lack of pre-school facilities for those in their early years of childhood, and post-16 opportunities for continuing and adult education.

7. The arrangements made for religious education, especially for those children whose parents avow specific religious beliefs.

8. The autonomy of teachers — at all levels of education.

9. The approaches to learning, and the teaching methods adopted, at the primary level.

10. The absence of a common curriculum in both primary and secondary schools.

11. The lack of overtly vocational courses for children during the compulsory years of secondary education.

12. Highly specialized first degree courses at universities, which require the study at secondary schools of a narrow range of subjects by

those children who express an early interest in applying for entry to them, resulting in the exclusion of those who make inappropriate options.

13.   A flourishing and influential system of independent and private schools.

A comparative *perspective* has been shown to be uniquely useful, because it has highlighted England's educational peculiarities. Of course conformity is not necessarily right, nor oddity always wrong. But eccentricity does invite attention, which suggests that all the items on this agenda need reasoned reassessment.

However, I consider that the central educational issues are contained within items 8-13. It is for this reason that, in the chapters which follow, a comparative *analysis* is made: first, of these crucial education practices (Chapters 3 and 4); second, of those critical matters of policy and principle which permeate them (Part Two, Chapters 5, 6 and 7).

Notes

1.   In the 1960s the authorities in many cities in America 'bussed' children from one neighbourhood to schools in another so as to ensure that no schools were composed of one ethnic group (Havighurst 1966, p. 181). Many white parents opposed this policy. Havighurst (op. cit. pp. 55-58) showed that the main demographic trend in Northern American cities up to the mid-1960s was towards residential segregation — by race and by social class — with white families moving house to largely all-white neighbourhoods with all-white schools. During the mid 1970s, I was told by officials and teachers of the Atlanta Public School System that this phenomenon was then in process in their District.

2.   The central problem in the tortured history of the relationships between Church and State in France was the powerful nineteenth-century ultra-montane tradition adopted by many Roman Catholics, who saw the Vatican as their ultimate superior authority. This relegated the temporal government of the French State to a subordinate position. French secularists were therefore adamantly opposed to the State subsidizing Catholic education. They also raised questions about the loyalty and patriotism of Catholics in France, which had serious political, even constitutional implications. Fraser (1971, pp. 62-71) discusses the Church-State issue in France and describes the passage and terms of the Debré Law. King (1979, pp. 127-131) outlines the secular versus Catholic issues in French education and indicates how the Debré Law has been implemented.

3. Spender and Sarah (1980) survey the main sexist mechanisms in education in England, and Mahony (1982, pp. 470-471) reports that her own research shows that these are intensified in mixed-sex classrooms.

4. In addition to the document cited, the Council published a wide range of other reports in 1982, e.g. *Adults: Their Educational Experiences and Needs. Adult Education and the Black Community* (Little et. al.); *Basic Science Education for Adults. Adults' Mathematical Ability and Performance. Use of Mathematics by Adults in Daily Life* (Sewell); *Continuing Education: From Policies to Practice.*

CHAPTER 3

SCHOOLS AND CLASSROOMS

1. Teachers

Although the teaching force in each of our countries is a unified occupational group, it is in each case highly diversified and stratified. The first obvious instance of this is in the primary or secondary school teacher labels, identified in Chapter 2. The differences here are intensified by the fact that such teachers used to be trained in separate institutions, and the structures and content of their courses still remain different. Broadly speaking, more stress is laid on subject content in the preparation of secondary teachers, and more on 'pedagogics', 'methods' and educational studies, particularly that of child psychology, in the preparation of primary teachers. There are clearly two very different models of teacher implicit in these differences of priority.

In recent years all countries have attempted to raise the status of primary teachers by upgrading the institutions where they are educated, making their courses longer and more rigorous, and thus producing more equivalence between their qualifications and those of their secondary counterparts. This has applied to the *école normale* in France, the *Pädagogische Hochschule* in the GFR and the *teachers' colleges* in the USA. In the USSR the pedagogical schools, which used to train pre-school and primary level teachers, are being rapidly dismantled, so that shortly, with only rare exceptions, all teachers will be educated at pedagogical institutes, whose status is equivalent to that of other specialist institutes and universities. All entrants will be recruited at age 18, on the completion of their secondary education, though the courses of study for primary and secondary teaching will vary along the lines indicated above.

In the secondary schools of all our countries, teachers are always grouped departmentally according to their subject specialisms, each of which has a head of department. There are some similarities between the levels of status bestowed on such departments; with the possible exception of the USA, teachers of orthodox academic subjects being afforded the highest regard. The USA and France are somewhat anomalous because two rather separate groups of staff exist in their secondary schools: the specialist guidance counsellors in the former and the ancillary *censeurs*, responsible for discipline, in the latter. In all our countries, teachers with particular seniority can be identified: school principals, directors or headteachers, and their deputies. However, as I show later, the precise nature of their responsibilities varies.

Most teachers in all countries are female; the ratio in England of approximately 60-40 being the lowest; that of the USA and the USSR, at about 75-25, the highest[1]. (This Soviet figure is worth commenting upon, for it is one of many indications that clear and rigid conventions regarding male-female occupations exist there. The notion of occupational parity between the sexes has been assumed merely because women there are represented in jobs, such as engineering and heavy manual labour, which in the West are traditionally all male.) In all countries, however, the percentage of women teachers declines as the age range being taught gets older, and they are markedly under-represented in the most senior teaching and administrative posts.

The legal and contractual position of teachers does vary somewhat. In France they are national, and in the GFR regional, civil servants; and in both countries they can be assigned and reallocated to any school for which they are appropriately qualified anywhere in the country or *Land,* by the French Ministry or particular *Land* Ministry of Education. These points also apply to teachers in the USSR, though the term civil servant is not used there. In all these countries, as in England, the qualifications teachers hold are nationally recognized. National salary scales exist, with differentials being paid according to the level of qualification, the experience and the seniority of individuals. However, different from England, very specific conditions of service are laid down. For example, in the USSR payment is made according to specified weekly classroom contact hours, with overtime paid for work in excess of these and extra payments made for marking children's work; and weekly and annual periods of in-service training during vacations are mandatory. In America, although teachers are bound by regulations laid down by the State Board of Education and the State Legislature, they are hired by a particular School District, and they can be assigned to any school within it and subsequently redeployed at the discretion of the District Superintendent. No agreed national salary scale or system of teacher certification exists, though interregional agreements make variations in the former and non-recognition of the latter, rarer than they once were. However, the contracts which teachers sign can often be very precise about the duties expected of them. The achievement of permanence of tenure by those appointed with only minimum qualifications is always conditional upon their continuing with part-time in-service courses.

In all four countries, teachers belong to one of several trade unions or professional associations. In the USSR they are all members of the TUWEHSRE, as are university teachers and all other workers in this employment sector, such as librarians, laboratory technicians, the cooks who supply meals, and those who clean the buildings. In addition to the many services it affords (see Chapter 2) this Union also publishes a variety of journals which disseminate ideas, and within the general theory of the role of trades unions in the USSR it acts as a filter in the flow of ideas, both upwards from the grass roots and downwards from policy makers and administrators. In the USA, the GFR, and France, teacher associations tend to represent far more sectionalized interests, and in Europe at least they act in defence of the conditions of employment of employees in negotiations, even conflicts, with employers. In the USA the style of the American Federation of Teachers comes close to this defence of labour position, whilst the NEA, with many university teachers and education administrators amongst its membership, has tended to concentrate on the promulgation of educational ideas. Other teacher associations — by region (e.g. the Memphis Teachers' Association), by level (e.g. the Los Angeles Elementary School Teachers' Association), by subject (e.g. the Kansas State History Teachers' Association), by ethnicity or religion (e.g. the Black Teachers' Association; Association of Jewish Teachers; Association of Catholic Teachers) — abound. Each of these associations, and other similar ones, represents the particular interests of its members where and when it can, and sponsors educational ideas through journals and conferences.

There are obvious similarities in what has been said here with the membership and work of teachers' unions and associations in England. The most obvious differences highlighted so far are the lack of specificity in teacher certification and conditions of employment, and the absence of mandatory in-service training requirements.

In their study of occupational structures in modern societies some sociologists distinguish some groups from others on grounds of 'professionalism', showing, for example, the origins and history of the idea, and the emergence of new professions (e.g. Tropp 1957). In this literature (e.g. Banks 1968; Liebermann 1956; Musgrave 1965) professional people are considered to be a discrete group because they:

1. Provide a definite and essential social service.

2. Are familiar with an esoteric body of knowledge.

3. Have received a long period of training.

4. Emphasize intellectual techniques in performing the service.

5. Emphasize the concept of service, rather than profitability, as the basis of their relationship with clients.

6. Have established codes of professional conduct, or a set of ethical principles, which govern relationships with clients.

7. Have established codes and conditions of service, and accept as a group broad responsibility for judgements made and acts performed.

8. Have professional organizations to enforce codes on all members and to represent their interests with respect to fees, salaries and other conditions of work.

9. Have freedom to practise their profession.

10. Receive the recognition and esteem of the public.

11. Control entry to the group by existing members.

Clearly Soviet teachers would reject the term 'profession' out of hand, and would argue that most of these criteria apply equally to most if not all other workers. Many of them can be said to apply, for example, to Western workers such as plumbers. It is for these sorts of reasons that other critics of 'professionalism' have pointed out that the service component of the term has been used to gloss over the monopolistic features of many professional associations (notably doctors and lawyers), which they have ruthlessly exploited to gain inordinate financial advantages for their members. On the other hand, this service idea has often been used by employers to make certain groups (e.g. nurses and teachers) accept poor financial rewards for their work. It is nevertheless reasonable to suggest that many teachers in our countries, including those in the USSR, would describe and defend their work in most of the above terms. Certainly this could be claimed for points 1-8, which can therefore be seen as those perceptions which are shared by teachers. Similarly, in no country does point 11 apply. So, the rest of this section will pursue the varying positions of teachers with regard to public esteem, and the extent of their autonomy.

It is not the intention here to dwell upon differences of status as between different types of teacher, for the significance attached to teachers according to the level of their work and the subject they teach has already been mentioned. Instead we will attempt to show the degrees and forms of regard with which teachers are held in our various countries. Because teachers provide a service which is public, their client-relationship is important, and their direct and indirect clientele is an extensive one. It ranges from the children they teach to parents, employers, and the public at large, particularly the citizens of local communities. In addition teachers have to take account of the wishes and directives of the administrative agencies who, technically, employ them, and the opinions and attitudes of colleagues, not least those with seniority. Judgements of teachers will depend upon what it is that they are expected to achieve, and the degree to which they appear to come up to those expectations. Clearly there are a variety of depictions of purpose or goals, and many ways, some notoriously unreliable (such as rumour or gossip) by which judgements are made. The opinions held by parents are often coloured by their own memories of schooling. Employers often decide according to their partial evidence regarding the mastery by school leavers of certain limited skills which are required of young employees. Citizens often use the appearance and behaviour of local school children in the neighbourhood as evidence of their teachers' competence. Much also depends on the bases upon which teachers claim their authority:- because they are authorities in a particular subject area or on how best to get children to learn something; or because they have powers — those formally invested upon them by the schooling system in being teachers, and those of selection and ascription implicit in their work. In their relationships with children and colleagues personality and charismatic qualities are often crucial, while organizational competence and disciplinary skills impress administrators. We can now discuss the status of teachers in our various countries in these general terms. The particular features of the interactions between teachers and children are taken up more specifically in Section 3 of this chapter.

Salaries are often used as a guide to the status of occupational groups, but due to the complexities of making cross-national comparisons in standards of living it is not possible to approach matters thus. One UNESCO study (1968) suggested that teachers everywhere, including the USSR, had a relatively lowly status in these terms. In every other respect, however, the opposite is the case in the Soviet Union. Because teachers are such vital agents in the process of achieving communism they are constantly applauded and supported, not least by public acclaim from senior political figures at Party Conferences, and so on. The Soviet media are used systematically to this effect. For example, in the weeks prior to 1 September the press and television constantly refer to the exciting and important activities about to be embarked upon by children at the opening of the new school year, all organized and provided by dedicated and skilled teachers. The Parents' Committees are in no sense vehicles for the receipt of parental opinion about teaching or schooling, but are instead used to reinforce and explain the work of teachers, guaranteeing its effective impact and also increasing parents' esteem for teachers. At the same time, schools are crucially important to all families. Failures of learning or cooperation can have serious consequences (see Section 4 of this chapter), while success in these respects brings important all round advantages. Soviet teachers, then, are quite unambiguously *in* authority; and they are authorities about things that really matter, through which they acquire much power in their relationships with their clients. Taken together all these things ensure them general esteem and high status.

The American picture is rather different because many of these factors do not apply, and in general the regard with which teachers are held there is more lowly. This is partly because wealth is an important index of status in the USA — as illustrated by the oft put question 'Well, if you are so clever, why are you so poor?'. In a society where, traditionally, women have not been highly regarded except as sex symbols or as mothers, any profession largely composed of them suffers accordingly. Similarly, no broad consensually and centrally held sense of purpose or direction exists, so that those things teachers claim to know about are not necessarily admitted as being important. Again the neighbourhood or community pattern of schooling, and the powers which parents have in electing the School District Superintendent and influencing what goes on in schools through their PTAs, have also tended to undermine the authority of teachers. On the other hand, educational qualifications are known by all to be important to children's life-chances and the contractual powers which teachers can wield through their instructional role over children eager to gain their high-school certificates is considerable. Conversely of course, teacher incompetence makes such children impatient and hostile.

The contractual basis of the teacher's authority identified here is relevant to France and the GFR. In French schools, while it is true that general skills and a common curriculum are taught in the years 6-15, teachers are also involved, particularly in the orientation cycle, with sifting and sorting children according to the various courses on offer at the next level. Through this, they acquire considerable power. At the second cycle, any course that children follow has important career consequences for them, so that again teachers gain importance as the agents of the successful acquisition of necessary knowledge. The same applies to the GFR, for although, as in France, the courses are diversified, each is still highly relevant and very important, even if only in a limited utilitarian sense, to those following them.

One other general point which applies to all teachers in all four countries is the consequence of the fact that the content of what they teach is decided by outside or superior administrative bodies — the central Ministries of Education in the USSR and France, the *Länder* Ministries in the GFR, the Superintendent's office in the USA. This means that, whilst teachers may dislike what they have to teach and might prefer to do other things, in their negotiations with children they do not have to explain or defend why they require certain things of them. Their authority is not undermined by criticisms about the relevance, interest or value of the content of learning, for they can quite properly deflect these by pointing out that this is prescribed from above, and they are only the agents of its successful acquisition. It follows that their competence in the eyes of all their clients, and as far as their superiors are concerned, is also measurable. But they all have one common advantage, namely that they are officially recognized as having themselves mastered the subjects which they teach.

All these points suggest that teachers in England are potentially very vulnerable. Like their American counterparts, they rarely receive public acclaim (though, contrary to popular and professional opinion, their salaries are not now immodest, particularly when compared to those paid in the 1950s and early 1960s). In recent years they have been criticized by employers, and made responsible for the apparent, though not actual, decline in standards — in achievement and of behaviour — amongst children. In comparative terms, this is partly because it is not always clear precisely what they are experts in or expert at, for they have no official and detailed designations in these respects. What is more, they have to answer personally charges of irrelevance or questions of purpose, and can be written off completely by those children who are not, or cannot be, persuaded about these matters. Not surprisingly then, in the absence of clear pedagogic criteria of their worth, they tend to depend on 'charisma' in their dealings with children, and on organizational proficiency in their attempts to impress their seniors, who in turn have no better ways of judging them. In such a situation it is entirely understandable that autonomy becomes very important to teachers.

A comparative analysis of teacher autonomy is most revealing, and to this end the taxonomy in Figure 6 indicates most of those factors which need to be taken into account in all or any of our countries. Where particular forces can be shown to affect the work of teachers, then their autonomy is to that extent limited or curtailed. We will refer to this taxonomy in the discussion which follows, and it is also relevant to the points made about teacher autonomy in England in Chapters 4, 5, 6, and 7.

INTERNAL

	FORMAL	INFORMAL
A G E N C I E S	• Governing body • Head teacher • Type or level of school • Authority or responsibility structure • Bureaucratic style • Decision-making system • Subject taught • Career structures • Support structures — pastoral, disciplinary system	• Work situation — school size, buildings, resources, timetable, etc. • Definitions of 'professionalism' • Views of 'teaching' and 'good' teacher — general consensus; senior staff; significant sub-groups • Views of learning and children
	◄ **TEACHER** ►	
C L I E N T S	• Children — classes taught; formal school groups, e.g. pastoral, extra-curricular	• Interaction with individuals, sub-groups • Peer groups and their interests, conventions, attitudes
I N F L U E N C E S	• Other on-site facilities — community centre, adult education, youth club, etc.	• Ancillary staff, e.g. caretaking, school meals, cleaning, etc.

Figure 6   The web of forces acting on the teacher

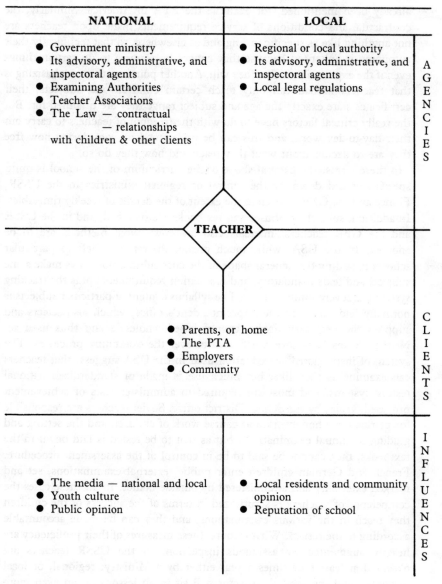

EXTERNAL

NATIONAL	LOCAL	
• Government ministry • Its advisory, administrative, and inspectoral agents • Examining Authorities • Teacher Associations • The Law — contractual — relationships with children & other clients	• Regional or local authority • Its advisory, administrative, and inspectoral agents • Local legal regulations	A G E N C I E S
TEACHER		
• Parents, or home • The PTA • Employers • Community		C L I E N T S
• The media — national and local • Youth culture • Public opinion	• Local residents and community opinion • Reputation of school	I N F L U E N C E S

Some of the constrainers of teacher autonomy in other countries have already been mentioned, for example the PTA in America. Similarly, the contractual and conditions of service requirements made upon teachers are not anything like as specific in England as elsewhere, so that technically their autonomy is enhanced because they cannot be *required* to do certain things even if the expectation is that they will. Another point worth reemphasizing is that teachers abroad can only teach certain children and subjects; their certificates state exactly the age and subject range they are qualified for. But the really critical factors have to do with the freedom of teachers to carry out their day-to-day work, and this can be understood by considering how free they are to decide about what they teach and how they do so.

In these terms, the general shape of the curriculum of the school is quite specifically laid down by the central or regional ministries in the USSR, France and the GFR — even to the extent of the details of weekly timetables. In addition, subject syllabuses and textbooks are specified, and in the USSR and the GFR teachers' manuals also lay down what methods are to be adopted. In the USA, while much greater discretion is left to particular schools regarding the general shape of the curriculum, State laws make some subjects and texts mandatory, and graduation requirements plus the tracking system put severe limits upon it. The syllabus content of particular subjects is normally laid down by the Superintendent's office, which also selects and supplies the necessary textbooks, purchased wholesale and thus used so. Neither do teachers have much control over the examining processes. The system of institutional accreditation used in the USA suggests that teachers can examine as they like; but much use is made of standardized national testing systems, and most are required to administer tests of achievement provided, again, by the School District office. Soviet teachers are responsible for marking the homework and course work of children and the setting and grading of annual examinations, but as that to be tested is laid down in the textbooks, they cannot be said to be in control of the assessment procedure. French and German children enter public, external examinations, set and marked externally and administered by outside bodies. In all these cases the competence of teachers is scrutinized in terms of the success of the children they teach in the various examinations, and they can be made accountable according to the results. What is more, these measures of their proficiency are heavily augmented by assiduous inspection. In the USSR teachers are observed at least four times a year either by a Ministry, regional, or local inspector, and the school's director will sit in on lessons on an even more regular basis. The judgements made, and the reports subsequently written, are based on a list of about 10 quite explicit headings. Inspectors elsewhere are invariably equally rigorous, and those of the GFR's *Länder* Ministries, the French Ministry and *départements*, and the American School Districts are extremely important because of the authority they wield, the degree of compliance they require, and the consequences for promotion of their reports. One last point is that careful, even legal guidelines (described in a later section below) exist in all these countries to cover teacher-pupil relationships regarding the enforcement of discipline. The inescapable conclusion which must be drawn is that, comparatively speaking, the visible constraints upon teachers in England are minimal and their autonomy is consequently enormous. Serious attention must, however, be given to what is by far the most important discussion of teachers in England of recent times, namely that provided by Grace (1978).

From his penetrating study of teachers in inner-city secondary schools, Grace suggests (op. cit., p. 218) that there are many 'invisible constraints' which limit the freedom of teachers in this country. These are: the activities of the examination boards; the way knowledge is defined as valid by those other than themselves; the general ethos and conditions under which they work; what being a good teacher or being a professional is taken to imply by the senior staff of schools. He found, in fact, (op. cit., pp. 209 and 217) that the great majority of teachers in his sample had a sense of autonomy in their work situation. However, a minority — those who had attempted some radical changes — felt the limitations placed upon them by those factors (op. cit., pp. 216-217).

While the opinion of this minority must have some validity in the sense of what some teachers in England actually think about their autonomy, in comparative terms at least, they appear to have a singularly poor case. For example, teachers abroad do not have the opportunity to opt for one out of several examining boards (on a single subject i.e. unitary basis; with a range of syllabuses on offer); to choose one of three testing modes; and to enter candidates for one, or other, or both of two different but overlapping levels of examination. What is more, teachers in England can become external examiners or moderators themselves and in some cases, while under the moderation of other sympathetic colleagues, are free to set and mark the assessment procedures. Two other complaints also fade into insignificance when considered from the perspective of teachers elsewhere, whose conditions of work are even more prescribed, and where definitions of knowledge are demonstrably externally imposed.

The position of the classroom teacher vis-à-vis the headteacher and senior deputizing assistants must be considered more carefully, for the headteacher's position in England is also singular and odd. The English headteacher's counterparts abroad are primarily administrators who implement policies decided by people who are their superiors. In the USA and France this can mean that many school principals or *proviseurs*, while having trained for and being well qualified for administration, have minimal teaching experience. Conversely, the Soviet school director, as the City Soviet's pedagogical supervisor, is periodically required to give model demonstration lessons for the benefit of his staff. Heads in England are in a very different position, for they too are singularly autonomous, and the origins and evolution of this tradition have been expertly documented by Bernbaum (1976). Despite legal niceties and the Taylor Report, they are still seen as responsible for all aspects of their school, a situation often captured by suitable nautical similes. Because of the 'employer' feature of this role, they are potentially vulnerable, which explains the many instances of sour clashes between them and the teacher association or union branches at their schools. On the other hand, their role also suggests that they have considerable power over their staff. In practice though, they tend not to interfere in the details of subject content or the methods which teachers employ. This may be because they feel incompetent to do so, and delegate such matters to heads of department whose professional integrity they respect. But it is also true that were they to do so they would bring their own autonomy into question.

Two other factors complicate matters further. First, as secondary schools have increased in size, so the tasks of internal administration have become more complex, leaving little if any time for tight pedagogical supervision. Second, 'the more diffuse approaches to teaching and learning which have recently been developed in classrooms has made for greater uncertainty about actual learning achievements', (Grace 1978, p. 107). Taken together, these trends have led heads to judge their teachers in terms of whether they hinder or facilitate them in carrying out their administration work. Teachers thus impress by how friendly and cooperative they are; how well organized they appear to be; how well they keep time; or how efficient they are at form filling and similar routines. But above all, they are judged by whether they appear to keep order. So, many become very chary of admitting to disciplinary problems because, by taking the time of senior staff and presenting them with problems, they feel they may draw critical attention to themselves. They may also, of course, find that such bureaucratic referrals are counter-productive, particularly if handled ineptly by senior staff who are perhaps unsympathetic to the problems and who do not know the children well. The children in turn can be aggrieved and can interpret the process as an admission of failure by the teacher, hence making the task of developing future relationships between them even more difficult. All this explains perhaps why so many secondary schools appear to have an ethos of being busy about incidentals rather than businesslike over fundamentals, and how certain quite unwarranted and disruptive behaviours by children gradually become conventional.

This discussion has now moved from demonstrating the scale of the autonomy of teachers in England into a discussion of some of its consequences, and whether it is proper or not. It is as well, therefore, to outline the major arguments about these matters. On the one hand there appear to be many advantages to be gained from our teachers' autonomy, which is why many abroad are envious of it. Thus, increased teacher motivation, flexibility, experimentation, vitality, and the opportunity to treat children in a way appropriate and relevant to their individual interests, needs, motivations, concerns and personal learning preferences, may accrue. Comparative examples, such as the intermittent resurfacing in America of the rights and wrongs of teaching evolution, and those documented in Chapter 5 with respect to the GFR, show that teachers do have the right to be protected from ill-informed, even malevolent pressure groups. On the other hand, there are serious dangers in a situation in which children are at the mercy of teachers who, because their competence is not specified, may or may not be enthusiastic, fair, or up to date with the subject they teach. Certainly beginning teachers find the vaguenesses about syllabus and pedagogical techniques bewildering, and a version of professionalism in which each practitioner does what and how he or she pleases does them a serious disservice. Ambiguity must also lead to teachers facing serious role conflicts, though Grace's findings (1972) show that, while many recognize the conflicting demands made of them, they do not find this a difficulty; for they resolve things by deciding, because of their autonomy, for themselves and on their own terms (op. cit., p. 108). While this is entirely understandable, it does not mean that it is defensible, for many settle for far less than they should. It is also likely that through their autonomy teachers do themselves a disservice in terms of their status and the esteem in which they are held by their clients and others. What is more, it greatly affects their dealings with children, with whom they are required, because of it, to negotiate everything. At best, these exchanges can be fruitful; at worst, they descend into conflict and hostility in which children become the teachers' main constrainers.

The critical points of the argument, then, appear to be these: Grace (1978) maintains that the nineteenth-century constraints upon teachers, which he so expertly identifies, continue still, but in more covert and invisible ways. Thus, the idea of the autonomy of teachers is perpetuated by those with power — as a gloss to cover this over. Musgrove and Taylor argued trenchantly in 1969 (and there is no reason to suggest that things are noticeably different *yet*) that 'the freedom of teachers is the profession's glory; it is the people's shame'. Chapter 7 will suggest that these two positions are in no sense irreconcilable, for both can be shown to be central elements in explaining the purposes and functions of education in England. However, the claim made here for the moment is a more limited one, namely that whatever the reasons, and with the consequences temporarily put to one side, few if any limits are placed upon the work of teachers here, *as compared with teachers abroad*. Those that do exist are quantitatively fewer and qualitatively less significant than elsewhere. Teacher autonomy cannot ever be absolute; it has inevitably to be somehow bounded. Some discussions of it which appear to neglect this fact (e.g. Young 1972) remain puzzling and partial. So this comparative analysis, focused specifically on limits, does show substantively the nature of teacher autonomy in England.

2. Children

Childhood

It is now widely accepted that notions of childhood and what was involved in being a child in the past were very different, in European and American societies, when compared with the present; and that differences also exist about these matters between contemporary societies. The three publications most influential in establishing these facts were those by Mead (1930), Erikson (1950) and Ariès (1962), though Bronfenbrenner (1972) has been an important recent addition. The conclusions drawn from these and other such studies have been various, but include the suggestion that childhood is a 'post-Rousseauesque' invention put to a number of uses, some romantic and others coercive. There are therefore certain advantages to be gained by stating in terms of first principles some notions of childhood which all five countries share; for it is an incontestable fact that in each of these societies, whether artificially or not, whether inevitably or not, the category 'child', and the concept 'childhood' do exist.

They do so mainly because the relatively new divisions of labour and specializations — by skill, trade, or occupation — which have emerged through the industrial and commercial changes which have occurred in all our countries have been augmented by the increasing significance which is now attached to chronological age. Here there are at least three broad compartments: people's working life; the years which precede it; and the years of retirement in old age. Certain legal rights, such as property holding, marriage, or the vote, are granted at specific ages. There are certain ages set for compliance to the criminal law, and the principle of diminished responsibility is applied to the young because it is felt that they cannot reasonably be held totally responsible for their own actions. The words 'baby', 'infant', 'child', and 'youth' are commonly used to describe the continuum from total dependence to total independence. But they also imply a process of evolution to maturity in which changing expectations of behaviour and capacity can be expected which require, in turn, increasing rights, duties, and responsibilities. There are, nevertheless, clear, if decreasing, imputations of inferiority attached to each of these stages, with no rigidly defined categorical points at which individuals can be said to have moved from one to the next. Obviously the extension of compulsory schooling, an important reinforcement of juvenility, seems to lengthen this procession to adulthood, already protracted by some of the economic factors already identified. Some of the psychologically inspired approaches to learning used in our countries during these years of immaturity will be discussed in Section 3 'Teaching and learning' below. But some attention must be paid first to the contrasts in the general attitudes adopted towards children in our various countries.

It is particularly appropriate here to juxtapose those of the USSR with those of our other countries, each of which has been broadly influenced by 'progressive' ideas about children, though the detailed interpretations and applications of certain central tenets have been different in each of them. The emergence of a novel and coherent set of educational ideas occurred towards the end of the nineteenth century, and the American progressive movement had its origins at this time in Dewey's pragmatic school of philosophy, which began with abstracted epistemological exactitudes, but which included important ideas about children and childhood. Its European counterpart used Rousseau as a beginning and took inspiration from the views and practices of Pestalozzi, Froebel, Montessori and others. Thereafter, in the 1920s and 1930s, through the transatlantic traffic of personnel and ideas, some of them formalized in various progressive education associations, mutual exchanges occurred through which certain terms or words came to be used in common.

As a result a shared general model of child and childhood emerged. Perhaps the key concept was that of *growth*, and it is important to recall that much use was made of Rousseau's acorn and oak tree analogy, and that Dewey's original academic training had been in biology. Children were seen as growing through various stages (later defined and refined by Piaget) to maturity, and the use of this botanical metaphor implied that they brought of themselves, and from themselves, certain faculties, attributes, capabilities, and interests. While many of these were shared or common, some were particular to individuals, for example, needs, and had to be treated with integrity. In addition growth required freedom; and for the young human organism, experience, particularly through various concrete types of activity and play, was crucial.

There are parallels between Dewey's Dynamic Principle and Marx's theory of Dialectics, for both centre upon the interrelationship between the individual and experience. Both therefore preempt previous philosophical concern about which came first and which should be given precedence. However, so far as the individual is concerned, the Soviet version of 'child' is much nearer to the Lockean *tabula rasa* with each particular slate thought of as being roughly the same size. Consequently, while individual differences and preferences are recognized, they are not considered important, and the child becomes overwhelmingly the product of experiences. Here, after Pavlov, language is seen as critical because it is the mechanism which makes sense of and orders experiences, yet simultaneously (and thus dialectically again) gives new meaning to them.

So we can now clarify the most important differences between these powerful and influential models of child and childhood. In the progressive tradition, child development should be as untrammelled and self-directed as possible, though guiding and facilitating are necessary and richness of experiential provision essential. In the Soviet view it is these inputs of experience which are critical, their quality and variety being decided upon with the clear end of a communist society in mind. Here the distinguishing human characteristics of cooperativeness and selflessness are fundamental. In progressivism, experience is not measured thus, for it is believed that societies are essentially loosely bound confederations of free individuals. Qualities are brought out of children in the one pedagogy; they are instilled into them in the other.

Adolescence

Put at its crudest, this particular age or stage is seen as those years of personal trauma experienced by all, triggered off by the physical changes which take place at puberty, and contributed to by the development of greater cognitive capacities, in which the individual searches for a sense of personal identity. This is often done through experimental thoughts and actions designed, consciously or otherwise, to test oneself, sometimes through the responses of others. It is seen as a particularly emotionally tumultuous and traumatic period because previous certainties are eroded, particularly as the threatening understanding dawns that the transformation into adulthood is imminent. At the same time adolescents are frustrated by those adults who do not respect their dignities in inter-personal relations, and resent not being granted certain adults' rights, many of which they cannot afford financially. Some psychologists argue that this stage is inevitable for all children in all societies, and always has been because of human psychological make-up; and that cases of archetypal adolescent behaviour, such as moodiness, unpredictability, aggression, temporary regression to child-like behaviour, and the rejection of adult conventions, can readily be documented in the past and have been constant themes in literature.[2] They therefore tend to recommend that children be treated sympathetically; everything should be done to ease and ameliorate their passage through these transitional years of ambiguity and limbo.

Some sociologists argue that the way modern societies are organized actually exacerbates the problems and pains suffered by adolescence. Others go further, however, and charge that particular types of society generate this period of turmoil, and that the problems are symptoms, individually suffered, of a deeper malaise within them.[3] They point to certain past periods of time or specific contemporary cultures or subcultures in which adolescence does not occur. Both State and corporate capitalism, in seeking to protract childhood so that the labour they recruit can be suitably tooled up with the skills and attitudes necessary for the work-place, induce the condition of *anomie* in youngsters, who turn for comfort and salvation to their own peers. In this process they develop values antithetical to those who threaten them, notably adults, and their solidarity is expressed in their separatist costume, appearance and language codes, musical and literary tastes, and cults of hero worship. Because these expressions are so forceful and vibrant they merit the label 'youth culture'. Two divergent explanations of this culture can be suggested. It can be seen as a coherent opposition by youth to the oppression they recognize and have not as yet succumbed to. Here it becomes either the laudable but shifting search for genuine alternatives, or the final celebration of freedom which will soon be lost. Another explanation is to regard youth culture as an artificial orchestration by certain vested interests for their own financial benefit, in which ever changing fads and fashions are therefore important.[4] Genuine originality is rapidly diluted and trivialized by commercialization; genuine sentiments are standardized and ritualized; vulgarity, even brutality and things similarly unethical, are tolerated. The hedonism of instant diversion and entertainment deflects youngsters from present and future realities, and thus they are initially contained but ultimately exploited.

Whatever the truth, there can be no doubt that schools are seriously affected in most of our countries by the culture of youth, particularly as it has now acquired an international dimension. It is therefore comparatively proper to consider in some detail the one country where its impact has been least, even minimal — the USSR.

It has not been possible for the Soviet regime to exclude the impact of Western youth culture from the USSR completely, for during the last decade at least, Western music and clothes have been popular among youngsters there. However, the potential conflicts of values which might have developed have been deflected and contained by sponsoring limited, controlled, and thus acceptable forms of its expression. Many schools have their own music 'groups', for example, who perform Western popular music publicly at Pioneer Palaces or the YCL's Palaces of Culture. Similarly, on the basis of Makarenko's work in the 1920s there has been a keen appreciation of the significance of peer-group norms, and positive steps have always been taken to sponsor these in directions seen as positive, to harness them to the fulfilment of the school's ends, and never to allow them to develop autonomously.

The Soviet Youth movement (Octobrists, Pioneers, the YCL) plays the most significant part in this process, for not only does it provide the main leisure and entertainment opportunities for youngsters (themselves carefully planned and circumscribed), it also impinges on the day-to-day life of children in schools. Group identity grows from the fact that individuals are always members of a Pioneer 'link' of four. A school class is made up of clusters of such links, and schools in turn are amalgams of classes. School and Youth movement rituals reinforce these related corporate loyalties, and generate through them the desired moral ethos. The optimum size of schools is decided partly by how well these processes can be successfully initiated, and clearly most children do have a sense of pride in *their* school.

The curriculum and disciplinary arrangements (see Chapter 4 and Section 4 below) also heavily reinforce conformity. The work that is required in classrooms is made very clear, and the marking system used each day to grade it brings immediate achievement rewards, particularly as the expectation is that all children are capable of succeeding. Rules of conduct are laid down in exact detail and positive recognition is given to exemplary behaviour through public compliments. What is more, what with school attendance, afternoon youth activity, and evening homework, children are kept very busy; with special arrangements being made to this end in vacations as well.

However, Soviet educators themselves admit that this regime does cause some problems in the years immediately following full-time education. The transition from school life — in which few decisions have to be taken, and where what has to be done at any particular time is rarely in doubt — to that of adulthood is often a difficult one. What may therefore happen is a delayed adolescent phenomenon, in which crises of identity — less exuberantly expressed but none the less critical for individuals — occur later, particularly for those who do not succeed in achieving quite as much as they had hoped for, or had been led to expect, in their level of employment. But it must be stressed that during the teenage years in the USSR there are few observable manifestations of the Western adolescent phenomenon. This is partly because they are not tolerated but mostly because, through the positive steps taken, they are not generated. Conformity is not just rewarded; it is also rewarding, comforting and comfortable. There is of course the possibility that, however successful such strategies are, they are in fact the systematic and unscrupulous application of the techniques of indoctrination. This charge is considered in Chapter 7. But it is worth pointing out that the general effects are not only important to children, but also to teachers. The cohesion of purpose, fully supported (rather than eroded) by the media, by families, by peer group values, makes their situation very different from that of teachers elsewhere. In England teachers have to contend with many contradictory influences acting upon children, which often undermine their position and what they stand for.

Other categories

Children can be variously perceived, 'seen', and thus understood — for example, according to their gender; their regional, ethnic, social class or cultural backgrounds; their abilities, aptitudes or interests. In some countries certain of these labels are deemed variously irrelevant, improper, unimportant, or invalid, and for many different reasons. These are discussed in terms of the equality principle in Chapter 6. Meanwhile it should be realized that important consequences ensue from the use of some of these labels, for they not only indicate the user's frame of reference, they are also the imputations of regard by which teachers decide how to treat children. It is not uncommon in England to hear teachers say: 'Well what do you expect, she's a girl'; or 'He's black'; or 'They're London/country kids'; or 'After all her father's left home'; or 'His parents are both doctors'; or 'They're a bright lot'. It is one thing to find out about children's background so as to be able to teach them better; it is quite another to use this information as a basis for judging them or writing them off. It is likely that in other countries different explanations based on other stereotypes exist and are similarly used, though no conclusive evidence of this is available. However, studies by Rosenthal and Jacobsen (1968), and Rist (1970) do indicate that the expectations of American teachers with respect to the ability and social class of children can determine what happens to them.

For these reasons it is worth dwelling on one abiding preconception which is deeply seated in the common sense of teachers in England, namely intelligence. Despite the fact that they rarely know the exact IQ of particular children, particularly in secondary schools, they nevertheless perceive children in terms of 'intelligence'. It is not just that they use such words as 'bright', 'average', 'thick', or 'dumb'; they also tend to lump children into three (never four or five or two) discrete groups, and in arithmetical numbers according to the normal distribution curve of intelligence tests, irrespective of their *actual* abilities. This happens despite the fact that the general intake of some schools is quite unrepresentative and untypical nationally. It is salutory therefore to recount why Soviet educators reject the concept of intelligence. Their rebuttal takes the following form:

1. They report that Western psychologists claim to have discovered a new human faculty called intelligence, which they find difficult to define precisely but which, with suitable refinements, they understand to be a central cognitive capacity. Further, despite its elusiveness of definition, intelligence can be measured by suitably invented tests.

2. They point out not only that intelligence thus becomes a capacity to do intelligence tests, but that an assumption has been made that human *faculties* are distributed amongst the population according to the statistical law of normal distribution which applies to human physical characteristics, such as weight, height, strength etc. Thus, when tests of intelligence were piloted they were found acceptable only if they succeeded in producing test scores amongst the sample groups used according to this familiar curve.

3. They argue that this was a totally unwarranted assumption, for human faculties, whether spiritual, affective, creative, or cognitive, are not necessarily commensurate with physical attributes. Thus, for example, even Christian theology never postulated that the righteous were numbered in terms of a bell-shaped curve.

4. They maintain that, whilst the triangular shape of the disproportionate distribution of wealth and power amongst people in feudalism has shifted, it has done so only to capitalism's hexagon, and this latter is clearly reflected in the basic assumptions underlying intelligence.

So $\bigcirc$ equals

As such it is ideologically rather than scientifically founded.

5. They charge that intelligence became a necessary new way of defining and measuring merit given the increasing unacceptability of birth. But because of its ideology, not only was social stratification not challenged, support was given through it to its existing shape. What was more, a happy way of accommodating those from the lowest ranks, newly found to be of worth, was available. Given the geneticist foundations of intelligence, those with it could be solicited to invigorate the élite and guarantee its vitality, efficiency, and continuation.

We may not agree with this line of argument, though its coherence is impressive, but it does show clearly that all conceptual categories through which children are understood are founded on certain premises. Such foundations need to be considered carefully, for very important consequences of treatment arise from them. The tripartite structure of post-1944 compulsory secondary education was developed on these fundamental assumptions made about intelligence and its distribution. Despite the new institutional arrangements made after 1966, much that goes on in comprehensive schools is still governed by them. The whole character of mass education in England would have developed quite differently had some alternative initial view of children been adopted.

3. Teaching and learning

In this section we examine the differences which exist between our countries regarding teaching and learning. In addition, the way in which the activity of teaching is seen as relating to that of learning is not entirely held in common, and again these differences will be considered. A cogent argument exists which suggests that it is not proper to consider teaching and learning as two discrete entities because they are organically interrelated and should therefore be discussed as such. Marxists also find error in the dichotomization of the two terms, and prefer to highlight their dialectic interconnections. In the Welsh language, *dysgu* is both teaching and learning. However, for heuristic purposes we will begin with the activity 'teaching' and then consider how it interrelates with ideas about learning.

Because the teachers in our countries are formally invested with certain responsibilities by the system which employs them, because they opt to contract themselves to fulfil these, and because of the requirements of the schooling context, their work does contain certain shared features. For example, at its most general their role is to implement the purposes and functions cast for schools by the particular society which they work in, and these are discussed in some detail in Chapter 7. However they share certain common *tasks* which have to be performed in all classrooms and it is possible to list these as follows:

1. **Instructional tasks**   These involve the establishment of the actual content to be learned, often broken down under such headings as skills, techniques, facts, terms, concepts, processes. There are decisions to be taken about the methods of teaching to be used (e.g. explaining, demonstrating, questioning, discussing), and there are the actual activities designed to promote learning which children will be required to do (e.g. listening, experimenting, writing, drawing, copying, imagining). It is even possible that some teaching skills are shared internationally (e.g. ways of asking questions and of giving instructions).

2. **Organizational and administrative tasks**   Here decisions about and actions regarding the use of the time and space available have to be made; the classroom furnishings have to be organized; the equipment and materials needed by the teacher or children for particular activities have to be arranged.

3. **Assessment and evaluation tasks**   These have two levels. Judgements are made, sometimes subjectively, sometimes on the basis of some form of evidence from the work done or via the results of tests or examinations, of what and how much children have learnt and are learning. At another level this evaluation of

children can be used by teachers in deciding how effective they are in their teaching.

4. **Disciplinary tasks** It is not necessary to subscribe to Waller's idea (1932) that classrooms are inevitably arenas of conflict between teachers and children, though his analysis still merits careful attention. However, even where classrooms are places of mutual cooperation and where the joy of learning is expressed, disciplinary tasks are endemic to the work of teachers. Definitions of what a well-disciplined classroom is like vary, and certainly the instructional and organizational efficiency of teachers, the degree to which they can generate interest and excitement, the extent to which children are motivated to learn, and the personality traits of teachers are all quite crucial elements in its achievement. But even so, teachers do still have to establish certain conventions of classroom behaviour; some for reasons of safety, others so as to produce an atmosphere conducive to learning for all members of the group. Rules are required which have to be enforced; and while the processes of explaining them and negotiating them may be protracted, the punishment of those who infringe them is inevitable.

5. **Pastoral and welfare tasks** Teachers endeavour to help children who, perhaps temporarily, have personal problems of some kind. They will do this mostly perhaps because they wish to help individuals suffering distress, but partly also because such difficulties inhibit the child's attempts to learn. In an extended form, because the sources of the problem may lie outside the school the teacher here will become something of a social worker, moving out into homes or the community in his or her aiding endeavours.

Whilst it is true that these tasks are shared by all teachers, some of them will be approached very differently, depending, for example, on the ages of the children being taught or the subject matter to be learned, but also on the views about education and learning held in a particular country or indeed by an individual teacher. Some teachers see certain of their tasks as far more significant than others and so define their work almost exclusively in terms of one or two sets of them, to the exclusion of others. Examples of this which have already been referred to are worth reiterating. In general, the specialist subject teachers in the French *lycée*, holding the *agrégé* qualification and thus only teaching 15 hours per week, are almost certainly overwhelmingly devoted to instructional and assessment tasks. The children they teach are the select few, and are likely to be well motivated. Any disciplinary difficulties are referred elsewhere. They see few reasons to concern themselves with pastoral or welfare issues. Their approach to instruction is primarily in terms of dispensing esoteric knowledge, of which they are acknowledged masters. They tend to judge their pupils according to their achievements in acquiring this knowledge and are likely to consider information about their backgrounds, problems, and so on, as irrelevant.

For the high-school teacher in America the instructional and assessment tasks are also paramount. Although they may take an interest in the children they teach, separate guidance specialists are available to them, and as most teach students who have opted to do their courses — many of whom will at least be extrinsically well motivated — the complexion of the disciplinary difficulties they experience will be coloured by these factors. On the other hand, all tasks are expected of Soviet teachers. They are contractually obliged to visit the parents of children in their homes as and when necessary, and are similarly required to do a certain amount of unpaid 'social' work in the community (e.g. sitting as magistrates; working for the Party; helping with Pioneer activities). All teachers are expected to be involved in pastoral work, and while their instructional and disciplinary tasks are also crucially important, both are rigidly defined for them.

In the sections that follow in this chapter further issues relating to assessment and evaluation, and discipline are taken up in detail. We must now focus on how the classroom teachers in our five countries interpret their instructional tasks. They are considerably influenced by what views they have about how children learn. Many definitions and explanations of learning exist and whilst none are by any means entirely adequate, some general theories — those of behaviourism in the USA, those of developmentalism in England, and those of cognition and thinking in the USSR — have been highly influential.

To the observer there are many similarities between Soviet pre-school classrooms and those catering for the early years of childhood elsewhere. The equipment, designed to develop motor skills, physical confidence and balance, the ability to differentiate, categorize, weigh, count, and recognize shapes, is often identical. Practical play activities which are also very similar to those used elsewhere are organized. However, in many respects these are only surface similarities. The daily timetable of events is specified for all pre-schools by the Ministry, and very specific reasons exist in terms of expected learning outcomes for each of them. The materials, and the uses they are put to by children, are very heavily teacher directed. Tasks and expectations of behaviour are all carefully graded from simple to more complex, so that even at this age the approach of imparting to children specified achievement skills is most noticeable. The main aim is to develop those abilities and understandings relevant and preparatory to the work of the primary classes of 10-year schools. This includes getting children to cooperate, and constant use is made of giving positive public recognition to examples of good behaviour.

It must be stressed that the impartation model of learning which infuses the whole of Soviet schooling, including higher education, begins at this very early stage. In art work, for example, materials appropriate for very young children are selected, and structured activities with them are organized. All children are first taught exactly how to execute a particular skill, such as holding a pencil, drawing a line, using scissors, mixing paint; and exercises are designed which ensure that they master and refine them — for example, various types of brush strokes in painting; various ways of folding and sticking paper or card. They then proceed to use these skills on a set activity — painting a landscape, say. The whole group of children is provided by the teacher with precisely the items of equipment which will be needed, and is then taken through each set step. As a result they all produce more or less the same picture, which contains what they have been required to put in. Whilst this is obviously a rigid process, it is nevertheless a good example of the Soviet view of learning, in that all the children do master the specified skills because each child is carefully taught them. Further, Soviet educators argue that without these skills no child can progress to more complex, and eventually original, activities; and that much time is wasted by allowing children either to learn things by trial and error themselves, or worse still, to fail to learn entirely.

The primary classes of the 10-year school in the USSR bear little resemblance to those in our other countries. Classes are quite large, often as many as 36 children, who sit at double desks arranged in rows; the teacher operates from the front of the class; the walls are bare of work, though rooms are usually decorated with pictures and plants. Lessons are formal, and children do a great deal of reading and writing work, with textbooks and exercise books as their main materials. The reading, writing and arithmetic exercises or drills which have to be accomplished are again carefully structured and graded, and are suitably introduced by explanations and instructions to the whole class by the teacher, who is also most assiduous about marking. There is no hint of the integration of activities, or of children being allowed to work at their own pace. Whilst the atmosphere is formal, with very specific rules and standards of behaviour, classroom relationships between teachers and children are friendly and praise is generously and again publicly given. For three years then, of the 24 weekly classroom hours, between 16 and 18 are given over to the task, approached thus, of teaching all children the skills of numeracy and literacy. (The remaining time is devoted to art, singing, physical education, and nature study.) The argument is that the work of the secondary specialist classes cannot be done without these basics, and Soviet evidence suggests that all but about 5% of children (who are required to repeat a year if they do not come up to the necessary standard of their particular age group) master these skills by age 10.

This general stance to learning is also apparent in the secondary classes. Much attention is given initially to the basic and necessary facts in a particular topic, with special technical terms being carefully identified and defined. Next, significant concepts and processes are taught, and then children are required to use the information they have acquired. All lessons follow a similar format, beginning with a period of recapitulation of the work of the previous lesson, during which individuals are asked questions or are required to go over their homework, often on the blackboard. Next comes an explanation of the new work of the lesson, and then homework is set. Teachers spend much time dispensing knowledge and explaining ideas with the help of those audio-visual aids useful to such processes. So, in science lessons children rarely if ever do experiments themselves, but they do watch many demonstrations by teachers. Language laboratories are provided in most schools, and fluency in speaking a foreign language is stressed, but much time is spent teaching grammatical and syntactical rules, with their exceptions, together with points of colloquial or idiomatic usage. Little music making apart from singing occurs, but an ability to read and write musical notations is required. Physical education, which takes place in well equipped gymnasia, is very much of the Swedish drill variety, and the whole group of boys or girls (for they are taught PE separately) use each piece of apparatus, and thus practise a particular physical skill, in order. They are under strict direction from the teacher, who will demonstrate precisely what is required before beginning the activity.

A useful way of illustrating the relationships between teaching and learning in the USSR is provided in Figure 7 which summarizes the training programme for a secondary specialist teacher of English at the famous Hertzen Pedagogical Institute at Leningrad.

There are implicit here very clear models of both teaching and learning. The teacher is someone who is an expert in a particular subject, for although

Note: Figures indicate hours per week, throughout the year.

Subject	Year 1	Year 2	Year 3	Year 4	Year 5	Total	Sub-total
English	19	19	12	12	10	72	
History of English Language	—	2	—	—	—	2	
English Lexicology	—	—	2	—	—	2	
English Literature	—	—	—	2	2	4	
Area Study	—	—	—	2	2	4	84
Latin	2	—	—	—	—	2	
German or Spanish	—	—	10	10	10	30	32
General Linguistics	2	—	—	—	—	2	
Theoretical Phonetics	—	—	—	2	—	2	4
History of CPSU	4	2	—	—	—	6	
Philosophy & Dialectics	—	2	1	—	—	3	
Policital Economy	—	—	2	—	—	2	
Marxism	—	—	—	2	—	2	13
General Psychology	2	—	—	—	—	2	
General Pedagogics	—	3	—	—	—	3	
History of Pedagogics	—	—	2	—	—	2	
Methods of English Teaching	—	—	—	2	—	2	9
Teaching Practice	—	—	—	6 weeks	8 weeks		
Weekly Hours Involved	29	28	29	31	24		

Figure 7 Summary of 5-year teacher education programme for teachers of English at the Hertzen Pedagogical Institute, Leningrad

pedagogics, methods, and school practice are attended to, the overwhelming amount of time spent is on the acquisition of competence in the subject matter. Learning is the passive acquisition by children of knowledge, dispensed to them by experts. While some children may learn more slowly than others, they are all thought of as being potentially capable of being made expert. This last point has one very important consequence for teachers. Although some children are recognized as experiencing learning difficulties because of some unfortunate extraneous factor such as inadequate parental support, generally speaking if any do fail to achieve, then it is the teacher's fault. Given this model of child, no other explanation is possible. Soviet teachers therefore cannot resort to some of the excuses used by teachers elsewhere.

Soviet educators reject most Western theorists of learning — Piaget and other developmental psychologists because the empirical basis of their claims is deemed unscientific; while the premises of others, notably Bruner, are seen as quite unrealistic. They also point out that the ideas of American 'progressivism' were tried in the 1920s by Krupskaya and Lunacharsky but were found wanting and rejected because children just did not learn enough. In establishing what to teach to a particular age group, and how, the Academy of Pedagogical Sciences conducts its own controlled teaching experiments in ordinary classrooms before the Ministry of Education makes any changes in the syllabuses or the teachers' handbooks of methods. In addition to this sort of content analysis, the general view is that a continuum exists in any content, beginning with skills, proceeding to facts, information and technical terms, then to concepts and their application. Creativity is greatly prized, and very broadly defined — for example it is as applicable in physics and engineering as it is to literature or the arts. But the assumption is that creativity is only possible *after* this hierarchy of understandings has been achieved.[5]

Judgements about the success of this approach to learning are notoriously difficult to make, for lack of the appropriate and reliable evidence. Most Western visitors to Soviet classrooms are impressed with what they see, in the sense that children appear eager, enthusiastic, exceptionally well motivated, confident, and on the observable evidence, competent and even accomplished. What must be stressed, however, is that estimations should always be made in terms of Soviet frames of reference, namely their views of what mass education should be.

The general appearance of American schools and classrooms is very different. At the primary level, open-plan classrooms are now very common, partly because they were found to be less expensive to build. Activity methods and group work, often involving team teaching, are much in evidence, with a great variety of work going on simultaneously. In high schools the specialist subject rooms or areas are usually generously equipped and sumptuously furnished for practical work by children. Workshops, studios and laboratories exist to this end; work on quarterly projects in the humanities and social sciences are supported by a wealth of materials provided by resource centres and libraries with full-time librarians with specialist qualifications for school work; the choice of activities in physical education is usually immensely varied, and the quality of the facilities and the coaching available are excellent. These features are the legacy of the growth, experience, and activity notions of the early progressive education movement, and it might seem that teachers, far from being dispensers of information, are facilitators of the self-directed and controlled learning of children.

However, there is another level of operation at work, for two crucial concepts from behaviourism became superimposed upon American 'progressive' ideas about learning, namely those of 'objectives' and 'planning'. Thus all activities are invariably 'programed'; much use is made of linear step-by-step instructional materials, even teaching machines, most of which are commercially produced and used in all the schools of a particular District. Here the special interests or idiosyncrasies of individual children are discounted, for they are seen as irrelevant in this version of learning. This is certainly the approach used for activities designed to equip children with basic writing, spelling, reading and computational skills. High-school textbooks are similarly carefully, even minutely staged, with the activities which need to be accomplished stated, as well as the knowledge content. Teachers therefore operate within a stimulus, response, reinforcement, conditioning frame of reference when organizing activities, and they are often required to enter their aims and objectives upon complex and finely subdivided matrices, again provided by the school's administration. Children's progress is constantly monitored and recorded, which is justified and explained by the intrinsic rewards which they therefore receive, with positive motivational outcomes. In all this, the activity methods adopted are carefully contrived and controlled, with pre-stated, measurable learning outcomes being involved. Those things which are not amenable to such specification and measurement tend to be discounted as unsuitable or unnecessary. Teachers here are instructional experts in that they are responsible for devising and then carefully managing and supervising those processes which produce learning thus understood. Children do often master a very broad range of topics. However, those who are slow to respond, or fail to achieve, tend to be explained away as lacking diligence and therefore having only themselves to blame. Nevertheless, as in the USSR, those children who are prepared to take on trust the validity of the procedures which they are asked to go through, and who apply themselves assiduously to the tasks set, are able to make noticeable achievements.

The validity of these generalizations about American classrooms is supported by the approaches adopted to the compensatory education programmes of the 1960s, for most of them attempted to break with this general approach to teaching and learning. It is true that some projects like that of Bereiter and Engleman (1966) stayed with a highly structured, strongly teacher directed mode of operation, concentrating heavily on the development of very specific skills, but these were the minority. Most projects were characterized by such words as 'free choice', 'self-expression', 'self-direction', 'natural', 'spontaneous', and were often supported, as in Silberman (1973), by reference to practices in England. They were conscious attempts to try and improve learning by rejecting traditional styles. Thereafter, however, a simultaneous decline occurred both in funding and in confidence in such approaches, with a consequent return to older ways.

It is now possible to make some comparative sense of teaching and learning in England, though this is no easy task, for the situation here is very confused. For example, while primary schools have undoubtedly been greatly influenced by 'progressive' ideas, the evidence of the HMI survey of Primary Education in England (DES 1978b) from their sample of 542 schools, suggests that such practices are nothing like as widespread as had often been assumed. At the secondary level, an impact has also been made upon classroom activities by the percolation of progressive ideas, and by, for example, the Nuffield (sciences) and Schools Council (history, geography, and the whole curriculum) projects. But it is more difficult to know what *exactly* goes on in classrooms in England because of the autonomy of teachers. For this reason, consideration will be given first to what a *theoretical* version of teaching and learning in England might appear to be, and then to the ways in which it is implemented or practised by teachers.

To begin with it is useful to point up those very general parameters of teaching and learning which do undeniably exist. One way of putting this is that first educational principles, second processes, and third evaluation must be involved. Another construction would be that due account has to be taken of the content to be taught or learned, the methods of teaching which are employed, and the learning activities which are organized. Teachers are therefore inevitably involved in planning, doing and reflecting. From this starting point it is possible to rehearse some of the arguments which might be used in England to criticize Soviet and American approaches, and to show why they are both deemed inappropriate here. So far as the USSR is concerned, it could be said that teaching and learning there appear to be totally dominated by considerations to do with subject content; that 'methods' are defined exclusively in terms of teaching techniques. Further, that the learning activities used appear inert, with rote memorization being overstressed and with children learning a lot *about* science, history, and so on, but never *doing* any of these subjects. Similarly, the English view is that children should not be viewed as passive recipients, for they bring much of themselves to the learning processes, and thus the 'discrete continuum' mode of analyzing the content to be learned seems unrealistic.

With regard to America, the contention might be that behaviourism is manipulative and thus unethical, and that its methods define learning as joyless and tedious, little account being taken of what happens in children's actual learning interactions. Again, by beginning with pre-stated objectives, and through the myopic pre-planning of everything in their terms, learning becomes rigidified, with the unpredictable and uncountable being excluded. This is a negative picture of what learning is *not* like so far as we in England are concerned. The other more positive side of the coin must now be described.

Many publications have appeared in the last 20 years in England stating and debating the 'progressive' approach to teaching and learning. Probably because of Dearden's tincture of iron (1968 and 1976) it is no longer possible to wave unexplicated slogans such as 'spelling is caught rather than taught', 'readiness', being 'beside the child', 'child-centredness', or 'interests'. Indeed very complex and subtle interpretations of many of these, and other terms, are emerging. For example, the key ideas in one of the best recent discussions of the primary curriculum, provided by Blenkin and Kelly (1982), are 'process' and 'a unified curriculum', both of which comply with key 'educational principles'. So proper account is taken of all the dimensions of teaching and learning alluded to earlier. Here such factors as time, space, place, structure, materials, skills, topics, subjects, and concepts are all realities. Through the flexible and sensitive practice of their art, teachers at one moment recognize and stress content, at another the best activity to promote it; but then are also capable of redefining it according to how children respond or react. They build into activities devised to generate the understanding of ideas, the acquisition of skills, and are all the while conscious of and carefully checking children's successes or otherwise. Here the teacher is sometimes instructor and provider; at others guide and facilitator; and always organizer. Similarly impressive justificatory explanations are used at the secondary level for the new orientations to subject teaching used in the projects already mentioned. For example, children are encouraged to learn by *doing* scientific experiments, by constructing history themselves from source material, by conducting geographical or sociological surveys, and by making music. They are required to learn those principles, procedures and concepts central to the contemporary study of mathematics, rather than those of the past. It is recommended that foreign languages should be acquired, not by learning and applying the rules of grammar, but via the direct method of teaching through constant oral usage of the language in ways close to those in which children learned their first language.

In each of these examples the approach to learning and teaching is infused at all times by central educational principles. The learning content and the methods adopted are expressions of these principles, and must therefore be congruent with them. The principles emerge once education is seen as that which develops children's understanding, their critical awareness, and their autonomy. It has essential, intrinsic value rather than instrumental aims. Such a synopsis does insufficient justice to the complexity and subtlety of all these ideas, for they represent a unique and highly sophisticated version of the relationships between teaching and learning.

On the other hand, whilst these are the theoretical intentions, what *actually* goes on in classrooms bears only a superficial resemblance to all these ideas, though it is true that some teachers are able to put them into practice often to startlingly good effect. More typically, however, in observing many primary classrooms it becomes clear that although they often appear lively, busy places, with a hive of disparate activity going on which children appear to both enjoy and be happy with, careful scrutiny shows that there is much pointlessness, underachievement, entertainment and containment as well. When asked, children in secondary classrooms often appear unsure about what they are supposed to be doing and why. Children at both levels often indulge in the tasks arranged for them in a desultory way showing little involvement, and at times employ the equipment or materials provided entirely to their own devices which, by chance, may at times be highly original, but which are often rather pointless and occasionally actually malevolent and destructive. In these situations the original ideas and intentions are being inadequately and improperly executed. When pressed to explain or comment upon what is going on in their rooms, teachers often display either their very partial understandings or even complete misunderstandings of them. Some illustrations seem appropriate.

Too many primary schools still timetable their days into activities which distinguish some as 'work' and others as 'play'. This split not only does violence to the intended learning relationships between these two concepts, it also effectively defines some things quite wrongly. False connotations of superiority and inferiority are acquired from these labels. There is fun in writing and mathematics; painting or music involve very hard work. Similarly, while the provision of sand and water for children to 'play' with is common practice in infant classes, in their interventions into the uses to which children put these materials many teachers display little understanding that the acquisition of important concepts (like volume, weight, flotation, etc.) are meant to be fostered by them. Activities are generated which are intended to permit self-expression or to develop aesthetic sensitivities, but children are often given little help with the fundamental skills necessary, and whatever they are able to do with the clay or paint or wood or scrap material is accepted uncritically, though many of them are frustrated by their lack of success. Teachers often talk in Piagetian terms, yet display no real understanding of them, or of the fact that many of them are now seen as highly questionable. Some, in conversation, indicate that they consider they employ certain 'modern' activity learning methods merely because they hope thereby better to achieve the acquisition by children of very traditional basic skills. They seem not to appreciate that very radical alternative objectives are in fact intended by these methods. Others, when asked for explanations for the inadequacy of a child's progress by its parents, account for this in terms of 'readiness'. Yet they display no appreciation of the fact that, while a child may not yet be 'ready' for reading or for a particular mathematical topic, it is their professional task to work out ways of getting it to be so. Intervention is necessary and teachers are the people who are supposed to be skilled in precisely these sorts of techniques. This is what parents, quite properly, expect of a school. For parents to be congratulated upon having a pleasant, happy, well-adjusted, cooperative, well-liked child may be a pleasant experience, but it is of only partial relevance and can also amount to being fobbed off.

These sorts of problems are by no means confined to primary schools. For example, the way in which many secondary schools organize field-work projects or school journeys, including those abroad, remains very unsatisfactory. In some schools it is not possible for all the children to be involved, which immediately raises questions of logic. If the enterprise is really important, why are some children excluded? In some cases this occurs for financial reasons — invariably parents are expected to subsidize the costs involved, and many are not prepared to admit their impecuniousness, so agree to their children's non-participation. Because of inadequate planning and the lack of clarity about the purpose of the exercise, what the children who are involved actually do, or positively learn, is largely of their own making.

Without doubt, most teachers, particularly at primary level, are excellent at organizing and managing classrooms; they treat children, most of whom thoroughly enjoy going to school, in a humane way. But the suspicion remains that teachers operate methods of working which have become expected of them, without really grasping their full implications. At the primary stage few of them really know enough about mathematics (cf. arithmetic) or science, or what it might mean to be a poet, historian, musician, painter, dancer or athlete. There is also, of course, the question of whether they can reasonably be expected to know.

This therefore raises a very serious issue: whether it is possible, in ordinary schools with current teacher-pupil ratios, for the average teacher to operate the ideas of the English progressive education literature; for it must be stressed that herculean demands are made upon any of those who try.[6] It may be that Soviet and American practices reflect a much more realistic appreciation of what is possible, feasible, and reasonable in the context of mass public schooling. Meanwhile, what appears to happen in many classrooms in England is that attempts are made to implement a partially understood version of teaching and learning which, while conceptually elegant and convincing, is too complex to be amenable to general application by the calibre of people recruited to teaching. The exact mechanisms involved are not entirely clear, but what appears to happen is that those responsible for teacher education take up certain ideas (Froebel, Dewey, Dalton, Bruner) or research evidences (Piaget, Bernstein). They then interpret them and pass them on to student teachers, who are required to organize their classroom practices accordingly. There are at least four points in this chain of events where distortions, perversions or mutations can occur.[7]

However, matters cannot be left there, for there are a number of ways in which it could be suggested that this situation has the effect of making schooling in England singularly *élitist*. Thus, if in our classrooms diffuse techniques of teaching and learning mean that children do not understand what is going on, what they should be doing, or why, then the educational processes which they experience serve only to mystify. In an unstructured, open-plan situation, devoid of obvious limits, and with insufficient clarity and precision of perceivable purpose, the children who benefit most are those who can, from their own resources (whether cognitive or familial) make sense of things. This is why such a climate can be detrimental to those who are anything less than outstanding in their abilities and achievements. Many teachers argue that if children at a particular developmental age cannot understand something, then that topic is deemed inadmissable, because they are not prepared to require its rote learning. However, it is the case that some things are not amenable to anything but memorization — a concept which has, most unfortunately, become equated with sterility. Further, those children who are not able to understand what is involved in a particular problem (e.g. 'What is the area of this room?'), because they are not given at least a standard formula for its solution cannot even get an answer to it. A class of children is often asked to embark on an open-ended project which involves, say, selecting a topic, researching it in various books which they are expected to hunt out in local libraries, and writing it up, with suitable pictures or illustrations. The idea behind this approach is perfectly defensible in some ways, in that children are given experience in using research skills, and are not inhibited by someone in authority telling them what to do or think. They can define the issues, discuss them, and present them in their own terms. They become themselves producers of knowledge. Yet it remains the case that those who are already capable of analytical thought, who have access in their homes to books and encyclopedias, and have a member of their household who can help them to discover information, refine and marshal their ideas, and so on, are at a distinct advantage. Those less blessed will inevitably produce less satisfactory products, and some find the scale of the tasks involved so overwhelming that they manage almost nothing. Thus can the least endowed become hindered rather than helped. At the same time it should be noted that this style of approach, often used in CSE course work, is closely modelled upon that of the university researcher. But such persons are able to operate as they do only after many years of preparation. This point also applies specifically to the way in which many of the secondary science courses were conceived, for they defined science, and thus what should go on in school laboratories, as being that activity which is conducted in, and by, university science departments (cf. David Layton's *Science for the People* 1973).

Further élitist effects of the universities can be seen at work in the history of the Schools Council's N and F proposals for examinations at 18+. The excellent case made for introducing breadth both in content and in those capable of presenting themselves as candidates at these proposed levels, was negated by the universities' insistence that they would not countenance changing either their traditional position of teaching only the élite, or the way in which they organized their highly specialized degree courses.

It does seem clear, then, that the approaches to teaching and learning in England are, comparatively speaking, novel and adventurous. An entirely convincing and elegant set of progressive ideas, very different from those which were developed in the USA, have emerged; with radical implications for mass schooling. Serious doubts remain about whether they have been put into practice in classrooms. It follows that the quality and autonomy of teachers in England need careful scrutiny; and this scrutiny must include their initial preparation and their continued inservice education. Two serious risks are involved in recent developments. One is that, far from *reducing* élitism in education, there is the distinct possibility that it has been and is being intensified. The other is that the unwarranted claim will be made that the principles of English progressive education cannot be applied to a mass system of schooling. This will lead to a rejection of the way teaching and learning has been formulated and the work of schools will be re-stated in terms of those activities which are achievable by the calibre of existing teachers. The danger here is that schools will develop in noneducational and essentially reactionary ways.

4. Discipline

In Chapter 2 we argued that certain codes of behaviour are necessary in all schools. Some of these will exist for reasons of physical safety — to cover the movement of large numbers of people through the building; or in specialist teaching areas such as workshops, laboratories or gymnasia, where particular hazards may be encountered and also in all other types of classroom. Others will be required if learning is to be maximized. It follows that school rules are therefore necessary and are usually formally laid down by those in authority. Clearly, mechanisms of enforcement are also inevitable, for children do not, of their own volition, abide by a rule merely because it has been promulgated to them; and it also follows that the punishment of transgressors becomes similarly inevitable. So it is worth looking at those rules which exist in the schools of our foreign countries, and the disciplinary mechanisms used by them.

All children of whatever age in all the schools throughout the Soviet Union are required to abide by a list of 20 rules (see Grant 1979, p. 57). They are very wide ranging, and cover the behaviour expected in the classroom, on the school premises, in homes, and in neighbourhoods. They are also very specific, covering the exact details of such things as posture, how and when to answer a teacher's question, when to stand or sit down, how to proceed with homework, even what to do on a bus or train. They are also a series of clear statements of the Soviet view of proper ethical attitudes, involving qualities such as diligence, respect and duty. In addition, they remove all ambiguities for both teachers and children about what is expected. These general rules are augmented by guidelines appropriate to particular age groups, specifying subsidiary expectations of behaviour and certain domestic tasks, such as tidying up and shoe cleaning, with increased demands being made as children get older. They display the evolutionary stages in Soviet notions of moral education.

Such specificity and precision does not exist in any of our other countries, though in the GFR, to ensure that parents are completely aware of their legal rights, all schools are required in law to apply certain rules. For example, the age at which children may leave the school premises, if they are not timetabled, is established by the relevant *Land* Ministry, and the exact steps which teachers have to take before a child can be excluded from a classroom, or suspended from school, are laid down. In the hand-books issued to all students in American high schools, there is always a detailed section containing the general rules of conduct required. These invariably include such headings as automobile parking, absence, truancy, dress codes, conduct on the school bus, and the procedures required of school administrators if they wish to temporarily suspend a student. In addition, rules are laid down to cover behaviour in corridors and public areas of the school; responsibilities with regard to the disposal of trash; the situations in which a student's locker or person may be searched; the consequences in cases of proven vandalism, theft, smoking, cheating, profanity, disobedience, fighting, and harrassment. More significantly, School Districts often make regulations to cover exactly how a teacher may, and may not, punish a student. In many, every teacher is required to provide each class they take with those rules of classroom behaviour they expect, and although the details are left to their discretion, those which appear unreasonable are publicly identifiable. What is more, in the case of a child identified as being 'tardy' because it has consistently infringed classroom rules, and therefore referred to senior staff, exact statements regarding the nature of the alleged offences can be made, mutually understood, and discussed. The guidance and counselling staff provide formal mechanisms for the enforcement of discipline, and children who cause teachers inordinate difficulties of noncooperation can be referred to them.

While it is true that this branch of the school's faculty is sometimes viewed with suspicion by the instructional staff, it is often the case that counsellors do use a wide range of techniques which are most useful to teachers and students alike. In particular, they employ diagnostic tests designed to uncover physical, cognitive or affective malfunctioning, some of which may be very minor but none the less important if unrecognized. Interviews with parents may be arranged, and through discussion detailed advice or suggestions about the most beneficial pedagogical approaches to particular children may be made available. The internally agreed code of practice which high schools have in these matters results from initiatives taken by the School Principal, who often discusses the issues involved with the Policies Committee of the Student Senate, the PTA, even community interest groups.

The existence of a separate disciplinary staff in French secondary schools has already been mentioned. The *censeur* is assisted by a number of *conseillers d'éducation* — usually one per hundred or so of children — who are in turn helped by *maîtres d'internat* or *pions*, most of whom work on a part-time basis and are often quite young. They may even be students in higher education. Each school has a representative body of students — *conseil des responsables* — made up of elected delegates from each class, with whom the school authorities negotiate, explaining and seeking support for their actions. While there is a high degree of formality, even legal nicety, in these arrangements, this does not guarantee success, due particularly to the youth and inexperience of the *pions*. But at least parents and children are fully aware of their rights and responsibilities.

The most rigorous enforcement mechanisms of all are those used in the USSR. Parents and teachers are made fully aware, through the documents to this effect provided for them by the Ministry of Education, what disciplinary procedures they should adopt. The first step is that children should be required to obey the rules. Transgressions must immediately be noted and drawn to public attention. The initial punishment recommended is the withdrawal of adult love, attention and regard. However, examples of good behaviour must be publicly applauded, and as soon as the child is old enough to understand them every opportunity must be taken to explain the reasons behind a rule, and why breaches of it are serious matters. Soviet educators argue that it is from this process of total obedience, and the understanding of reasons that self-discipline and moral autonomy eventually emerge. The way in which examples of misbehaviour are handled merits careful description. The first thing that a teacher does is to require an explanation of an individual's failings from the other members of its 'link', who are asked what steps they have taken. Thus, whilst children can expect immediate help from others with those aspects of their work which they are finding difficult, they are also almost certain to be chastized by them; for the misbehaviour of one immediately reflects on three others. In addition, repeated examples of poor behaviour are used to bring shame upon a whole class, and children are then brought before the Pioneer courts, whose officials are their peers, and where cases are publicly debated and remedial actions stipulated. In this way peer group pressures are systematically used to promote conformity.

Many Western observers see this process as inciting children to 'split' upon each other, and Bronfenbrenner's evidence (1972) suggests that Soviet children have no compunctions whatsoever about reprimanding each other about poor behaviour and if necessary also informing adults. But many of the behaviours involved are reprehensible, even immoral and intolerable. The Western condonement of silence and group concealment by children often causes serious malpractices to go undiscovered and discourages the development of group responsibility. It is not surprising, perhaps, that through these processes most children in the USSR do conform, but in extreme cases two further steps are open to the school. First, teachers can visit parents in their homes, accompanied if necessary by a member of the school's Parents' Committee, and explanations can be required for a child's continued recalcitrance. Second the trade union officials at the place of the parents' employment can be informed, and they too can intercede — publicly if necessary — requiring the parents to give an account of themselves.

Some of these strategies would be viewed with repugnance in England, but certain general comparative points relating to rules and their enforcement are worth making. The behaviour conventions expected of children, and school discipline in general, express in part those moral and ethical values perpetuated by our schools. In the countries discussed above, many of these are attended to by administrative agencies outside the schools, who establish broad norms and lay out clearly the rights and responsibilities of parents, teachers and children alike. So far as specific schools are concerned, clear regulations usually exist about behaviour in the school at large, the procedures by which miscreants will be treated and, more significantly, what is expected of children in classrooms.

In England, however, while it appears that certain attributes are, perhaps quite properly, widely valued and encouraged — punctuality, diligence, neatness, acquiescence — none are universally required or unambiguously specified. Even the rules devised independently by specific schools, which apply unconditionally to all children throughout the building, tend to limit themselves to necessary but relatively minor matters such as which side of the corridor to walk, or which staircase to proceed down; out-of-bounds zones; lateness; payment of lunch money. They invariably stop short of specifying the classroom behaviour which is required if those learning purposes shared by children and teachers which schools exist to sponsor are to be achieved. This omission is not normally explained by the inability of teachers to cooperate to the extent of producing an agreeable set of conventions along the above lines. Rather, it is argued that such rules, however well grounded, would inhibit to an unacceptable extent the individual freedom of teachers to operate in ways which they prefer. However, particularly at the secondary level, the result is that children are confused by the constantly changing demands made by different teachers — in what is requested, and the degree of compliance required. Teachers have to struggle alone to establish what they desire in their particular classroom for their own good, or indifferent, or even indefensible reasons. The bargaining between the parties becomes protracted, sometimes endlessly, and is often duplicated in class after class. Mutual frustration and time-wasting occurs from these attempts to resolve ambiguities. The general ethos degenerates into one of conflict and confrontation, with classrooms governed by rules which nevertheless do inevitably evolve, even if accidentally, from the residues of battles fought and truces negotiated. So it is no surprise that the punishments inflicted for misbehaviour can be construed by children as arbitrary and unfair, thus contributing to the escalation towards defiance. Certainly many punishments seem singularly inappropriate in terms of the school's *raison d'être*. How must school be construed if punishment — pain and discomfort — is inflicted on children by their being made to stay *longer* at it, in detention? How can the work of the English department fail to be denigrated when one of the activities it exists to joyously sponsor — essay writing — is given as punishment?

Much is lost as a result of this drift. Schools miss the opportunity to make clear to children exactly what they think are the central purposes of their attendance, and to explain the various sorts of good reasons for those rules necessitated by such purposes — itself an educative ethical exercise. The further possibility of involving pupils themselves in rule making — requiring the learning of those proper and important lessons of cause and effect, of constructive negotiating, and of personal responsibility for misbehaviour — is not countenanced. Thus are general and wide-ranging disservices done, and dysfunctions generated to be unnecessarily, pointlessly suffered by people inside, even outside, schools. Unless, of course, we admit that there *are* no proper purposes, or that no good reasons or valid aims exist. This possibility will be returned to in Chapter 7.

Three other general points emerge with some force. First, parents in England are rarely aware of their precise rights; are often uncertain about when teachers can be said to have treated their children unfairly or arbitrarily; and have no established channel of recourse in the event of improprieties. Second, children in turn are not required to accept, as they properly should, full responsibility for those of their actions which are palpably unreasonable, for no agreed statements of these exist. Too often, when such realizations dawn, things have gone too far, and it is too late for rectification. In the meantime, teachers have to cope with behaviour which few adults in different contexts would be prepared to tolerate. Third, the lack of adequate liaison between the educational psychological services, the social services, and schools means that there is a lack of diagnostic expertise which, if available, would undoubtedly uncover flaws both in teachers' pedagogy and children's personalities and propensities.

To conclude this section, it is worth considering some specific examples of ill-discipline, and some of the explanations given for different types of misbehaviour. Teachers in England know very well that the dynamics of their interactions with their pupils during their early meetings — the first few days in a primary school; the first four or five lessons at the secondary stage — are quite crucial to the subsequent climate of classroom discipline. A mutual exchange of signals takes place between the two parties, and children are most adept at interpreting those of their teachers. They also set about, sometimes quite systematically, to test their teachers out by seeing what they will tolerate, or 'what stuff they are made of'. Much, of course, will depend on the personality qualities which the participants in these negotiations have, and the kind of work to be embarked on. However, the observer can readily detect that the bargaining takes the following broad form.

Teachers attempt to make quite clear what their expectations are. They draw attention, through noticing and praising them, to various examples of good behaviour, and they rebuke those guilty of improprieties — publicly if they feel that a general example must be made. The next step will invariably be the issuing of warnings, even threats, to persistent transgressors, and then punishment of some sort will be resorted to. Clearly these stages can be collapsed or protracted according to the competence of the teacher, who bears in mind several consequences of his or her actions in responding to a particular incident — for example that children have a sense of fair play. But failure to negotiate any one of them will result in a deterioration in the ethos of the classroom; for it is the negotiation of these stages that makes the teacher's reputation, and establishes the quality of classroom relationships. Similarly, some forms of behaviour become conventional and the future realities of classroom life are laid down.

The technical incompetence of teachers during these processes can easily produce behaviours which are dysfunctional to learning. For example, student teachers very commonly give insufficiently clear or exact instructions, which can result in answers to questions being shouted out simultaneously, or in children chattering so much that an unacceptably high level of noise is produced. Again, because they genuinely do not know exactly what to do when set a task, a few children may move around the room, so distracting others. A teacher's lack of dynamism, or failure to set work which is within the children's capacity, can mean that classes do not listen, or do not do the work assigned to them. Such beginnings often degenerate into 'messing about' or horseplay primarily because point and purpose have been lost, and children proceed to fill the lesson time, quite understandably, on their own terms. At this stage it is much more difficult to rectify things, for they have become normal by convention.

Most teachers, of course, do manage to negotiate these stages satisfactorily, though rarely without some trial and error. However, where, as in some of our foreign countries, clear general rules for all classrooms are specified, many of these pupil behaviours do not emerge in the first place, which makes life far less fraught for all concerned. It is for precisely this reason that experienced teachers who have already made their reputation in a school tend to have few problems. Because of what they have been told through their own grapevine, classes never even 'try on' certain things. Without some general policy, and in schools where a very high percentage of such staff do not exist, there is the serious risk that some quite indefensible behaviours become conventional in many classrooms, are tolerated, and so begin to be seen as normal and unexceptional. Children, when asked, say they dislike these conditions, though because of their loyalty to their fellows they rarely take the initiative in making their frustrations known, and tend instead to vent their anger on teachers, so making things worse.

Recent concern has been widely expressed about behaviour of quite another kind — namely that which is called 'disruptive' — and the studies by Lawrence (1977, 1980) and Lawrence, Steed and Young (1981) are particularly valuable because they began by discovering how teachers themselves experience and define this term. In addition, the opinions of the children were sought. Further research, as yet unpublished, into classroom conditions in six European countries suggests that these behaviours are experienced by teachers there as well. In France, for example, they found a marked increase, since about 1968, in such things as alcoholism; extreme lateness in arriving at lessons; defiance by children who totally refuse to obey teachers; but in particular, vandalism and violence by children towards each other and teachers. Their evidence suggests that in France such things are likely to be more prevalent in big schools, and in large towns, and particularly among the 14-16 age group, though much concern is also expressed about violence in primary schools. In the GFR, vandalism and bullying were also the most common manifestations of disruptive behaviour mentioned by their respondents, though rowdy behaviour and truancy are prevalent. The schools most affected are those of a non-selective variety at the secondary level in large towns. In inner-city areas, sporadic waves of this kind of behaviour occur and schools are not usually permanently subjected to them.

It is of some interest to identify the explanations for this type of problem. In England they come under five headings. First, as has already been suggested, there is teacher incompetence. Second comes the institutional inadequacy of schools. So, just as Hargreaves (1967) argued that the actual composition of teaching groups by streams generates 'delinquescence' in some classes, so the claim is that other but similar structural arrangements made by some schools generate disruption. Third, some vaguely formulated psychological or neo-psychiatric explanation is given, where the fault is thought to reside in the personality of a particular child. This can take the form of social or emotional maladjustment or cognitive malfunction. The fourth explanation is provided in terms of some social problem which the child has, which is external to the school but which is brought into the school and may even be compounded by the way the child is treated there. Here, the upset caused by a family bereavement, the separation of parents, malnutrition or housing deprivation are often cited. Finally, some macro-sociological theory is often used, where, for example, a group of children are seen as the victims of the clash of cultures and values which exists between the school on the one hand and their homes or their out-of-school friends on the other. Here, the children are seen only as specific cases of broader societal contradictions; in particular, for Marxists, those of Western capitalism. Lawrence, Steed and Young's evidence shows that many of these ideas are adhered to in France and the GFR as well, and they are certainly familiar in the American literature on this problem. However, in the USA, while broad sociological explanations have been offered, there is a marked preference for some psychological explanation, siting the fault in the child and requiring some form of remedy in those terms, often on the basis of behaviour modification techniques.

It would appear that in France over-simple explanations in terms of the constitution of the child have been superseded and a formal distinction is at times made between maladjustment and children exhibiting disruptive behaviour. There is mention of school-based factors, such as the raising of the school leaving age to 16, the rigidity and irrelevance of what schools offer, and the fact that all children are required to do the same work, so that lack of ability or boredom causes many to disrupt classes. But the preferred factors would appear to be environmental ones, such as the high level of unemployment, the violence shown on television, and the anonymity of crowded conditions in housing, particularly those of the *Habitat à Loyer Modéré* (dwelling with controlled rent). In addition, children from one-parent families and the general decline of cultural and moral values in society are often mentioned, as is the difficulty of achieving collaboration between some parents and the school. In the GFR, low intelligence and unemployment are considered as causes, though the most common explanations seem to be the lack of socialization, guidance and supervision provided by families, and the trigger effects of multiple defects where a child cannot handle a constellation of problems.

The research, then, promises to be of considerable interest and importance when published, and will merit closer attention than that given here, particularly because of its novelty, for no other international investigation of this issue has been attempted before.

It does appear that many countries are experiencing similar problems to our own over extreme forms of misbehaviour by some children, and similarities exist between them in how they try to understand and explain them. But two cautionary notes need to be sounded. First, a few respondents in France and the GFR were conscious of the danger of assuming that everything was better in the past, and that things are worse now than they once were. What may be occurring, however, is that a sharper perception of the issues now exists and greater publicity is given to them, particularly with the general thrust towards taking mass schooling seriously. Most claims about the decline in standards of behaviour heard in England are entirely unsatisfactory because the historical evidence necessary to support them is extremely scant and notoriously difficult to interpret. Yet it is true to say, for example, that the realities of secondary modern classrooms, where the vast majority of children in England were educated in the days of tripartism, were rarely publicly illuminated. There is evidence of the chronic disciplinary difficulties — involving truancy, insubordination and fierce hostility — which faced teachers in the years immediately following the 1870 Education Act. The public schools were no exception. The militia had to be called out several times to quell the rioting boys of Eton College during the first two decades of the nineteenth century, and any boy there (the playing fields apart) who could survive the nightly unsupervised incarceration in the Long Room dormitory might well have found Waterloo something of a picnic. It was because he had some success in improving such conditions at Rugby that Arnold was such an exception and a pioneer of new methods, though even in his time it appears that Flashman had his moments! Second, a comparative perspective on discipline, as with any other issue, needs to look out for local factors in problem perception, analysis and solution.

5. Assessment

Many important changes have taken place over the last three decades in the assessment and examining procedures used in England. First came the replacement of the School Certificate examinations by the GCE Ordinary and Advanced level system — and eventually the introduction of a variety of new questioning techniques in O level, even A level papers. Next came the debates which cast doubts on the validity of the 11+ examination and caused its gradual, though by no means complete, dismantling. Then the CSE was introduced with the intention of providing an examination for those secondary school children thought incapable of O level, so giving them some goal to work for. Teachers were given more control over the procedures involved, hence the three modes of examining which were developed and offered. At present, steps are being taken to introduce a common 16+ examination. Marked changes have taken place in the assessment procedures used at the other levels as well; for example, unit degrees have been introduced by some universities, while those awarded by the newly founded polytechnics become validated by mechanisms devised by the CNAA. More recently, attention has been focused on the 16-19 age range with the introduction of the CEE, and the N and F proposals; whilst the Mansell Report (DES 1979b) made very important recommendations, currently in process of implementation, regarding the assessment of courses for certain groups of full-time students staying on at colleges, who were uncertain about what they wished to do, and for whom no obvious examined course existed. In addition, the examining of vocational courses has been reorganized through BEC and TEC.

During these years the debate about examinations has been heated, primarily because two highly controversial themes have consistently run through them. First, concern has been expressed about educational standards, some people arguing that they have fallen, with the intention of bringing into question certain recent changes in educational organization (e.g. comprehensive schools) or of practice (e.g. 'modern' methods of teaching). Second, discussion has focused on the constricting and inhibiting effects that examinations have on the work of schools. Here, one claim is that examination requirements define not only the content of courses but also the teaching and learning process. Inevitably, questions are raised of control — over knowledge, and over the future careers of children. Prior to a comparative commentary, an attempt must be made to map out the major issues; for the fact is that all our countries do have systems of examining or assessment, and although they differ markedly, certain principles are held in common.

1.   The purposes of assessment

It is invariably argued that assessment is necessary for several broad social and economic reasons — for example, a society can only function, not only justly but also efficiently, when certain things are properly learned by all its citizens, and when the various occupational groups are composed of those whose expertise is both proven and relevant. Selection is seen as inevitable, and precision in its achievement crucial.

2.   Forms of testing

(a) **Achievement tests**   The search here is for evidence of how much of the content of a particular body of knowledge a child can be said to have acquired. This content is often itemized thus: the acquisition of facts and terms; the understanding of concepts, principles and relationships; an ability to manipulate and use the information thus defined.

(b) **Tests of originality and creativity**   Here evidence of something more than cognitive dexterity is sought.

(c) **Tests of capacity, potential and aptitude**   Here the assumption is that, irrespective of how or what they have been taught and the level of their current achievements, children have certain propensities (for reasons which are not always clear) that can be discovered.

(d) **Diagnostic tests** Here attempts are made to discover why it is that certain children achieve what they do, and to provide teachers with clues about how those who are underachieving may best be helped.

It is evident that, apart from diagnosis and selection, certain other things are involved here. Tests of achievement are in fact qualifying procedures. Their authenticity rests on their predictive accuracy, and competitiveness may also be implied. However, such tests can be used for purposes of evaluation as well. For example, children's test scores can be used by outsiders to judge teachers. On the other hand, self-critical teachers, as they reflect upon the efficacy of their work, constantly seek out ways of knowing how well they are doing and how to do even better. Some of their procedures are, quite properly, somewhat subjective. They take account of how interested or involved the children appear to be. Others are far more systematic, as when they elicit oral replies to questions designed to discover what children have remembered from past lessons, or when they listen to the conversations of children, from which they can learn a great deal about their interests, or levels of understanding. They often consider the children's efforts at doing classwork assignments, or read their homework with similar intentions. Here then, the evidence provided by more formal assessment procedures can also be a quite vital aid.

The subjectivity of teachers' judgements merits more protracted consideration because they can have unfortunate consequences due to their unreliability. Teachers have, of necessity, to make judgements about the children they teach and some of these will depend on very nebulous factors, such as their perceptions of their appearance or personal qualities. On occasions they will be the consequence of totally unwarranted stereotypes which teachers have concerning social class, ethnicity, gender or home background. These opinions of children, however ill-founded, can colour the way in which teachers interact with such children and these quite informal mechanisms can then directly affect their judgements of their worth, ability and actual levels of achievement. It is for these sorts of reasons that Hextall (1976) has drawn attention to the fundamental importance of teachers' routine marking procedures, through which children come to be assigned to different levels of courses. There is a sense in which he makes an urgent plea therefore for teachers to set about this aspect of their work more rigorously. It is also worth stressing that, because of the partialities, even prejudices of teachers, more neutral, objective forms of assessment are recommended. Certainly in the nineteenth century, examinations were seen as a way of removing nepotism and corruption in the recruitment of civil servants and undergraduates, and in the granting to the latter of their degrees. Examinations were seen as the mechanisms which ensured justice, through the sponsorship of merit. This leads to the next set of general principles.

3.   Modes of formal examining

(a) **External examinations**   — set, marked and administered by some impartial, neutral bodies.

(b) **Internal examinations**   — set, marked and administered by those who teach the courses, though usually moderated externally.

(c) **Institutional accreditation**   — where an external body, after proper consideration, grants examining powers to the teaching personnel, whose examinations then become internal.

4.   Methods of examining

(a) **Timed**

Objective tests   — 'objective' refers to the marking, which can be done mechanically because the answer is pre-determined. They test the candidates' ability to recall and recognize, but they can also be used to test reasoning and understanding.

Essays   — designed to test the candidates' capacity to marshal thoughts, their powers of judgement, concentration, and literary fluency. Access to books or other reference material may be permitted, to reduce stress and minimize the need for memorization.

(b) **Untimed**

Essays, theses, dissertations or projects   — often requiring the definition of a problem or the formulation of a hypothesis, the collection of data, and the presentation of an argued analytical conclusion.

(c) **Continuous assessments**   — where candidates are judged throughout the whole period of the course of study, rather than at its conclusion. A variety of actual types of examination may be used.

(d) **Orals**   — conducted with, (and upon), or without, a previously completed examination of some kind, e.g. (b) and (e).

(e) **Practical or performance** — timed or untimed and usually concerned with scientific, aesthetic or physical activity.

The literature on assessment in England[8] shows the uses and abuses of these modes and methods. Although distinctions can be drawn between judgemental processes, the formal testing or examining of courses, and various types of evaluative procedures, it is clear that they are by no means three discrete stages, for they are essentially interactive components. While some American case studies exist (e.g. Rist 1970) which show these subtle interactions at work, no comparative research exists on them, so that what follows is limited to a description of the formal assessment procedures used in our foreign countries.

In the USSR, most examinations at all levels are conducted orally, because this form of testing is believed there to be the most rigorous and efficient. Blackboards are used where writing (e.g. of a mathematical proof) is necessary. This work is done under the eye of the examiner and, in schools, in front of the whole class. This system has the subsidiary effect of requiring great verbal fluency, personal confidence and speed of thought by candidates. Apart from post-graduate degrees, where it is conducted upon a dissertation, the questioning takes a variety of forms, but the aim is to cover fully all aspects of the course content and the stress is always on achievement acquisition. Psychological tests of cognitive capacity or potential are eschewed for reasons already identified (see Section 2 in this chapter) though some use is made of predictive aptitude tests in the recruitment of certain specialists such as pilots. There are examinations, such as those used to recruit children for the specialist secondary schools, and university undergraduates, which are, in practice, highly selective and competitive. However, the expectation in schools is that all examinees can, indeed must, perform satisfactorily, and the marks awarded are not controlled by some pre-determined curve of distribution. In the 10-year schools, apart from annual examinations in the subjects of the curriculum, the work of children is continuously assessed. A common marking scale, from 5 to 1, is used everywhere and for everything, with 5 used to denote excellence, 3 as a pass, and 2 and 1 being unacceptable grades. The grades which all children get for each of their weekly assignments are entered on their record cards, which they have to carry at all times, and which they have to show to their parents. An annual average mark for each subject is computed and any child whose general profile falls below 3 is required to repeat the year. It is on the basis of this evidence that the Certificate of Completion of Extended Secondary Education is awarded, and those with particularly notable achievements in particular subjects are recognized.

These procedures are carried out by teachers, though because of the centralization of control over syllabus content and the actual content of that to be tested, it is claimed that objectivity in marking and comparability of standards nationally are achieved. However, one phenomenon is worth mentioning: namely that many university departments complain that too many of their entry candidates who have been given very high grade profiles by their teachers are found, upon examination, to have been seriously over-marked. Soviet educators also say that the grade of 3 is too often resorted to by teachers. This is explainable, perhaps even understandable, by the fact that teachers draw attention to their own inadequacy if they use 2s or 1s, because few other explanations for failure by children are admissible.

The Americans have been most inventive in the development of testing procedures, and it would be safe to say that almost every item in the schedule provided earlier in this section is currently used there. In particular, all kinds of psychological and objective tests have been developed for use in industry, business and commerce, and there has been no absence of controversy about them. Spring (1972) usefully charts the major stages in the debate about IQ, for example, beginning as long ago as the First World War when the apparently reliable predictive quality of Yerkes' work on IQ tests was used to assign those drafted into the services to particular military niches. Where education is concerned, the American approach to learning, involving planning and the detailed specification of objectives, also generated innumerable testing devices; and it should be stressed that many of these are refined, diligently constructed, and appear to have a high degree of reliability and validity. They should not be too lightly dismissed, although it could be argued that the curriculum in the schools of the USA has become effectively determined by measurement procedures, where that which cannot be counted is discounted.

In addition to this characteristic feature of American procedures of assessment, several other notable aspects and inventions can be identified. The first of these is the accreditation of institutions, through which high schools, colleges, even universities are certified as being competent to examine their students and to grant particular awards. Complex criteria are used by external bodies, and always involve measures of the quality of campuses and faculties (i.e. the teaching staff). Having been certified as efficient, but with periodic rechecking always being involved, institutions are permitted to devise their own internal examining procedures. However, their awards, at whatever level, always involve the use of the credit system, which in turn always includes the specification of hours of classroom attendance. Teachers at all levels are required to inform their class exactly what they have to do to earn credit for the course, which may include reading particular texts, the passing of quizzes, and the sitting of timed tests of various kinds. But to augment this continuous assessment, the most common requirement is the submission of an untimed 'paper' of some kind.

Conventions of marking or grading have become nationally recognized and used (i.e. A, B, C and F, where A is excellent and F means fail). These are always converted into numerical equivalents, and because of the use of pluses and minuses for each grade given, it becomes possible to rank the average performance of students. Nationally standardized objective tests of subject matter are widely used as well, so that grade equivalence is guaranteed and a particular student can be placed in a very fine national achievement percentile. All these procedures tend to be governed by a normal curve of distribution of marks, which means that they are endemically competitive and sometimes fiercely so. Students who gain High School Certification have an automatic right of entry to the State's system of higher education, whilst interregional agreements mean that they can gain access to colleges or universities other than local ones. The most prestigious universities — some State, some with ancient private charters, certainly those of the Ivy League — have their own entrance requirements, though access can be gained to them at the Graduate School level by those whose under-graduate record elsewhere has been shown to be exceptional. There is a close correlation between attendance at some of these Schools (e.g. the Harvard Law School) and entry into élite positions, especially political ones.

The French Cartesian, intellectual, rational tradition is perhaps particularly amenable to formal examination, and certainly in no other country are examinations quite so dominant and important a feature of school life. They are a Napoleonic inheritance, and perhaps had Chinese mandarism as their inspiration. They continue to flourish because they are seen as the central democratic mechanism through which socio-economic, even political positions are ascribed on the basis of ability. It follows that a rigid and publicly recognized hierarchy of qualifications exists according to which level of examination children, students and adults have passed. During the first orientation cycle of secondary education, pupils are variously and constantly assessed and a *dossier* of their achievements is built up. Thereafter, each educational route leads to a specific terminal test — one of the several *baccalauréat* awards, or the technician's certificate (the *brevet*), or a vocational studies certificate (*brevet d'études professionelles*) or the vocational skills certificate (*certificat d'aptitude professionelle*). At the university level, three levels of degrees are granted: the *license*, the *maîtrise*, and the doctorate. Professional, vocational and technical qualifications granted at other institutions of higher education are similarly scaled, including those of teachers. Those few who pass the fiercely selective *concours* and gain entry into the most prestigious *grandes écoles* — the *Ecoles Normales Superieures*, the *Ecole Polytechnique* or the *Ecole Nationale d'Administration* — must sign a 10-year contract which requires them to take State employment upon graduation.

All examinations which lead to any of these nationally recognized awards are externally controlled, and are set and marked in conditions of great secrecy by the agents of the central Ministry. At the school level, they are sat by candidates throughout the country at exactly the same hour. Some features of the system have acquired considerable notoriety, not least the chronic strains and pressures which are induced in pupils. Most remain competitive in the sense that, irrespective of the performance of a particular entry, a pre-determined percentage of candidates always have to fail — a practice which generates much hostility. For example, whilst the overall pass rate in the *baccalauréat* has increased in recent years from 50% to about 67% (King 1979), according to figures published recently,[9] the pass rate for the *agrégation* fell from 14.4% in 1964 to 4.8% in 1979, whilst the equivalent rates for the *CAPES* were 38.4% in 1964 and 4.7% in 1979. Such apparent arbitrariness is reflected also by the fact that while all examinations are achievement orientated, some seem to be designed to discover what candidates do *not* know, rather than what they do. Chance can also be involved — for example in some orals used at university level, where candidates are tested on their knowledge of set texts, they are often asked to choose by some random method one text only, and are then questioned solely on it. This practice is seen as ensuring that all aspects of a course have to be covered, though of course it by no means guarantees this, for very negligent students can sometimes be lucky. In general, it follows that, because of the relatively high failure rates at all levels, including those at the university degree level, the entry for any examination includes many students who are resitting.

These descriptions of our foreign countries lend no support to those radical arguments sometimes put forward in England in favour of the abolition of examinations. However, because they are educationally so necessary, and socially so important, enormous care is needed in their construction and use. One danger is that they can come to dominate the curriculum, not merely in terms of prescribing the content taught, but also in the whole orientation of particular subjects, the actual teaching and learning methods used, the quality of teacher-pupil relationships, even the general ethos of schools. For example, the use of timed written papers in music, English and modern languages, means that those activities not examinable in this way, such as making music, writing creatively or speaking French, become unimportant. All this suggests that continued attention needs to be paid in England to the examining processes, to make examinations more reliable. Even greater imagination is called for in devising better, more valid and relevant methods. This is particularly important for secondary schools, with the impending introduction of a common 16+ examination.

On the other hand, teachers in England certainly do have to evaluate and assess not only their own work but that of the children they teach, and to avoid this reality is quite irresponsible. Careful attention to these matters is therefore a matter of some urgency. A comparative perspective suggests that the following aspects of assessment and examination need reconsideration.

1. *The informal assessment procedures used by teachers*

   (a) How they come to judge children, and how this affects their perception of children's achievements, abilities and potentialities.

   (b) How they mark, grade, or comment upon the on-going classwork and homework set (e.g. whether the criteria they use are apparent to children and whether it is clear why something has been marked wrong). Without such clarity, pupils have no way of knowing how to proceed to improve their work; they remain mystified, and the real teaching and learning potentialities of evaluation are lost.

   (c) The need for greater expertise in the setting of internal school examinations in the early years of secondary schools, by which children get consigned to particular courses.

2. *The information available to children and parents about the system of public examinations*

Entry to higher, further and vocational educational courses in England is governed by a labyrinth of regulations, and most employers make certain requirements regarding the qualifications they expect of potential employees. In most of these cases particular subjects are specified and, what is more, success in a broad, balanced range of them is required. However, quite different from any other countries, our public examinations are run on a unitary basis. This means that many choices have to be made by most secondary school children after only three years or so of attendance, and few of these can subsequently be altered. Because they lack information and guidance, many children make their options without understanding the consequences.

3. National standards of achievement

Although some standardized tests do exist and are used, their relative absence in England makes us a comparative exception. Serious doubts exist even about the comparability of standards between GCE examining boards. This situation can be explained historically, and certain liberating advantages accrue for schools. But there are also risks involved, namely that teachers have insufficiently high expectations of children, who in turn can remain complacent about their work. The inexactitudes involved cause some very sound courses to be widely undervalued, and some qualifications gained (e.g. CSE) to be unrecognized. Moreover, charges of declining standards, although often quite unfounded, can gain credence for lack of measured rebuttal.

4. Specialization and narrowness

These words apply to the assessment of academic GCE A level and university degree courses. In all other countries the demands made upon students at equivalent stages are much broader, and narrow specialization into science or the arts or languages, etc., and then into a single subject, is delayed much longer. While this point is well understood, and has often been made in England, and while it is part of our tradition of scholarship, nothing has been done about it because of the independence and power of our universities. The knock-on effects upon schools remain serious.

6. Summary and conclusions

We have seen that teachers in all our five countries have certain shared characteristics and are required to carry out many tasks in common. Those aspects of their work situations and conditions of employment which are local to a particular country have also been identified. The status of teachers in each society has also been considered.

We have discussed the models of childhood and the approaches to learning which are adopted in our foreign countries, and various interpretations of adolescence. The validity of certain English ways of categorizing children was questioned, mainly because of the consequences for children of making certain broad assumptions about them. Particular attention was paid to the concept of intelligence and the use of IQ tests. We have seen how and why teachers in the USSR, the USA and England make very different connections between 'teaching' and 'learning', which have marked consequences for their classroom practices. We have discussed the different approaches to discipline and assessment in our five countries, and I have argued that schools in England need to work out agreed policies for classroom discipline. Those aspects of the assessment and examining procedures used here which need *re*consideration are summarized on pages 99-100.

Our comparative analysis has shown conclusively that teachers in England have a remarkable degree of autonomy. While there are many potential advantages in this situation, serious risks are involved. We have seen that more complex theories of learning and teaching have been developed in England than elsewhere which have important implications for schools, but that what goes on in classrooms often bears little resemblance to the spirit, point, and purpose of these ideas. I have argued that what teachers actually do, represents their attempts to relate theory and practice and that many of their current efforts are unfortunate perversions or distortions.

I have therefore suggested that these developments may be causing more rather than less élitism in our schools. I have argued that the principles of English progressive education have radical implications for schools, but that unless the quality of teachers is improved, then the conclusion will be drawn that they are not applicable to a system of mass schooling. These issues are considered again in Chapter 7, where further reasoned conclusions are drawn.

Notes

1. Grant's figure (1979, p. 48) for women teachers in the USSR is 73% of the total. He gives further details about women in various types of teaching posts (op. cit. pp. 48-9) i.e. at the primary and secondary levels; in different subject specialisms; at the assistant director, and director levels; and in teacher education.

2. Several psychological theories of adolescence — including those of Freud, Rank and Erik Erikson — which take this position are outlined by Dacey (1979, pp. 3-37). Whilst the alternative 'Environmental' theories of Ruth Benedict and Margaret Mead are mentioned by Dacey, he sees adolescence as an inevitable developmental stage, and discusses various theories from social psychology and psychoanalysis which seek to explain it.

3. These, and other sociological analyses of youth cultures, are discussed in Hall and Jefferson (1976, chapter 1, pp. 9-75).

4. Each of these interpretations is discussed by Brake (1980, pp. 155-161).

5. This approach is used even in the special music schools, where the most precociously gifted are trained. Initially total technical mastery of a particular instrument is required, and some of the virtuosity displayed by the children I saw was extraordinary. Interpretation or composition comes only thereafter.

6. The fact that a Dean of Education found that teaching in an infant school involved 'the most difficult and complex tasks of his teaching career' (Blenkin and Kelly 1982, p. 7) does not augur well for students and teachers.

7. The title of Brearley and Hitchfield's book *A Teacher's Guide to Reading Piaget* (1966) is highly significant here. Staffroom talk about language in secondary schools is often conducted in terms either of the Bullock Report (1975) — itself heavily impregnated by Barnes et al. (1969) — or Bernstein (1973, 1974, 1976). However, the language policies of some schools are garbled versions of Bullock. Similarly, Bernstein's 'codes' are often misunderstood, causing unfortunate effects on the way in which teachers perceive and treat children from working class backgrounds.

8. Norwood Report (Board of Education 1943); Beloe Report (Schools Council 1968); Wiseman (1961); Montgomery (1965, 1978); Nutall and Willmott (1972); Lewis (1974); Macintosh and Hudson (1974); Hoste and Bloomfield (1975); Wyatt (1975); Schools Council (1968, 1974, 1975, 1978); Downey (1977); Pudwell (1980).

9. *Le Français dans le Monde* November-December 1980, No. 9.

CHAPTER 4

THE CURRICULUM

1. Introduction

This chapter is designed as a bridge between the relatively descriptive preceding chapters and the more contentious ones which follow. This is not a matter of convenience, for inevitably the topic of curriculum encapsulates most educational issues. Mundane sounding but still significant concerns, like school structures, the use of space and time, and the provision of materials, resources and furnishings, are involved. So are most of the matters already treated in Chapter 3 — such as teaching styles, theories of learning, modes of assessment or evaluation, classroom discipline — and these will be incorporated appropriately in the discussion which follows. However, the curriculum includes additional contingent and quite critical matters such as forms of interpersonal relationships, scales of moral and ethical values, types of interpersonal relationships — and, inevitably, even more fundamental issues — such as those of educational purpose, principle and function — are also involved in it. This chapter is a lead into the consideration of these matters, for it cannot escape raising them. As a result, a certain amount of repetition, or the reworking of recurrent themes is unfortunately unavoidable.

2. Common problems, trends and solutions

The comparative literature (e.g. Ryba 1980) suggests that countries share, and themselves recognize, several general though very difficult curriculum problems. Some of the points made below may be familiar, but for the purposes of this analysis it is necessary to reiterate them in outline. The first problem stems from the dramatic explosion in human knowledge which has undoubtedly occurred during the twentieth century (Holmes *in* Bereday and Lauwerys 1958). A common index of this phenomenon is the growth of human scientific knowledge which is estimated to be doubling every ten years. Given the sheer scale of this growth, questions of the following kind arise in many countries — 'How can school knowledge be kept up to date?'

or 'What, out of this knowledge, should children be taught?' or 'What principles can inform our decision to include or exclude some of this knowledge from the school's curriculum?'.

A second factor which tends to compound the first is the concurrent explosion in human expectations regarding education. That is to say, since the early 1950s citizens have increasingly demanded for their children access to more and more schooling, and specifically to those high-status knowledge areas traditionally provided only for the élite. An OECD publication put it this way: '... all European school systems are responding in one way or another to the political pressures for greater equality of opportunity and for less specialisation.' (Centre for Educational Research and Innovation 1972, p. 12). There is a recognition here by the clientele that extended schooling in some subject areas provides the best chance for social and economic mobility and access to the good life.

Arising from this pressure, a third problem emerges, namely that most countries have had to face up to what the curriculum in mass education can, must or might look like. Thus, is mass education a general 'liberal' education for all? If so, where does vocational education appear? Or has the former always implied the latter anyway? Must mass education, to meet the equality principle, mean a common compulsory curriculum for all, and if so, for how long, and what should it include? On the other hand, should the equality principle find expression in treating differing individual needs differently, by organizing an extensive optional or choice-based curriculum? But who is to decide who has special needs? Can the differentiation inherent here avoid élitism? But, how can students with a profound depth of specialist knowledge in one or two subjects, so necessary for creative and frontier research, be provided for?

A fourth problem, logically connected with what has already emerged, concerns resources. Even in relatively rich countries the provision of more and better education makes it necessary to find new financial resources, and sometimes this involves difficult priority choices, within the educational sector and between education and other social services.

A fifth argument' poses an even more complex problem and raises further dilemmas. The postulation is that the curriculum of schools is insufficiently relevant, mainly to the needs of society and the economy. In short, most children are not provided with the skills, knowledge, experiences and attitudes needed in the world of work which they enter when they leave school. Neither does the school help them enough in making realistic decisions about their future employment. A commonly heard rejoinder to this view is that because of the rapidity of technological change it is impossible to anticipate what knowledge or skills will ultimately be most helpful to students, particularly with a 40-year working life in prospect, during which they may have to be drastically retrained at least twice. Better, the argument goes, to recognize that the most certain prediction is that the future will see a marked increase in the leisure time citizens are going to enjoy. The curriculum should focus instead on preparing for this by developing in them worthwhile interests, sustained by life-long continuing education. But the relevance argument does not rest there. It is also suggested (King 1974) that the curriculum is irrelevant to the needs of individual children, as perceived by them, and thus they become alienated from schooling. Such perceptions are, however, very varied and may not only be in direct contradiction to what the schools are offering, but to social and economic requirements as well.

This dilemma illustrates nicely another fundamental difficulty, the parameters of which are very clear and broadly agreed upon. That is, that what children are taught should take account of (i) societal needs; (ii) individual needs; and (iii) the nature of knowledge. Such a statement is all very well, but what weighting should be attached to one or another factor? Various countries proceed with this weighting process differently, depending on local factors which are often subtle and delicate.

A seventh identifiable problem compounds matters further because, it is argued, countries must recognize the consequences of the increasing economic and political interdependence of nations. This argument is applied particularly forcefully to the EEC context, but also recognizes cross-continental — First to Third World — relationships, and thus the need to develop curricula for international understanding. Sometimes this is couched in very basic terms, for example, the need for more foreign languages to aid the geographical mobility of future labour forces, or, in similar vein, the need to harmonize curricula, examinations, etc. across educational systems. Another version presses for a curriculum for international understanding in which at least a beginning is made by removing the overtly ethnocentric and nationalistic character of most history syllabuses and geography textbooks (Merchant 1967; Dance 1970). The most cogent arguments are those put by supporters of the International Baccalaureate, particularly Peterson (1972).

What has already been said throws up a number of miscellaneous related issues which must be mentioned. There are serious implications in it for the work of the teacher. Given even the knowledge explosion point, inevitably his or her traditional role as an authority becomes less tenable. More seriously, teachers occupy a completely central and quite critical position in the classroom and outside it, negotiating directly with children and others about the problems outlined here. Sometimes doubts are therefore raised about their claim to be in authority. Questions also arise about methods and systems of evaluation and assessment. Given the apparent need for curriculum innovation, there is an obvious need to look at the sources of such innovation and its effective dissemination.

The final problem is probably the most important, for in a sense it overrides all the others. This has to do with questions of politics, control and power. It has already been demonstrated that even one curriculum problem can raise questions to which there are several possible answers which are contradictory and irreconcilable. In this situation, which is applicable to many countries, the curriculum has to be seen as a political matter, and decisions about it emanate from the national patterns of power and control discussed in Chapter 5.

In England the problems of curriculum are not necessarily couched in quite the above terms, yet it is difficult to deny that many ring true for us. Certainly notions of mass education, curriculum relevance and matters of control, power, and thus teacher autonomy and responsibility, are most germane. A more detailed set of reflections on our domestic scenario is delayed until the final section of this chapter.

If we turn next to what could be identified as common trends and solutions, a beginning can be made at the primary level. All countries continue to give a heavy priority to teaching children the basic skills of numeracy and literacy (i.e. reading, writing and arithmetic computation). Much stress is also put on the physical health and well-being of children and to beginning the process of the socialization of the child away from an exclusive dependence on its family. But the English primary school curriculum tends to be much more extended in terms of content than abroad. While art, music, nature study, and so on are given nominal attention, with the exception perhaps of the USA, very little time is devoted elsewhere to the wide range of activities (including science, environmental studies, history and thematic work) which are familiar features of most schools here. Similarly, comparatively speaking, we are unorthodox in our use of time, space and the way we group children for learning. Many foreign experts, notably the Americans (e.g. Silberman 1973) have urged that their countries follow in our steps. Another feature at this level is that the process of the assessment of children in most countries is limited to the testing of their attainment in the various curriculum areas. Objective testing does occur in the USA, but is rarer in Western Europe and positively rejected in the USSR. Finally, at the end of this stage of schooling, Western European countries — as was seen in Chapter 2 — have followed the earlier lead of the USA, Sweden and the USSR in deferring selection as late as possible through the establishment of some form of 'common' secondary school; a movement which has vital curricular implications.

This provides a useful bridge to a consideration of common developments at the secondary level. In all countries there has been a noticeable, even dramatic decline in classical studies (Latin and Greek), perhaps to make room for the increased time given to mathematics and sciences. But more noticeable has been the trend to establish a required, common curriculum for all children, ranging from the three-year orientation cycle in France, to seven years in the USSR. The Soviet Union's requirements are probably the most extensive in scope, though France comes close to its degree of detail, and even in the USA the State or Local School Boards of Education commonly lay down requirements that all children be taught some subjects, and specify precisely what texts and textbooks must be used.

In general the justifications proffered for these developments are two-fold; first, that the State, for security and national cohesion reasons, has the right to demand of its future citizens a mastery of a basic core of knowledge; second, that selection or sorting is endemic to curriculum differentiation and such a process runs contrary to equality of educational opportunity. On the surface there is a remarkable similarity about what is included everywhere in the compulsory core list of subjects. They are, in descending order of commonality: mother tongue and its literature; mathematics; natural and physical sciences; modern foreign language(s); history; geography; art; music; PE. It is also significant that this curriculum can be described thus, using the very orthodox labels of discrete subjects. Notions of integration or combined studies are not unheard of in the USA, under organizing titles such as 'Social Skills and Culture' or 'Man and his Environment', but they are uncommon elsewhere, or provided late as an elective subject, often to the least able. In the Soviet Union they are rejected totally, for here it is argued that the major cognitive achievement in the history of ideas has been to isolate properly separate modes of thought, though the need for children to see the relationships or interconnections between disciplines is admitted and sought.

Another interesting trend is the way in which many countries have set about solving the explosion of knowledge problem. What they have done is to identify the central skills, concepts, ideas and methods of particular subjects and to teach these to children, rather than continuing with an encyclopedic coverage of all the known knowledge of a particular field. This principle of selection has informed not only English science and mathematics projects like

Nuffield and SMP, and the Schools Council's projects in history and geography, but also the changes in subject content in France, under Haby, the USSR's new syllabuses (Markuschevitch 1969) and the various curriculum projects of the 1960s and early 1970s in the USA.

Developments in England are not dissimilar to what has been identified so far in this section. The move to comprehensive secondary schools and our usual practice within them of having a more or less common curriculum for the first two or three years, in mixed ability classes, followed by electives constituted on the setting principle, to supplement a limited core of subjects, all bear comparison with the above. However, in terms of control over content and teaching methods, the considerable power exercised by external agencies in other countries makes an enormous qualitative difference.

3.　Singularities and differences

It is now necessary to draw attention to the differences between countries in curriculum matters. Three levels of analysis will be considered: problem recognition, problem analysis, problem solution. A good beginning can be made by pursuing the idea that, arising out of what has been reported so far in this chapter, a series of stark, interrelated and entirely necessary questions exist which all discussions of curriculum at each of the above levels have, through the inevitability of logic, to address themselves to. The questions look like this:

What are children taught?

What do children learn?

Why are children taught this?

What should children be taught?

What should children learn?

How are children taught?

Why are children taught thus?

How should children be taught?　Why?

How do children learn?

How should children learn?

Who are children taught by?

Who do children learn from?

Where are children taught?

Where do children learn?

Where should children be taught?

What is learning?

What is childhood?

Do children differ?   Or; what proper criteria of differences
between children should be recognized?

Are any of the following criteria relevant: chronological age,
maturation, stage of development, mental age, ability,
attainment, aptitude, interest, needs, social class, background,
gender, ethnicity, experience, culture, family background.

So, should children who are manifestly different be taught different
things and in different ways? Or, despite their differences,
should all children be taught the same things, but in different
ways?

The following valid generalizations emerge from a consideration of this battery of questions. Due to their complexity, ideally the curriculum should be broadly, widely, maximally conceived. It would seem that a minimal conceptualization (e.g. listing the subjects on the school's timetable, or the identification of the formal offerings taught by it) is inadequate because it omits the many informal experiences children have — what they learn from, say, the covert, hidden, but implicit value system of the school; from their peers; even from people outside the school. Similarly the division of labour in some analyses of curriculum between philosophers (what? and why? questions) and psychologists (how? questions) seems antiquated. Other distinctions can also be deemed misleading. To separate content from method is unsatisfactory because, for the pupils, the method may well be the message; it is what they *do* in 'lessons' which governs how they come to define the content, irrespective of its formal label by, say, a subject title. To treat some concepts as discrete entities would also appear fallible — for example, teaching and learning; the elements within the teacher's activities of planning, teaching and evaluating. Finally, the questions suggest that the claim that objectives and assessment are somehow neutral and separate from process is false.

In fact, however, these questions are *not* universally recognized or raised. For example, some would ask, 'Who's asking these questions? Teachers; curriculum mongers; parents?' Or, 'Which of these questions do children raise?' Thus, in practice, attempts are made to order the complexities by assuming that some questions must be paramount or that some follow logically from others. Two well-known examples should suffice. First, let us consider the well-known claim, in some of the progressive or child-centred literature, of the overwhelming centrality of the learner. Thus, what is taught, this argument goes, must be governed by the nature, special features, qualities, etc. of those who are being taught, or who are doing the learning. Second, a powerful-sounding case is put in the work advocating an objective model of teaching and curriculum (e.g. Bloom 1956) that it is aims, or goals, which should govern all. Plausibility is enhanced by the exhaustive and comprehensive-sounding categories of objectives identified in taxonomical form. In both these cases, order is achieved; ambiguity is reduced, even if many essential considerations are denigrated or lost in the process.

A succinct way of developing this point further is to attempt to state the questions in composite form, so as to produce an all-embracing summary of the crucial issues. One such summary might be: 'How, where, and from whom should which children be taught and learn what?' Other reformulations are possible, indicating the priorities and partialities of the questioner. Such composites can be transposed into statements about the curriculum in terms of what is, what can be, or what should be. It is quite clear that these variations, either in question or statement form, rest upon some prior, conceptualizing, framing, ordering, device at work. Comparatively speaking, this is precisely what occurs.

So, in some countries it will be found that some questions get priority — will be seen as preceding others; some questions will not be recognized as serious, and will even be deemed illegitimate. Thus the local Epistemological Style, containing a formula of connected guiding principles, will produce a check-list of questions, probably convertible to composite form, summarizing the way in which the curriculum is deemed problematical — if at all. Similarly the composite statement profiles — different for one Epistemological Style as compared to another — will in effect be a summary of local curriculum analysis and contain those solutions to the problem deemed necessary, perhaps containing the implication that urgent changes in policy or practice are needed.

One warning note of reservation must be sounded about an omission from the discussion of the curriculum in various countries which follows. The idea has been expressed that the curriculum should be defined and understood maximally — to include its covert, often hidden features, many of which are inculcated by day-to-day interactions and classroom events. Unfortunately, no comparative studies of this kind exist, even where such data might have been expected, that is, in the comparative study of school subjects and their matter. Halls (1970) does describe clearly what foreign languages are taught in various European countries and gives the precise reasons why they are selected. The importance of Dance's work for history, and Merchant's for geography has already been alluded to. Davies' study (1982) of physics teaching and the training of physics teachers is encyclopedic. King et al. (1974) uncover extremely important information regarding how children aged 16-19 react to, and what they think of, what they have been taught — though not with subject based precision. The negative findings in Husén's attempt (1967) to study the efficacy of the schools of 12 countries are also important. He set out to measure their efficiency by testing the attainment of children in mathematics, which, naturally perhaps, he presumed to be if not entirely culture proof, at least far more so than any other subject. What emerges, however, is not only that *school* mathematics differs from place to place according to what is included, depending on the purposes in mind, but something further. That is that *mathematics* has various definitions, partly because what is deemed worthy of research, even the abstract symbolic language invented and traditionally used by practitioners, is specific to and bound by time, place, culture and custom.

None of this is to say that the sort of comparative curriculum studies envisaged here are impossible, or that what has been done is of no consequence. But few have set out so far to uncover the variously expressed, subtle, hidden ideological mechanisms at work. Such studies would need to include comparisons of not only *what* is taught — lists of subjects, syllabus contents — and *why* — justificatory arguments expressing purposes — but also *how* it is taught, who by, what children actually learn, and what they think of what they have learned. Thus would the informally inculcated moral or ethical values be revealed. Extensive periods of observation would be involved, by field workers with appropriate linguistic and pedagogical backgrounds, capable of extrapolating many half-hidden meanings. What follows here, then, is an attempt to look at the curriculum of each of our foreign countries as perspicaciously as possible, but without data covering some fundamental matters. Use can and will be made of evidence like school rules or the varying identity labels of status and purpose inherently worn by teachers.

4.   The USSR — Marxist-Leninism

The Marxist-Leninist Epistemological Style, as described in Chapter 1, provides very clear ground rules which, when applied to the curriculum, mean that many of the common dilemmas identified above either never appear or quickly disappear. This can be demonstrated by rehearsing arguments of principle in terms of the ground rules, and describing the current practices that exist. For Soviet educators, the initial generalities of principle are these: given that the prime political aim of the educational system is to produce a communist society, it follows that the major curriculum determinant is that of societal need. The school curriculum must contain that knowledge which is worth while when so defined. Such a principle immediately identifies superior forms of knowledge and criteria for inclusion and exclusion, dispenses with charges of irrelevance, and includes concern for a type of education for international understanding. Further, even with finite resources, an overwhelming case for priority in their use can be made for education. The vanguard cadre model of progress towards communism eliminates ambiguities regarding control because politically all power is properly vested in the Party. The teacher is unequivocally *in* authority and *an* authority. Again, for the new society to be born, it follows that all children must have access to, and acquire, this general fund of knowledge. With very few exceptions (i.e. those who are measurably physically impaired) all children are thought capable of mastering this knowledge, for nature is seen as the result of nurture, of the moulding process of learning. Any differences which appear in the pace or speed with which children learn are explained in terms of differentiated diligence, which is rectifiable, and not through innate intelligence or aptitude.

Soviet educators would claim that their orientation has always been towards mass education; far from having to cope with a pressure of increasing demand for schooling, they have always positively fostered it. They also point out that their definition of the curriculum has also always been very broadly based, involving two far from discrete components:

1. The acquisition by pupils of the necessary knowledge of various subjects, broken down chronologically into their component parts — skills, facts, ideas, concepts, principles, methods — which leads, upon proper mastery, to originality and creativity.

2. An obedience to certain ethically founded rules which are then understood, accepted and internalized, enabling in turn the acquisition of proper moral values and attitudes which lead to actions and behaviour appropriate to a socialist citizen.

The curriculum, derived from these premises, is described as polytechnical education and the official timetabling of its knowledge components is given in Figure 8 (Novosti Press, 1979).

SUBJECT	NUMBER OF INSTRUCTION HOURS PER WEEK PER GRADE									
	i	ii	iii	iv	v	vi	vii	viii	ix	x
Native Language	12	10	10	6	6	3	3	2	1	-
Literature	-	-	-	2	2	2	2	3	4	3
Mathematics	6	6	6	6	6	6	6	6	5	5
History	-	-	-	2	2	2	2	3	4	3
Social Science	-	-	-	-	-	-	-	-	-	2
Nature Study	-	2	2	2	-	-	-	-	-	-
Geography	-	-	-	-	2	3	2	2	2	-
Biology	-	-	-	-	2	2	2	2	1	2
Physics	-	-	-	-	-	2	2	3	4	5
Astronomy	-	-	-	-	-	-	-	-	-	1
Draughtsmanship	-	-	-	-	-	1	1	1	-	-
Foreign Language	-	-	-	-	4	3	3	2	2	2
Chemistry	-	-	-	-	-	-	2	2	3	3
Fine Art	1	1	1	1	1	1	-	-	-	-
Singing & Music	1	1	1	1	1	1	1	-	-	-
Physical Education	2	2	2	2	2	2	2	2	2	2
Vocation Training	2	2	2	2	2	2	2	2	2	2
Optional Instruction hours	-	-	-	-	-	-	2	4	6	6
	24	24	24	24	30	30	32	34	36	36

Figure 8

A number of important comments must be made regarding this curriculum. Clearly it is more extensive than those of other countries, for not only does the central all-Soviet Ministry in Moscow specify the subjects to be taught in every school per hour per week, it also lays down, in absolute detail, the following:

(a) the syllabus for each subject, including the sequence of topics;

(b) the textbook or text to be used;

(c) the teaching and methods to be applied;

(d) the tests and examinations to be used for assessment purposes.

The universal application of the above is ensured partly by the central, regional, local and Trade Union inspectors who assiduously monitor schools, and partly because the role ascribed to school directors is largely that of the pedagogical supervision of teachers and includes the delivery of model lessons. There are two exceptions, however. One concerns those areas, usually rural and geographically distant, where the facilities of plant, furnishings, even staffing, are measurably inferior. Such inequalities are admitted but not condoned, and are seen as entirely temporary situations awaiting appropriate budgetary increases. The other relates to the adjustments in the regulations, to take account of the enormous linguistic variations within the USSR and to protect, even encourage, cultural diversity. Thus, in those regions which have an 'advanced' language, children are made initially literate in this mother tongue, which is in turn used as the medium of instruction for all subjects in secondary classes. Russian becomes the first compulsory 'foreign' language and schools provide 11 years of schooling to make up for time lost. Again, local examples are used to illustrate the content of many subjects, and syllabuses include local cultural features, notably in history and geography. This is the way diversity is recognized, and fostered.

The structuring of the curriculum implies a 'sandwich' type notion of learning, because the content of work in the initial three years of primary classes is almost exclusively aimed at getting children to master the fundamental skills of reading, writing and arithmetic; a logically necessary and discrete prelude for the successful study of specialist subjects. It is interesting that Western visitors tend to find the teaching methods used in all schools, for all ages, very traditional. They normally involve: (i) recapitulation of the last lesson or homework often via questioning; (ii) the presentation and exposition of new material by the teacher, using demonstration or visual aids depending on the subject; (iii) setting of homework exercises on the new work. This didacticism, however, fits the Soviet notion of instructing or informing the young; the model of childhood here is of inferiority, passivity, being made expert. However, exhaustive care is undoubtedly taken by the relevant planners at the Academy of Pedagogical Sciences. Detailed analysis is made of all the concomitants of the knowledge to be taught; comprehensive experimental teaching of a selection of classes in ordinary schools is organized to establish what age groups can be taught which knowledge elements, and this provides the basis for ordering the work. Certainly many visitors are genuinely, even breathtakingly, impressed by the levels of achievement demonstrated by all children.[1]

Similar rigour is applied to ensuring proper moral attitudes and behaviour (Bronfenbrenner 1972). Precise mechanisms derived from Makarenko are systematically applied. The basis here is the list of 20 Rules for Pupils which we have already discussed in Chapter 2. They are reinforced by the models of ideal behaviour demonstrated by various adults, especially teachers, and by drawing attention to heroes and heroines from past and present who personify the exemplary. The school is heavily reinforced in this process by the mass media; many occasions are devised for publicly praising and presenting accolades to good pupils and people.

Residual problems do exist, however, and are admitted by Soviet educators. Concern is expressed, for instance, about the indirect effects of the teaching methods, which can result in school being defined by children as tedious, and also in raising questions in their minds about the relevance of school knowledge, thus perceived, to life. This is often brought out acutely in the crises both of identity and self-organization which many youngsters seem to experience when they leave the cocoon of certainties of the school for the world of work. But without doubt the most acute difficulty arises over the implications of the knowledge explosion. Soviet epistemology suggests that Communist citizens need to know everything about everything. Partial solutions to this crisis have been found by extending compulsory education — children are shortly going to be required to begin at 6 — and by teaching more efficiently, hence the recent collapse of the time devoted to primary class work from four years to three. A more permanent cure may be forthcoming in their use of the proposal already mentioned, to teach those skills, concepts, methods, etc. central to given subject areas, instead of traditional Soviet encyclopedism.

Arising from this difficulty is another, namely how to provide children (some or all?) with a real depth of specialist understanding in one or two subjects, given the overwhelming demands already made upon them by the extensive core curriculum. This specialization is necessary for at least some, as a prelude to higher education which produces the creative frontier researchers that the economy needs. Some policies involving specialization, (e.g. the schools set up decades ago for the specially gifted in music, sport, circus, ballet, etc. and augmented by Kruschev towards mathematics and physics) have not subsequently been extended because they came to be seen as politically unacceptable, carrying too many élitist overtones. The current thinking involves the following steps:

(a) Allowing children to study optional subjects during years 7, 8, 9 and 10.

(b) Each 10-year school being specially equipped to teach in depth one of the orthodox school subjects. About one third of an age group will be encouraged to express their options by specializing thus, moving to another school should the one they currently attend not offer the option they want.

(c) Moving certain children to a professional trade school, which continues teaching the core curriculum but uses the option time to provide an extensive preparation for a particular skilled industrial or commercial trade. The notional target clientele for these institutions is again about one-third of an age cohort.

It is not at all easy, even for visitors conducting research in the field, to discover how exactly these choices come to be made. They must be to some extent the exercise of preference by children and their parents, partly influenced by those pressures of supply and demand in the labour market which they can recognize. However, the demand side is under the surveillance of the State, so that selection through tests of competence must also be involved. In many cases, children will be ascribed to one of the three routes because of manpower needs. Not only are some over-ambitious children debarred if they under-achieve, there are also checks against losing others with outstanding competence through their exercising under-ambitious preferences.

So, this policy involves differentiation and selection and is thus an agency in the division of labour; for routes to higher education, skilled or unskilled work will result from the pursuance of some options or none at all. Extensive part-time opportunities for continuing adult education do ameliorate, or make less inevitable, the life and work chances consequent upon these choices. But the argument is that in the end Soviet society has to face quite honestly its need for a differentiated work force, all of whose contributions are theoretically equally valued.

Criticisms of Soviet curriculum design and practice must be made with care. It is possible, however, to state three broad reservations from within a Marxist perspective. As a prelude we must be reminded of the tendency among Soviet teachers to over-mark children's work (see Chapter 3, Section 5). These actions mean that there must be many children, thus hidden from attention, who can hardly be said to have satisfactorily mastered their work. The second criticism is that the curriculum, in its theoretical mode of inculcating the knowledge and behaviour generally required of all pupils, produces many children who, manifestly, are masters — but of little beyond regurgitation of facts and rule following. There is serious doubt about whether they all understand what they are able to say, are able to use what they say they know, or whether they have an internalized ethical code which enables them to make autonomous choices and produce moral actions. If this is so, then this practice smacks of indoctrination, which is entirely antithetical to Marxist principles. Third, it follows that doubts must be raised about whether the curriculum is in any special way 'polytechnical' at all. Little evidence exists for believing that through it participants have been enabled to recognize the dialectical relationship between theory and practice; the falsehood of dichotomizing life and work; or the equality of manual and mental labour. What is highlighted in each of these three points as legitimate criticism, is within, internal to, the Marxist-Leninist Epistemological Style. The critique fastens upon inconsistencies between principle and practice; dissonance when basic ground rules are juxtaposed with more detailed elements of policy; the impossibility of certain strategies ever being able to produce certain broad, even laudable, aims or ambitions.

5. The USA and Liberal-Pragmatism

To establish the validity of an American, Pragmatic Epistemological Style — its existence, centrality, coherence and all-embracing impact — two generalizations normally made about the United States have to be disposed of. First, its tolerant societal pluralism, the endemic characteristics of a liberal, democratic capitalism; second, the variety in its educational provision and practice caused by the localism of its administration. We may begin by pointing out that for its continuation, capitalism, like communism, requires that a set of clear norms, or a code of conventional mental wisdom, be produced; and that this should then be recognized and closely observed by citizens. The extreme variations of geography, climate and ethnicity across America undoubtedly produce some expressions of cultural variety. Eccentricity is sought and treasured by many Americans. But it is tolerated only in limited peripheral forms, because most Americans are heavily conformist in the important aspects of their life style. Some conformities arise from the identity of goods purchaseable from the nationwide corporations, providers of cuisine and costume, housing and household goods, and legislators for proper habits in work, even leisure rituals. Other conformities are caused by the enormous exercise in effective persuasion mounted by the mass media. Again, while it is true that restless frontierism motivates the extraordinary geographical mobility of the American people, it is also the case they they move partly because they can rely on finding most familiar things at their new 'frontier'.

It is for these background reasons that, although some variations of details do exist in American education, similarity of provision between locales in fact becomes essential. While control may be exercised locally, there is an identity of intention behind the policies implemented. Educational practices also tend to be overwhelmingly similar, as was shown in Chapter 2. If it were otherwise, then the argument, put in its bland form, that the schools of America have always played a crucial part in the historical need to homogenize and harmonize the vast numbers of diverse immigrants into being Americans, could not hold. Neither could the more abrasive interpretation that such a need was invented and propagated by big business for its own convenience, and to ensure effective conformity, through perfumed repression.

The above typifications of American education are vividly demonstrated in the wave of radical critiques which began in the 1950s and developed with increasing velocity and ferocity in the 1960s and 1970s.[2] Their targets and prescriptions were varied, but the point they all made was the extreme efficiency of American schooling in inculcating the principles crystallized in my concept of Epistemological Style.

Let us look at why, how and when these general educational features developed. Two particularly critical factors must be mentioned. First, the outstanding significance, because of its inviolate nature, of the American constitution. The high sounding but very general precepts so boldly stated in it by the eighteenth-century founding fathers have very rarely been challenged. Indeed, due to their general character, few would want to, or could, find exception to them. But because of this very generality, these precepts have been used constantly to consolidate the conventional and to check change. The constitution was established, and has been used, as a guardian against the ephemeral. It is an agent of political conservatism — but it also inhibits changes in educational styles. The second factor concerns the origins and establishment of such styles in the first place. Here the key is the Pragmatic school of thought, avowedly socially practical, developed particularly through the work of Dewey (1899, 1916, 1922) and also of Herbert Spencer (See Lauwerys 1957).

During his teaching career, first at the University of Chicago (1894-1904) and then at Teachers' College, Columbia University, New York (1904-1929), Dewey gathered around him several distinguished colleagues such as Rugg, Kilpatrick and Bode. Between them they developed a highly original and complex school of philosophy. Pervasiveness of dissemination was guaranteed by the fact that all were active in the progressive education movement and its nationwide, organized actions groups such as the NEA. Thousands of student teachers and potential local educational administrators came into contact with these ideas through their attendance at Chicago and Teachers' College. They proceeded to practise the preachings of Pragmatism, which, once established, at first infused and then rigidified the cast of American educational thought. Gumbert and Spring (1974) provide a telling account of these processes, and also show how the original ideas later became mutated and were eventually used by corporations for their own purposes.

As to more recent, post-war times, the following list details other trends which have encouraged conformity:

— The consolidation of school districts, advocated in the 1960s by liberals such as Keppel (1966) in the cause of greater equality of educational opportunity, efficiency and cost benefits, has proceeded apace. A consequence of this reduction in their number, but an increase in the size of each, has been to erode distinctiveness and increase the similarities between local school districts.

— For similar reasons, and at about the same time, a large number of interstate agreements were concluded. These were aimed at coordinating research, development and planning in education for a whole region and thus included agreed high school graduation and teacher certification accreditation for the whole zone. Interregional similarities were in turn increased in both these matters by the activity of the National Accrediting Association and the National Association for the Accrediting of Teachers.

— The actions of Federal institutions have had similar effects. The role of the Supreme Court as a national norm setter is documented in Chapters 5 and 6, for through its judicial judgements it has required states to conform more closely over matters of religion and facilities for racial minorities. Federal legislation both on civil rights and to provide financing for compensatory education was also important. In the latter case, there were always strings attached to the provision of dollars, so ensuring that funded curricular packages, for example, became similar.

— Less official, but none the less formal national institutions, such as the NEA, the NAOPTA, and the teacher associations, have often championed systematic nationwide causes. But the great increase in the use made by schools, colleges and universities, of national testing services, which claim to provide overall guidelines of achievement standards, has increased the trend to conformity — for children are taught what the tests measure. Also philanthropic societies, such as the Rockefeller, Ford or Carnegie Foundation, have sponsored new syllabus programmes, which have been widely taken up. Of even greater significance has been the effect of the success which the textbook companies have achieved in selling their wares to one whole school district after another. Consequently the content of many courses has become identical nationwide.

To summarize: it can reasonably be claimed that due to these trends the American electorate mandates school superintendents in the fewer but larger school districts to administer or implement increasingly similar policies and practices, with decreasing diversity of aims and purpose. Thus has national identity been achieved by overwhelming conformity to the liberal, democratic, capitalist ideology.

This case becomes satisfactorily watertight if we also recall other traditional and common educational practices, each of which could be described as entirely novel American inventions: namely the elective, credit and grade systems; tracking; and a neo-behaviourist, objectives model of curriculum or syllabus planning. We must discuss each of these in at least outline form, by looking at how high schools operate in practice.

Some descriptions of the American high-school curriculum suggest that it comprises a very small, required core, augmented by an enormously varied programme of electives which individual students are free to choose from. Further, this is why the curriculum defies generality, for what schools offer varies; and the curriculum is as various as the choices made by individuals.

Certainly, by European standards the list of elective courses on offer is phenomenally long — often 150 or more — and fields of study are included which are excluded from our schools because they are thought inappropriate. It is also the case that because worthwhile knowledge in America is defined as that which is of most use to the individual's perceived needs, and because knowing *how* is preferred to knowing *that,* these study areas are not hierarchized so starkly into high, medium, low or no-status categories. To maximize individual choice, flexibility is provided by the credit system, which incidentally also permits the rectification of misinformed choices made earlier in a student's career. Thus, once a course programme has been successfully negotiated by compliance with its necessary attendance and assessment rubrics, credit is recorded to the student. Over six years, sufficient of such credits can be built up by quarter, semester and year to reach the total required for high-school graduation.

However, there is much greater standardization in the high-school curriculum than is implied in this depiction. So that flexibility does not descend to anarchy, and to insure against ludicrous differences in the standards of requirement and expectation, the grade system was produced. Nationally understood standards of achievement emerged, enabling immediate recognition of what might be meant by a student who claimed success in a specific study area to a certain grade level. Marking or evaluation scales — using A, B, C, etc. — became the overall convention.

An analysis of any of the high-school registration booklets which are issued to all students, and which they all have to negotiate, will reveal further commonalities. Schools make clear not only the total number of credits which have to be acquired, but put limits upon exactly how.

Thus, for example:

'Class of 1981 — students will need a total of 15 credits for graduation including the following:

1.   English — 3 credits; including Composition — 3 quarters, Language — 1 quarter, Oral Communication — 1 quarter, English electives — 4 quarters.

2.   Social Studies — 2 credits; including World History — 3 quarters, American History — 3 quarters, Basic Economics — 1 quarter, State and Local Government — 1 quarter.

3.   Mathematics — 1 credit.

4.   Science — 1 credit.

5.   Electives — 8 credits.'

Any inspection of the Electives offered in any high school will reveal that they are invariably taught under the aegis of departmentally titled fields of study, appropriately staffed by qualified specialists. In the following list, figures in brackets indicate, roughly, how many separate courses such departments usually offer: Art (8) and Technical Arts (16); Business Education (10); Counselling (3); Driver & Traffic Safety Education (1); English (50); Foreign Languages (15); Home Economics (15); Mathematics (20); Music (12); Physical Education (12); Sciences (10); Social Studies (35). Credits earnable for specific courses range from .25 to .5 to 1 or 1.5 even 2.

In most high schools, due to the impact of those who argued in the 1960s the need for much more academic rigour in the graduation requirements, very specific guidelines are provided regarding the choice of electives. Such guidelines are called 'tracking'. Two broad tracks are immediately obvious: one for College-bound, another for non-College-bound students. For the former there are usually three different, if parallel sets of lines. First, a Program for the Gifted and Talented. Second, an Honours Program for those destined for demanding in-State and out-of-State universities — (here, for example, students are required to build up their elective credits in 'French to grade VI; German to grade III; Algebra to grade II and Honours Geometry, Analysis, Calculus; in Science Biology II, Physics II, Honours Chemistry; in Social Studies, Philosophy to grade IV').[4] Third, a less taxing package for admission to most publicly supported in-State four-year colleges, where perhaps 10 units of credit must be earned in academic subjects — here the minimum is usually: English — 4 years; Foreign Languages — 2 years; Algebra — 1 year; Geometry — 1 year; Social Studies — 3 years; Laboratory Sciences — 2 years. About 40% of high-school students will proceed to higher education in some form on graduation, at whichever of these levels. Further, although some of these institutions, through their reputations (e.g. the Ivy League universities), or through the esteem they have won (the many internationally recognized State Universities), can afford to be very selective, traditionally the tertiary level of education has not defined the high-school curriculum through its entry requirements to the extent common in Europe. The Arts and Science Bachelor degrees are broadly constructed, leading only then to the postgraduate vocational schools of, say, law or medicine.

The non-College track is similarly layered, ranging from electives carefully constructed to qualify graduates for entry to skilled or semi-skilled technical or commercial trades, to programs (however euphemistically labelled, e.g. Alternative Learning Program for Sophomores) catering for slow learners whose basic skills are still defective, or for some students whose disaffection with the ordinary school diet leads to behaviour which means they have to be persuaded on to separate courses.

So, many of the electives may not be effective choices for given students. The counselling service available to children in all schools tended, according to Cicourel and Kitsuse (1963), to limit or at least delineate student horizons further. In any event, some courses have prerequisites attached to them, namely satisfactory achievement in a specific related field as a preliminary qualification for enrolment. In all these ways, then, the curriculum is not quite as diverse or different as our original definition might have implied.

Attention must now be directed to three qualitative ingredients of the American curriculum which combine to give it its distinctive, but again nationwide, general flavour. These are:

1. **Planning** after the style of two very early curriculum prescriptions, i.e. those of the NEA in its *Committee of Ten on Secondary School Studies* 1892-3, and its National Committee on Reorganisation of Secondary Education, 1918, bulletin 35, *Seven Cardinal Principles of Secondary Education.* Or, the **prestatement of objectives** (often remarkable for their quite extraordinary scope and usually presented taxonomically) after Bloom (1956) and Tyler (1949).

2. **Learning** conceived in behaviourist terms, after Skinner (1959, 1968), involving the programming of the content; seeing learning as changes in behaviour.

3. **Evaluating success** by the constant and fine measurement of 2, when matched against 1.

Samples to flavour abound: for example, the way textbooks are structured; that courses are called 'programs' with their teaching materials packaged accordingly; the tests and testing devices used by counselling services and the academic staff of schools alike; the categories used in the reports on children sent by schools to parents; even the way broadsheets from superintendents to schools, and the papers enunciating principles from principals to their faculty, are couched.

Even the ideas of Bruner (1960, 1966), so well known and respected in Europe — perhaps because of their dissimilarity to much American thinking — contain these elements, not least in his MACOS scheme. Renowned for the originality of its conception and richness of materials, it remains planned and structured and is objectives orientated. Perhaps this explains why the content and activities failed to work, for the expectation was that all children could study the same exemplifying phenomena like herring gulls and salmon, even when for many, such as inner-city pupils, they were divorced from their day-to-day experiences. It explains too, the insensitivity and anthropological error of placing Eskimo culture in a mid-way position on an animal-Man (sic) complexity continuum.

Nascent threats to the sacrosanct model of individualism contained in some of the above are denied or seemingly ignored. The charge that behaviourism denies people's dignity, seeing them as conditionable robots, is deflected. Claims that an objectives model of planning is prescriptive and inhibitive are rebutted by arguing that it is neutral and can be used by individuals to objectively delineate their own needs. Further arguments to support the overriding advantages of fine planning are put as follows: that all eventualities can be predicted and covered; that teaching is improved by having to state aims so precisely and by having to break down content into a set of step-by-minute-step stages; that through constant and instantaneous success and reward the material is mastered by all children.

Although American schools are required by the constitution to eschew matters of religion, they do not leave matters of morality, ethics or values entirely to individuals and their parents. It is worth pointing up some of the statements in school handbooks which reveal the hidden, but implicit and common value structures. So, although the advisory facilities of the school are carefully detailed, students are charged as individuals to be responsible for their own study selections, their own progress, their own achievements. Whose fault failure then? How, then, may the teacher's role be constructed? 'Student Discipline' invariably covers value-laden points like lateness, cheating, cooperative classroom behaviour, fighting, harassment, disruption, profanity, smoking, drinking, illegal drugs, sportsmanship, vandalism, theft, conventions of dress. Finally, the extensive lists of the many varied extracurricular facilities by way of clubs, societies, and teams provide further insights. For example, there are not only 'Cheerleaders; to promote school spirit and enthusiasm at all athletic events', but also 'a Chapter of the Future Business Leaders of America', and of the 'Distributive Education Club of America — the club is nationwide with competition in sales demonstrations, manuals, displays, advertising, and other areas of marketing and distribution ..... students learn to relate their classroom knowledge to the competitive world of business'.[5]

We can now see how the American Epistemological Style and its schooling devices described so far can, in its own terms, dispose of most of the general problems we began with — perhaps with even greater rapidity and *élan* than does even Marxist-Leninism. The curriculum, based on a small common core with a systematic range of electives, and aided by the credit system and an explicit model of learning, was devised for the purpose of providing mass education. Americans could claim that in its own way it is a coherent and original version of this notion. The knowledge explosion issue can be solved by using the usefulness and relevance to the individual's needs to select what is to be taught or learned. Increasing aspirations can similarly be met. The problem of relevance (i.e. to the individual student's perceptions) need not be admitted as a difficulty either, because curriculum design has always avoided it by providing choices and requiring individual responsibility in exercising them. The role of the teacher as a guide for making choices, and then as a systematic instructor once such choices have been made, is still comfortable enough.

What remains to be done in this section is to consider briefly how certain recent and residual educational issues somewhat specific to the USA have been conducted. This should add to the patina of our analysis, for we shall see how some problems are recognized and analysed, and how solutions are formulated in an idiosyncratic American style.

One such case concerns the way in which the issue of academic excellence developed. The USSR's sputnik successes in the 1950s were a series of challenges to the general viability and success of American society, and produced a telling impact on her credibility and prestige internationally. Critics (e.g. Trace 1971, *What Ivan Knows that Johnny Doesn't*) raised trenchant attacks upon the educational system and its part in producing this decline. Teacher education was particularly savaged (Bestor 1953; Koerner 1963) for preparing teachers who knew everything about Johnny but nothing about what Johnny ought to know. In short, they argued that high school and college graduates just did not know enough; the system produced too few scientific experts to man the necessary US counter space movements. The implication of this was that students should be taught more of those subjects traditionally seen as academic — math, the physical sciences, modern languages. Conant's best-selling and seemingly neutral surveys of high schools (1959, 1967) added fuel to the flames. Solutions advocated included the tightening up of graduation rubrics, the intensification of tracking, and the 'back to basics' movement for primary schools. It is worth quoting Blenkin's summary of one highly significant event of this period, the Woods Hole conference, 1959:

> Fundamental to the thinking of this conference was the now famous notion that
> any subject can be taught effectively in some intellectually honest form to any
> child at any stage of development (Bruner 1960, p. 33) ..... The style .....
> depended on academic experts within disciplines (notably the sciences) to
> structure the knowledge and expert planners and psychologists to relate this
> knowledge structure to the child's level of learning. It was intended that,
> having engaged experts to resolve the 'structure' and 'readiness' issues, the
> teacher's task would be simply to implement the curriculum development.
> (Blenkin 1980, p. 57)

There followed a proliferation of federal and independently funded projects
which tried to implement these ideas by redesigning and improving subjects
(Project Physics); or by discovering very able youngsters (Project Talent).
These influences did cause adjustments to be made to the curricula for
children and students all over America. But what is interesting is how these
national needs arguments, pressing for academic and intellectual rigour and
running counter to the well-established notions of individual needs and
useful knowledge, were accommodated. This was achieved by defining
acquiescence as temporary, and through certain redefinitions. Thus, changes
wrought for national socio-economic and political needs were tolerated, but
only while national defence and prestige was at stake and not after this crisis
was over. For the moment they were to be seen as curricular changes towards
internationalism, defined as the restoration of pride in America in the eyes of
Americans and foreigners alike. This again is why, during the 1970s, federal
activity first declined and then lapsed as older traditions could be resorted to.

Some attention must be paid to the deschooling movement and the voucher
system. For a time, enormous interest was shown in the ideas of Reimer,
Friere and Illich, by many people and in particular by radicals both of the left
and the right. This was so because, for very different reasons, they feared the
activities of national and federal agencies identified above. Deschoolers
restated conservative or traditional ideas in novel forms. They sought to
return to individuals and families their lost freedoms and liberties over the
content of education by enabling them to evade the reach of the powers of
government and the other agencies who were prescribing content. Having
made their point and having achieved sufficient retrenchment in the public
schools, again through the decline in federal activity, the movement declined.

It is worth emphasizing that every attempt has been made to discuss
American education in American terms. Critics and defenders cited have been
American writers, each successful or influential to the extent that they have
struck chords in an American style of educational thought and analysis.
Epistemological Styles are not immutable; but they are certainly tough and

crystalline — the fossilized remains of previous arguments and procedures. Pursuing this geological analogy, new layering does take place, and while weathering and cracking occur, even eruption or explosion never completely shatters the bed-rock.

6. Europe

The European scene can be dealt with more briefly, but the setting must include an appreciation of the following points. First, whilst the statement of the origins and features of the classical European Epistemological Style holds good for all Western parts of the continent, there are variations within it. There are marginal differences between the French, German and English versions of the common style and attention will be drawn to them in what follows. Historically the French and German traditions have been powerful models for other continental countries; the former percolating into Iberia, Italy and Belgium; the latter greatly affecting Scandinavia and the Low Countries. The English style was highly influential in zones originally called colonial territories, and more recently, partnerships in Commonwealth. Colonialism also accounts for the global impact of the European approach to education, most notably in Third World countries. (It is unclear whether, with poignant irony, the pursuit of the abstract leads to ruling the waves and distant shores and lands, or whether such a luxury can be afforded because of the wealth generated by the utilitarian activities of the lesser men, of industry, commerce, technology and merchandising.)

Second, it is important to reiterate that in Europe, while the existence of the three determining parameters of curriculum (i.e. the needs of society and of individuals, and the nature of knowledge) are recognized, it is the third of these which has been given greatest weight. And it is because worthwhile knowledge has been defined as the pursuit of objective truth that discrete forms of such knowledge have been evolved, ranked on a high, medium, low, no-status continuum. Of equal importance is the related, though by no means logically connected, extension, namely that only some people were and are capable of initiation into this esoteric world of largely pure, rational, propositional knowledge. Thus, irrespective of institutional arrangements, the curriculum continues to have élitist connotations. It is worth stressing that throughout Europe, and not least in France, Germany and England, certain groups of children, categorized by geography, gender, and ethnicity, but much more importantly, by social class, grossly underachieve. To put it differently, using normal indices and measures, children from working-class backgrounds are still differentiated out, by being selected for high-status academic courses less frequently than children from other classes, despite their numerical superiority. Officially there may be claims that a search for merit is being conducted to form the élite; in fact birth remains a major determinant in its perpetuation.

Third, given this description, the general problems we began with in this chapter may be highly specific European ones resulting from pressures to develop some form of mass education. It has already been demonstrated that American and Soviet thought sees them as having only tangential relevance or significance. European solutions to the problems would appear to be much more difficult to come by, given attitudes here to knowledge and people. However, let us now see how each of our countries has approached the issues.

7. France

In looking at how the French have defined and attempted to solve the central dilemmas of mass education, certain well-documented features of French education must be reiterated. First, there is the post-Revolutionary insistence on the recruitment of the élite by merit, as demonstrated by some people's success in education, with the post-Napoleonic pinnacle being represented by graduates from universities, with the general staff emerging from the minute few who completed their courses at the *grandes écoles*. Such a premise makes competition at all stages quite inevitable, so that, for example, examinations have always been governed by the existence of pre-specified pass, failure percentages. This competitive élitism is different in character from that of America because fewer people are seen as potentially capable of success, so enabling selection to begin much earlier. Further, the competition is about the acquisition of that necessary encyclopedic body of abstract wisdoms, labelled *culture générale*. Finally, such a system always functioned on behalf of the State, so, when post-war governments recognized that education could not only fashion national identity but also service economic growth, it was mobilized to facilitate this by producing, qualitatively and quantitatively, the State's manpower needs.

In front of a backcloth thus patterned, there has been a great deal of activity in the educational sector over the past two decades, much of which continues to affect the practice of French schooling and was designed to have important consequences for the curriculum. The compromise Berthoin legislation of 1959 and the more far reaching decrees of Fouchet in 1963 consolidated the institutional structure into the three clear levels of primary; first and second cycle secondary; higher and further. Thus, following five years of primary schooling, children moved to common secondary schools (*collèges d'enseignement secondaire*) and entered the four years of the orientation or observation cycle, with, in theory, a common curriculum for all. In principle, this period was and is designed with twin purposes in mind: namely, to enable pupils to recognize which of several educational and vocational prospects they would prefer; to allow teachers to begin the induction of all into the components of *culture générale* whilst at the same time providing them, through the evidence of differentials of attainment, with grounds for directing different individuals to different second cycle courses. The 1966-70 Education Plan quite explicity stated that this nationwide organization of the 11-15 year span was to ensure the democratization of education by delaying selection, giving everyone access to high-status knowledge areas and thus the rational ascription of children to appropriate niches. The secondary *collèges* were to provide a comprehensive counselling service to ensure informed choices.

The second secondary phase was, and continues to be, divided broadly into two. Children opting for, or assigned to, the two-year short cycle acquire the basic school-leaving certificate, *certificat d'aptitude professionelle*, which qualifies them for semi-skilled or unskilled employment. Courses are nevertheless varied, because certificates qualify holders for quite specific jobs. Those who embark on the long four-year cycle hope to acquire more prestigious certification. Some study for the *brevet de technicien* which is orientated broadly to one of the following employment segments: industrial-technical; socio-technical; hotel and catering; agriculture. Again, however, there is great variety in the detail of *brevet* courses as each, again, leads to specified employment in commerce or industry, though this time of a skilled nature. The most academically successful follow a *baccalauréat* course, which qualifies holders for entry into higher education and the professions. This second cycle, then, was specifically designed in all respects to be entirely vocational, to meet pressures for relevance, even to the extent of augmenting the five or so traditional *baccalauréats* with many new ones based in science, technology, even commerce.

This edifice looked impressive at first glance. Constructed and defended with the renowned French flair for elegances of form, it appeared neatly to match practice with explicit, consistent and congruent principles. Traditional élitism was not jettisoned, but fairness was injected into the system generating it. Mass education could thus properly be defined as treating differently those who were demonstrably, by attainment, unequal. The necessary instrumental and utilitarian functions of education had been made to work efficiently for mutual benefit, but without the loss of that which is intrinsically worthwhile.

The pursuit of excellence was retained, but it also accrued to the communal national advantage.

In the early 1970s, however, several reservations began to be voiced about the real extent of the improvements wrought, notably with regard to practices at the first cycle stage of secondary schooling. (Significantly, the way in which basic principles had been elucidated was not fundamentally challenged.) These criticisms had to be taken seriously, for the ethical validity of the French version of equality was entirely dependent upon propriety and fairness at this level. *Redoublement* (children repeating a year) therefore became a serious problem. The individual child's progress was, and is, monitored by yearly tests of attainment. Pupils failing these examinations were required to repeat the year (which incidentally could mean that the ascription of chronological age to various grades of work was entirely nominal). The trouble with the evidence was that it showed overwhelmingly that it was children from working-class backgrounds who were doing most of the repeating. King (1974), for example, maintained that in this period only 36% of working-class children were completing five years of primary schooling without repeating, though 76% of children from middle-class homes were doing so. A tactic adopted by middle-class parents to retain their familial advantage by perpetuating the social position of their progeny was also uncovered. What they did was to enrol their children in schools of religious foundation — largely Roman Catholic — and this in the context of nearly two centuries of Church versus State furore in French education. These schools tended to be conservative, with a reputation for the successful schooling of their pupils in the traditional high-status subjects.

However, perhaps the most crucial strictures centred upon the actual curriculum of the first cycle schools. It appeared that in practice no common curriculum existed during this so-called orientation period, for children at the *collèges* were always assigned, on entry, to one of three *filières* — or streams — according to attainment. The curriculum was rarely, if ever, identical between these groups or grids. Naturally, therefore, one *filière* track in practice led to a quite specific course or group of courses at the second cycle. Once the curriculum had become thus differentiated, for even the shortest of time spans and in even the most minor of ways, movement between grids became impossible. This was because students could not study in year 2 what they had not learned in year 1 because they had been given no opportunity to do so.

In general then, it was claimed that selection had not been effectively deferred. Assignment at age 11 remained crucial. Just how crucial could be seen by the fact that holding only a *certificat d'aptitude professionelle* in no way guaranteed employment; holders often found no match between their qualification and the actualities of the local job market. Even the elegantly postulated French version of equality became depicted as a mirage.

The Haby Law, 1975, and the Decrees of 1977 and 1978 set out explicitly to remedy some of these deficiencies and malpractices. Poujol's depiction of these developments (1980) merits careful summary. He argues that the law 'had five main objectives; first to improve equality of chances; secondly to give a well balanced schooling; thirdly to promote technological and vocational education; fourthly to educate for citizenship; and fifthly, to establish a school community with its own responsibility' (p. 187). He identifies other important guiding principles which, by implication, were very novel in the French context. For example: developing critical minds capable of interpreting information from the media 'to combine both "knowledge of" and "knowing how"; ..... more attention ..... to the psychological development of the child with a progressive, developmental approach throughout the four years of the course; ..... to study in depth a few selected themes instead of trying helplessly to be encyclopaedic'.

Several policies were devised to achieve these aims — like keeping the first cycle *collèges* small (about 250 pupils only); setting up Councils in every school made up of elected representatives from parents and pupils; providing textbooks free of charge. But the most crucial device was the entire reshaping of the curriculum. Poujol's summary of its current character is as follows:

Weekly Timetable Hours at Collège

	Years 1 & 2	Years 3 & 4
French	5 + 1 hour further help or enrichment	5
Mathematics	3 + 1 hour further help or enrichment	4
Modern Languages	3 + 1 hour further help or enrichment	3
History — Geography	3	3
Artistic Education	2	2
Technical & Handicraft Education	2	$1\frac{1}{2}$
TOTAL	21 + up to 3 hours further help or enrichment	$21\frac{1}{2}$

Weekly Timetable Hours at Collège (cont)

	Years 1 & 2	Years 3 & 4
Physical Education	3	3
Optional Sport	2	

The pupils in the third and fourth years have to take at least one of the following:

Latin	3 hours	Greek	3 hours
Second Language	3 hours	First Language enrichment	2 hours
Technology	3 hours		

The school year runs for 35 weeks.
An additional timetable may be offered in those *collèges* where pupils in the fourth year experience severe learning difficulties.

Two comments are essential. On the one hand, the claim now is that the old tracks or *filières* have effectively been abolished; all children between the ages of 12 and 16 follow an absolutely identical common core of subject matter. Further, the repeating (*redoublement*) phenomenon has been eradicated by the additional 'enrichment' provisions for children with special needs. Thus has equality been achieved. The common curriculum has been improved qualitatively by not only recasting the content of the traditional subjects — mathematics, French and modern languages, but also by redefining the other subjects. The humanities are now seen as 'economic and civic initiation'. The other major areas are to be seen as 'introductions into' physical and chemical phenomena; technology and handicrafts; the arts. Thus are the Haby aims, 2-5 as outlined by Poujol above, to be met.

On the other hand, the pattern of options required in years 3 and 4 appears to contradict all this. It is apparent that not only does curriculum differentiation occur here, but it is along entirely traditional high to low-status subject lines, which transparently lead to the clear second cycle tracks, with obvious consequences for further education, occupation and life chances. It is necessary and possible to pursue other residual criticisms of the qualitative features of the curriculum.

Manifestly, the curriculum in France is attainment-based. Courses are understood, described, defined and experienced in terms of what examination or certificate they lead to. In these terms then, the second cycle curriculum, for example, is extraordinarily differentiated; what is more, the status of the various certificates is heavily hierarchized partly because their content elements are deemed either pure or polluted manifestations of *culture générale*. Although there are by now 18 separate *baccalauréats*, many of the new ones are upgraded *brevet* courses, with a technological bias. They are held in much lower esteem than the traditional A, B, C, D, even T (technical) titles. (Interestingly, of these, the C *baccalauréat* has now ousted the classical-language-based A *baccalauréat* as the supreme award). The whole spirit of this curriculum, then, even in the terms of its own rationale remains jaundiced. It means that, in effect, a child in France is only as good as the examination he or she has passed. There is much resentment of this high-jump characteristic to learning.

In further pursuit of these qualitative features of the French curriculum, it is salutory to consider Archer's depiction (1979, chapter 8) of policy developments after the 1968 student protests as blind panic rather than careful planning. Despite the vehemence of these protests, often by students of school age, including charges of arbitrary selection, incompetent administration and indifferent teaching, little seems to have changed in the area of teachers and teaching. The Joxe Report, 1972 evidences a recognition of some malaise here. It found the general ethos of schools, in particular pupil-teacher relations, entirely unsatisfactory. It made several recommendations aimed at amelioration and humanization. However, it would appear that many teachers in France still see their role solely as dispensers of knowledge, so that they remain authoritarian in their stances and inflexible in their teaching methods. As a result, classroom activities contribute to giving the curriculum a certain spirit, which is further reinforced by the strict hierarchies within the teaching profession. Explicit and heavily guarded status differentials exist, in ascending order, between *instituteurs, licence* holders, and teachers with the *CAPES*. But by far the most prestigious teachers are those few who are members of the *Société des Agrégés*. They are the best paid, have the lowest teaching load, and usually see their work at a second cycle *lycée* as a temporary interlude, for they are qualified to teach at a university. However, they earn such accolades and exercise power because, through long training, they have become highly qualified subject specialists. The curriculum cannot possibly escape being defined by pupils in terms of what, inescapably, they read into this state of affairs, for it reinforces traditional hierarchies of knowledge.

In summary then, vigorous attempts have undoubtedly been made in France, through the power of the Ministry of Education, to fashion a publicly stated curriculum for schools. This is based on certain cogently presented principles involving notions of democratization, equality and corporate societal needs. Ironically, it is partly because of the inflexibility of centralism and the strictly hierarchic nature of the structures involved that these laudable ambitions have not been fully achieved.

8.   The GFR

In the curriculum of schools in the GFR there is less evidence of change — either in the general shape of institutional structures or the actual content of what children are taught. It is not that there has been an absence of ideas, nor a shortage of suggestions for change, because there has been a great deal of such activity. For example, as long ago as 1959 there were important recommendations made in the *Rahmenplan* which did precipitate some inter-*Land* coordination in the 1960s and 1970s, though on peripheral matters. Again in 1970 and 1973 important documents of a wide-ranging nature were produced by the Education Council of the Federal Ministry of Education and Science. The establishment of the *Bildungsrat* in 1969, through the sponsorship of the then Chancellor, Brandt, resulted in several publications including a report in 1969 and another in 1970. Together they were very comprehensive, covering all aspects of schooling and including a proposal for the complete reform of the secondary stage. Significantly, this included the idea that, after five years of primary work beginning at age 5, there should be a two-year orientation cycle at ages 10-12 as a prelude to four years of common schooling with a common curriculum, culminating in a new style *Arbitur I* achievable by all children at 16. This was to be followed by a two-year course for the academically most able, leading to an *Abitur II*, newly designed so as to interlock vocational and non-vocational elements. Finally, in 1973, a *Bund-Land Kommission* for education was charged with producing plans for a nationwide restructuring of schools, including what and how they taught.

These ideas have not gone completely unheeded, and some changes have been wrought. The prestigious *Gymnasia* have become more porous to children from working-class (*Arbeiter*) backgrounds, though they still only make up about 17% of the students at such schools despite there being about 37% of such children in the student population at large (Wilms 1977). All *Länder* have established selection at 12 instead of 10. Some, notably those under the political control of the SPD, such as Hamburg and Hessen, have set up common secondary schools, though hardly any are *Gesamtschule* (i.e. integrated comprehensives), the one at Gelsenkirchen being exceptional, for most are organized on strictly multilateral lines with children ascribed to one of three curriculum tracks on entry. Integrated colleges for 16-19 year olds, with open access and a wide level of courses (*Oberstuffenkollegien*) are even rarer. The percentage of young people achieving success in the *Abitur* has increased, though this often produces the acid rejoinder from some adults, of lowered standards. (Their usual claim is that the change, whereby points are earned on a unitary basis by subject to make up a necessary total, makes the current *Abitur* a softer option than that of their times, when a grade 4 or better had to be earned in all subjects.) However, schooling and the curriculum in the GFR retain their traditional styles and habits, despite the federal government's expressed hope of the early 1970s that radical reform would be complete by 1980. It can still be accurately depicted as a dual system: *Bildung* for some (i.e. the 20% or so at *Gymnasia*); vocational training and opportunities for the rest — highly skilled for the 15% *Realschule* graduates; skilled or semi-skilled for the majority (i.e. the 65% who emerge from the *Hauptschule*).

The usual explanation for this stagnation is that, due to the post-war constitutional arrangement whereby control over education was vested at the regional level with the *Länder* or city states, effective change can be blocked even when sponsored by the federal government, for its agencies have no power. Similarly, local initiatives by individual schools never emerge because they have to abide by the catalogue of detailed regulations covering all 'what?' 'how?' and 'why?' curriculum matters, produced by individual *Länder* ministries of education.

However, there is much more to things than this, for regional administration does not, ipso facto, produce conservatism. Why then, have there been so few regional initiatives; why have *Länder* politicians of education not been required to shift things by the power of the ballot box? The administration of education in the GFR looks American because it was planned thus. But perhaps because of fragmentation and inconsistency in respect of anything beyond this, the content and style of education remained what it had always been — similar to that of France and to the post-1944 tripartitism in England. In subsequent years (e.g. see Hearnden 1976) nothing seems to have necessitated a shift in the formula. Popular pressure for an alternative model of mass education based on radically different principles and procedures, the explosion of aspirations argument, has been very muted.

Hauptschule, class 9.

Times of Lessons	Monday	Tuesday	Wednesday	Thursday	Friday	Saturday
8.00–8.45 8.45–9.30	Maths	Biology	Sport	Crafts (boys)	English	Group work e.g. Sport, Cookery, Photography
9.45–10.30	Religion	History	German	Free	Social Studies	Physics & Chemistry
10.30–11.15	Geography	German	Social Studies	House-craft (girls)		
11.30–12.15	Options-Music/Art;	Social Studies	Maths		Maths	Free
12.15–1.00	Physics/Chemistry		English	Free	German	Free

Realschule, class 9.

Times of Lessons	Monday	Tuesday	Wednesday	Thursday	Friday	Saturday
7.55–8.40	German	German	French	English	Typing	German
8.45–9.30	French	English	English	Maths	French	Physics
9.45–10.30	English	History	Maths	Geography	German	Biology
10.35–11.20	Maths	Sport (Girls) or Crafts (Boys)		House-craft (girls)	Short-hand	Physics
11.30–12.10	Art		Textiles (girls) or Sport (boys)		History	Geography
12.10–12.50		Biology			Geography	Free

Figure 9   Weekly timetables in the GFR

Gymnasium, class 9.

Times of Lessons	Monday	Tuesday	Wednesday	Thursday	Friday	Saturday
8.00–8.45	History	English	Latin or French	English	History	Maths
8.55–9.40	German	German Latin or French		Maths	English	Latin or French
9.45–10.30	English		Physics	German	Social Studies	Physics
10.45–11.30	Maths	Maths	Art		Biology	Chemistry
11.35–12.20	Sport	Geography		Chemistry	Religion	Music
12.30–1.15		Religion	Free	Free	Free	Free

Figure 9 Weekly timetables in the GFR

This is either because parents have never developed enough political confidence or educational awareness to challenge the existing pattern of social stratification or, more likely, because of the existence of one central feature of German education, namely vocational training. This has always been taken seriously and continues to be readily available, indeed legally required for all youngsters on leaving full-time compulsory schooling. It follows that there are perfectly adequate compensations offered to those children not selected for the *Gymnasium* and its *Abitur* courses, for although they are debarred from the professions, they can see their long-term destinations in one of many trades. Further, with the Republic's post-war economic success, ensured initially by the terms of the Bretton-Woods agreement, 1946, and then sustained by the very priority given to efficient vocational training, the financial reward in most of these jobs has been very considerable. It is highly significant that those singularly tedious and low-paid tasks which exist in any economy are accomplished largely by migrant *Gastarbeiter* recruited from the poor southern countries of Europe, especially Turkey. Psychologically, all German parents and children, however low their status, can always identify a large group who are in all ways their inferiors. So, in this context, the dual system has proved a perfectly viable equation to solve the social, political and economic needs of citizens irrespective of the opinion of the State's federal agencies.

A more detailed description of curricula is now necessary. Some insights emerge from reflecting upon the entirely typical weekly timetables for 15 year-old 9th grade pupils in the three types of schools (See Figure 9, after Wilms 1976).

Despite the obvious limitations of this sort of evidence, several important points can be extrapolated from it. Apart from obvious things — the use of time, the fact that options are severely limited, and the very partial differentiation of provision for boys and girls — the reality of dualism emerges clearly. Although all children study German, mathematics, English, biology, geography, history, religion, art and music, and engage in sport, and this clearly represents a very considerably greater common element in the curriculum than in England, children at the *Gymnasium* are, in addition, required to do Latin or French; and for them physics and chemistry are not options as at the *Hauptschule*. Conversely, craft or housecraft, social studies and group work are not for them. Children at the *Realschule*, sandwiched between the two types of school, work at a collection of subjects which bridges the divide. The inclusion of shorthand and typing would seem to be clearly indicative of the occupational niche expected for them. Curiously, though maybe of no significance, they do no religion or music. It must also be remembered that for the children at the *Hauptschule* — 65% or so of the age cohort — this is the last year of their schooling. Their curriculum therefore represents what is deemed the necessary knowledge for skilled or semi-skilled employment and as a prelude to their statutory part-time vocational studies. Clearly the opportunities they have for access to the high-status subjects identified in the list of common subjects is limited. Students following the variously specialist *Gymnasia* courses will continue, nevertheless, with their study of these subjects for a further four years at least. During these years their timetables will be modified somewhat, with the peripheral subjects being dropped to allow more time for more specialist study of classical or modern languages, or mathematics and science. The three broad categories of children in the GFR thus have a highly differentiated access to high-status knowledge.

Of course this evidence indicates nothing of the qualitative or ideological qualities of the three curricula, which shows why comparative research into the detailed features of different subjects is so urgently needed. So it is only possible to ask some questions regarding ethos and values. What exactly goes on under the headings 'social studies' and 'group work' for the future men and women of lead? Again, although the fact that most subjects are studied by both boys and girls, usually in coeducational schools, is remarkable by English standards, are some subjects normally deemed the natural prerogative of either boys or girls? What role implications and gender messages are pervaded by, say, the craft-housecraft dichotomy?

The pattern of courses leading to the *Abitur* are not dissimilar to those of the major *baccalauréats* in France. The percentage of children, by social class, attending *Gymnasia* is also similar to the percentage in France attending *lycées*, though the nomenclatures used in this respect in Germany are a little confusing. Backgrounds with % figures are given thus by Wilms (1977): *Arbeiter* (worker) 17%; *Angestellte* (employee) 37%; *Beamte* (civil servant) 17%; *Selbständige* (self-employed) 24%. For many, the slog towards the *Abitur* is punctuated by repeating years, so that the average age at which young people achieve this status remains at about the figure given by King (1974) of 20.7 years. Privately funded extra coaching is very often required *en route* and is extensively supplied by those parents who can afford it; thus, if a long-jump metaphor is applied, some contestants are enabled to have several extra approaches to the launching board to enhance their chances. Another similarity with France is that, although some degree of specialization is required, the *Abitur* is broad in scope, covering the full spectrum of languages, mathematics and sciences, though with a minimal aesthetics component. This is very different from English sixth form A level work, which, comparatively, looks highly specialized, and seems to imply that general education is satisfactorily achieved by, and at, the GCE Ordinary level.

9. England

It is now important to identify carefully what this international analysis highlights with respect to England. There has undoubtedly been a great deal of activity on the curriculum front here over the last two decades. A very considerable literature has been produced by university-based experts, concerned with the analysis of problems from a great variety of disciplinary perspectives. Initiatives from official bodies such as the DES (1977, 1978a, 1981) and the Schools Council (1967, 1970, 1971, 1975, 1978) have taken the process further by recommending planned changes in what should be taught in terms of what a common curriculum might look like, and what the actual content of some subject syllabuses should consist of. These ideas have been augmented by the initiatives of curriculum centres or projects (Stenhouse 1975; *Ideas* Nos. 1 to 15, 1967-70. Smith, ed.) plus Local Authority advisers and Teachers' Centres who have made recommendations regarding teaching strategies and produced materials for use in classrooms. Teachers have been active too, usually proceeding from first principles and producing their own analyses and their own materials, developing teaching techniques and methods of assessment autonomously. They may have been influenced by seminal writings and have adapted such ideas to local situations.

We have already seen how some English developments appear to be quite similar to trends abroad (pp. 107-8 above). Our institutional framework has changed in directions similar to most other countries and many common secondary schools accepting all children irrespective of ability have been established nationwide. New subject areas, such as drama, theatre and film studies, social studies, environmental studies, and integrated studies, have been introduced to extend the choices open to secondary pupils, though it would be quite impossible to recognize or describe typically national patterning in such developments. Undoubtedly the CSE examination has also been very significant, partly by providing extrinsic goals for children with average attainment, but also, through the Mode 3 system, in allowing teachers more scope to develop courses directly relevant to the local needs and interests of their children. Superficially, all of this seems similar to some central features of, say, the American high school: an elective system and localized certification procedures. Justifications of an American type, relating to the thrust in the direction of more equal educational opportunity by meeting the children's individual needs and interests, have been woven into these processes. The trends have often been really radical in intent.

However, what we must show is how, comparatively speaking, the English situation is in fact different, more complex, but essentially more confused than in most countries. Even in the examples given above, similarities of degree, direction and pace are more apparent than real.

No acceptably accurate national description can be given of the primary school curriculum, except that in all such schools attempts are made to ensure that children acquire certain basic numeracy and literacy skills. Of the 3.7 million children who attend maintained secondary schools, about 3 million do so in 11-18 comprehensives (DES 1980). Let us *assume* that there has been a general move towards teaching and learning in such schools along the following lines:

(a)   mixed ability groups with a common curriculum for the 11-14 age group;

(b)   a system of options — based on individual choice, setted according to attainment, and mindful of one or other type of terminal examination — for the last two years of compulsory schooling.

Let us also assume that this pattern is grounded on the happy marriage of two international recommendations of principle:

(i)   after France and the USSR, equality: i.e. deferred selection through the non-labelling of younger children, plus access for them all to certain knowledge areas;

(ii) after the USA, freedom of choice and the expression of the preference of individual needs and interests for older children.

However, this general version of the curriculum in England just does not hold at all for a number of reasons. First, no national grade system exists in England. Different from the other countries cited, the attainment of children of a given age (including those at primary level) cannot be set against established achievement norms. The clear, nationally applied measures used elsewhere as indices of when pupils have satisfactorily completed a given year do not exist here. Second, the curriculum of English secondary schools defies even a remote generalized description compared with the other countries. This is because even when one school attempts to provide a common curriculum for all its children there is no guarantee that such a package is in any way similar to that of any other school. Though the subject labels usually look the same, what is actually taught under such orthodox titles as English, history, geography, even mathematics, will vary enormously according to the content, methods and approaches adopted not only by individual departments but by individual teachers. It is for this reason that the DES's publications regarding what a common curriculum might look like are meaningless; for although the general package is described, nothing is said about the content of specific parcels. This is in stark contrast to the detailed nationally or regionally established common curricula of the USSR, France and Germany, and the similarities achieved by custom in the USA.

Things are compounded further by the options systems in English schools. Few of these are devised using even similar principles, and in practice many are the product of arbitrary local staffing, timetabling, or site factors. Clearly they are not compiled with the cohesiveness implicit in *Bildung, culture générale,* or American tracking guidelines. The type of cohesion built into the School Certificate was jettisoned in the interests of freedom of choice when the GCE O level became a unitary examination. Yet such freedom of choice, based on individual needs or interests, is in fact inhibited by the requirements of higher education or future employment. Further, few children know or are told precisely what these requirements are. Those with parents who, perhaps through personal experience, do understand the consequences of dropping some subjects or opting for others, have a profound advantage. Neither can the argument be sustained that the external examining bodies bring cohesion.

The purpose of Mode 3 examinations at O level and CSE is to ensure variation of syllabus, as well as testing procedures. Even Mode 1 syllabuses contain large varieties of choice — for example the University of London Examining Board offers four separate options in O level mathematics alone. Its history examination offers tests of almost any period, not only in the past of Britain, but in that of Europe, even the World. In modern languages there are 112 different O level and CSE syllabuses to select from. Then it must be remembered that schools rarely use one examining board exclusively. Teachers commonly select those boards who examine what they prefer to teach.

In practice, the curriculum pursued even by arithmetically tiny groups of children even in one school is varied according to the following possible computations: the subjects they select; the level of the examination (O level or CSE); the examining board used; which syllabus is decided upon; which mode of assessment is employed per subject. Additionally, given this situation there cannot be much guarantee of national equivalence of standards, either between boards, or within boards. These points also indicate that the view often heard, that examinations in England inhibit the freedom of teachers and continue to define the curriculum, is something of a myth.

We must now recall that the autonomy of teachers in England is enormous (see Chapter 3). No equivalent exists here for the inhibiting, constraining and defining activities of administrative agencies elsewhere — central ministries in France and the USSR; regional *Länder* ministries in the GFR; locally elected School District Superintendents plus PTAs in America. This idiosyncrasy can be seen as one of England's outstanding strengths, since it ensures vitality. Responses to necessary change are rapidly forthcoming; novel schemes and improvements are constantly initiated locally. On the other hand, matters of enormous importance depend on the quality of teachers, as individuals and as a group. Quite specifically, children are at the mercy of the degree of imagination, enthusiasm, efficiency and competence of their teachers and the curriculum strategies that they decide to plan, implement and evaluate.

It may be the case that the problems of confusion identified so far in our curriculum scene are too complex for teachers to be expected to solve, for it is they who will have to do so given their present powers. Conversely it may be that some of the problems cannot be solved until the freedom of teachers, especially the inadequate ones, is curtailed; for autonomy can also be obstructionist. Of course this begs the question: 'If teachers are not to decide, who shall?' Similarly it is not enough to require teachers to be responsible without specifying to *whom* they are to be responsible. Even the Taylor

Report's accountability formula (DES 1977) to answer these questions is too bland, because it will not itself be able to resolve head-on collisions of principle and interest between the assembled parties.

Having attended to one English idiosyncrasy, two further very clear ones must be mentioned. One is the scant attention we pay to overtly vocational knowledge; the other is the very heavily specialist nature of those A level courses which constitute the entry requirements for higher education. In each of the other countries discussed, vocational preparation is very carefully provided for — the professional trade schools in the USSR; the rich variety of vocational tracks in the American high school; the *brevet*, even *certificat d'aptitude professionelle* courses in France; the mandatory post-15 vocational provision of the GFR. As to the requirements made of young people seeking higher education in these countries, as demonstrated in the *Abitur*, the *baccalauréat*, the American College-bound tracks, and the content of years 8, 9 and 10 of the Soviet Union's 10-year schools, they are far broader than ours. It cannot be denied that our insistence on narrow specialization post-16 has been criticized for decades and most recently in the debate generated by the Schools Council N and F proposals. It is also worth remembering that these discussions came to a halt because our universities would have nothing to do with them. They rejected the educational arguments of the merits of breadth, and the utilitarian ones of delaying commitment by youngsters, because they would have had to make internal adjustments in, and redefinitions of, undergraduate training. They insisted on retaining the traditional, though localized, strand in the English version of the European Epistemological Style — the achievement of a liberal education through detailed, narrow expertise in a very limited field of learning.

It might seem that the intention of this section has been to portray the totality of the English curriculum scene as one of amiable confusion, or tolerant inconsistency and gentle and harmless idiosyncrasy, explainable by the high degree of teacher autonomy, which has been hard fought for and rightly won; hence ensuring freshness and flexibility, and respect for children as individual persons. Nothing could be further from the truth. We must now seek more realistic interpretations; more abrasive, even radical depictions.

One such alternative summary of English curriculum development is provided by Blenkin (1980). She argues that: (a) we have inherited and currently still generally apply a nineteenth-century form of conceptualizing the nature of education and who should receive it, identified by Williams (1961); and (b) opportunities for change were missed in the 1960s when American planning notions were imported wholesale. Other critiques (e.g. Young 1971) contain a strong hint of conspiracy theory, and have to be taken seriously even if they fail to implicate specific conspirators or quite reveal the nature of their plots. What follows here is a view of the English curriculum scene when seen through the conceptual spectacles of Epistemological Styles.

We are undoubtedly the inheritors of the European tradition already outlined in Chapter 1. The assumptions about humanity, knowledge, even society contained within it are still pervasive. The tradition is still highly influential so that those curriculum reforms that have been attempted, often with radical intention, have been diluted and nullified. Recent innovations have been at best cosmetic.

A clear indication of the truth of this claim is that the curriculum debate in the UK has been conducted very largely in terms of the nature of knowledge. Pring's excellent and influential book *Knowledge and Schooling* (1976) is an interesting and exact case in this respect. The broad spectrum of English approaches to knowledge — a perfectly proper starting point for any curriculum analysis — is discussed carefully. The book takes in the R.S. Peters / P. Hirst version and criticisms of this position provided by sociologists; it considers pragmatism, notions of integration of knowledge, and child-centred approaches to knowledge. Pring even recounts how his attempts to apply curriculum theory in the classroom foundered because of the way the children in his class viewed the enterprise. Significantly, however, there is only one reference or mention given to what we have described as the 'societal needs' determinant of curriculum, and then in rather grudging, even disparaging terms (pp. 52-53).

Our over-preoccupation with the nature of knowledge debate, itself rather partial, has had the following results:

(a)   Despite the attention given in some of the literature to individualism and child-centredness, we still overwhelmingly accept the assumptions regarding the potentialities of children and how they must be categorized implicit in the IQ's bell-shaped curve. Teachers and others retain its fundamental tripartism and constantly 'see' children, of whatever age, in A, B, C terms (Keddie 1971). Through this process the old Platonic assumptions about children prevail. Similarly founded prescriptions about the general shape of society are not assailed.

(b)   Knowledge remains highly hierarchized on a high-to-low status continuum. We 'frame' knowledge (Bernstein 1971), using criteria recognized though not invented by Hirst, and we then ascribe worth to given bounded subjects according to their apparently pure, intellectual, mind forming qualities. This claim can be substantiated conceptually; but it can also be demonstrated by focusing on school practices. Subjects like mathematics, the sciences, modern languages, English, history, music, art and, more recently, geography and economics have high to medium status. Subjects like design and technology, social studies, and home *economics* (once known as domestic *science* as a first attempt at respectability by parasitic association) are low in prestige. They cannot be studied in higher education (cf. further education), indeed some are not admitted as being sufficiently respectable to merit examination at the Ordinary level of the GCE. Even if they are, they are viewed with great suspicion by universities and are sometimes not counted as valid partial entry qualifications. The full implications of this situation for those who opt for, or are consigned to, low-status courses are fudged. These optional courses may well have been developed to try and meet the individual needs and interests of children. But in our climate of hierarchized knowledge, we cannot also promote mobility, or access to power through knowledge (the other version of equality) by this system. By rejecting the idea of a required common curriculum of high-status subjects for all children, on grounds of freedom of choice, we exaggerate inequalities, and effectively perpetuate élitism. As we have seen, in the USA options or electives abound but subject hierarchies are far less apparent; the credit system permits early choice errors to be rectified and irrevocable selection is considerably delayed by a more porous higher education system; tracking requirements are explicit, much advice is offered, so that at least students know the name of the game they are playing. In Europe and the USSR, where knowledge is as hierarchized as in England, this is at least admitted; all children are theoretically given a chance to see if they can acquire the higher forms, and, most important of all, the implications for those who fail are recognized and alternative vocational routes provided.

(c)   Given the above hierarchies, it is perhaps not surprising that, in the English curriculum, scant attention is paid to overtly vocational knowledge. School work, in England's 'liberal education' tradition, should be above such mundane matters. But the absence of such vocational courses means three things. First, children not studying high-status subjects may be following interesting courses, but their post-school interests are not necessarily being fostered in ways which they can directly perceive as relevant; which may be why some become disaffected. Secondly, the economy is not being provided with a potential workforce which has acquired some knowledge appropriate to their work place. Employers complain about this; teachers respond that this is not the school's purpose; yet no very clear, unambiguous or consistent statements about what the school's purpose is, are forthcoming. Thirdly, vocational sorting does in fact occur, but covertly. High-status subjects are defended for their intrinsic worth, for their liberalizing, educative content. However, the collection of qualifications in these subjects is imperative for anyone contemplating employment in the well paid professions. In this sense, high-status subjects are themselves profoundly vocational. Their mastery has always been deemed an essential prerequisite for professional training.

10.   Summary and conclusions

We began by discussing those curriculum problems which appear to be common to all our five countries. We went on to describe some general solutions to them which each country has adopted. However, by focusing on the singular methods of curriculum analysis used in our various countries, we found that many of the generalities did not apply to them. We then described what the current curriculum theories and practices are in each of our foreign countries and what residual problems exist in each. Our discussion of each country was conducted in the terms of reference of each one's Epistemological Style and any criticisms made were also within the logic of these local modes of analysis.

At first sight, we found the curriculum scene in England to be more confused than elsewhere. It proved impossible to describe, with any reasonable degree of accuracy, what the general shape of the curriculum in England's school system is. I suggested three reasons for this:

1.   The absence of a national grade system to measure children's achievements.

2.   That external examinations do not produce any cohesion.

3.   The control exercised by teachers over syllabuses, teaching and learning methods and examining processes.

As a result, no common curriculum exists in England and this situation is most anomolous. In all our other countries a basic body of important knowledge is identified and attempts are made to get all children to understand it. We found too that England was the only country where vocational courses were not provided at the secondary level.

I then argued that beneath these surface confusions lie important and significant realities. First, the continued existence in England of hierarchies of knowledge. Second, that children are still classified according to categories implicit in IQ tests. Third, that all children are not given access to high-status knowledge. Fourth, that although overt vocational education is not provided, covert vocational selection does take place. I then made three further suggestions:

1. That recent curriculum developments in England have failed to alter these realities.

2. That a minority of children benefit greatly because their parents understand the realities.

3. That some people's interests are well served if the confusions continue.

Finally, our discussion has shown that the topic 'curriculum' involves many matters of principle and several questions about educational purposes. In subsequent chapters we look at these issues; in particular those of power and control in education, the equality principle and how it applies to education, educational ideologies and the purposes and functions of education.

Notes

1. This opinion was certainly expressed by my fellow members of three Comparative Education Society of Europe study tours to the USSR during the mid-1970s. All were very experienced teachers or senior educational administrators from a variety of countries, including America, Australia, Canada, the GFR and England.

2. For example, Freidenburg 1959, 1963; Friere 1970; Goodman 1956, 1962; Henry 1972; Herndon 1965; Kozol 1967; Holt 1964, 1967, 1970; Illich 1970, 1971; Reimer 1971.

3. This particular example comes from the 1978-79 registration booklet of a high school in Lakewood, Colorado.

4. Ibid.

5. Ibid.

PART TWO

POLICIES, PRINCIPLES AND PRECEPTS

Introduction

The chapters that follow are concerned with certain fundamental principles which are the foundations upon which schooling and education are organized and practised. The argument is that while common principles exist, they are not identically held to in our various countries. So we will look at how these principles are differently worked out and how the consequent local under-standings are used to identify, analyse and solve particular problems. The exercise in Comparative Epistemology, begun in Chapter 4, which used historical and anthropological stances, will thus be extended. There are two other themes which run intermittently but continuously throughout the chapters and which must be clarified at the outset.

(a)   Models of State

First, each of our countries has evolved and holds to a rather different model of 'the State'. It is neither necessary nor possible here to enter into the historical details of their origins and evolutions, nor to discuss conflicting philosophical theories of State. What must be indicated, however, is what version of State exists in each country, for this is an important frame of reference which partly delimits their approach to the issues discussed below.

In the USSR, the State is conceived of maximally and inclusively; it owns everything, pervades everywhere. It acts for the people, yet, dialectically, *is* the people. The Party is the State, and works for it. Theoretically, both Party and State will wither away once their work during the temporary stage of Socialism gives way to Communism.

The model of State in America is the direct opposite to this. The Constitution of 1787, and subsequent amendments, paid much attention to ensuring a nonintrusive and thus minimal State, designed only to look after those broad interests which the federal structure could not cope with, such as those of national defence and welfare. The arrangements made to govern those institutions of the Federal Government thus made necessary were full of checks against the emergence of oligarchic tyrannies and balances between proper but conflicting interests. In this sense, the American State represents a mechanism which safeguards free associations between individuals.

In Europe, positions some way between these two extremes are taken up. The GFR's constitution was modelled upon that of America, and the powers of federal agencies were purposely curtailed to ensure that no single political party could suborn them, as the Fascists had done. Nevertheless, it was intended that national interests should be guaranteed and defended, and that the vested interests of *Länder* or pressure groups should be curtailed. However, while Marxist ideas have made few inroads into conventional American thought, this is not so in the GFR, for during SPD periods of power (1966—1982), the State was more intrusive here in taking responsibility for those thought to be incapable of looking after their own needs. In France an even stronger model is used. The State itself is, to outsiders, a somewhat mystical conception, invoking nebulous notions of historical, cultural and national identity, made up of people whose spirit is somehow extraneous to them. It has many powerful central departments, which have always been energetically employed on its behalf and in its defence. Since the Second World War, a liberal version of State has been commonly and broadly accepted in England, mainly due, perhaps, to the consensual agreement which emerged from, and for, the Beveridge Report. This invokes such things as a mixed economy and relatively generous welfare services. In this, the way the clause IV debate was resolved at the time of Gaitskell, was important to Labour party attitudes, while the work of R.A. Butler in reorienting the stance of the Conservatives in the years following the loss of the 1945 election, was another crucial episode.

Politicians in all our countries — always deemed to represent The People, though variously enfranchised and mandated to do so — have common ways of implementing their policies, through similar legislative, judicial, fiduciary and administrative institutions. Technically, through one of several of these organs, they could alter the model of State traditionally adhered to. It is significant, however, that in recent times they have not done so, for the general model of State represents the consensus of political opinion held, or the limits within which political parties are expected to operate. It is also interesting that the constitutions or similar legal frameworks by which the

State was founded often contain important general precepts about how a given nation expects to organize itself. These are often most revealing and will be alluded to.

(b) Educational ideologies

The second theme has to do with ideology, a term which often carries connotations of specious invalidity and malicious intentions. In Chapter 4, however, the notion of varying Epistemological Styles was proposed; in Chapter 6, various profiles of the equality principle are investigated; in Chapter 7, differing patterns of argument about the purposes and functions of education are described. In each of these cases, each style or profile or pattern is based on premises or assumptions not amenable to total, permanent or objective verification, and for this reason they are each understood in what follows as being educational ideologies. However, they differ markedly from educational *doctrines;* for these remain no more than bodies of interconnected claims which, even in principle, cannot be shown to be true or false. Educational ideologies are relative cultural constructs, and are essentially local and temporal encapsulations, but when they are worked out, as they often are, with care, and when they are internally consistent, they provide perfectly proper ways of finding acceptable solutions to what would otherwise be impossible problems. It is in this entirely nonpejorative sense that the word 'ideologies' is used initially in what follows. But every opportunity is taken in Chapter 7 to investigate the possibility that each is no more than a convenient, alluring, persuasive, legitimising gloss, used by some for their own ends. Even if this is the case, however, it does not deny that they exist, that they are important, resilient, widely held and are fundamental to any understanding of a particular society. But it must be stressed again that they differ markedly as between the USSR, the USA and Europe, which in turn has its own local variants. Each has to be understood initially within its own logical terms, using the processes of empathetical imagination (getting inside the skin of a society, past or present) so central to the work of anthropologists and historians.

As described and used here, the idea of varying educational ideologies (whose components include epistemological styles, equality profiles, and patterns of purpose and function arguments) is an extension to, and perhaps a refinement of, three previously proposed methodologies in the comparative study of education. These are Hans's 'factors' (1949), Mallinson's 'national character' (1957), but most especially Holmes's 'normative patterns' (1965).

The idea of varying educational ideologies owes much to these established modes of analysis, but supplements them with what Lauwerys urged (1959), namely that consideration be given to the philosophical dimension. On the other hand, the assumption often made, that philosophy is the pursuit of objective or necessary, and thus culture-proof truth, is rejected. Here instead it is the cultural and historical specificity of varying philosophies which is sought, and differences between them highlighted. Again, as in Part One, the object is to gain a better insight into the way arguments are constructed and used, and to what ends, in England, through a comparative analysis of them.

CHAPTER 5

THE ADMINISTRATION OF EDUCATION — POWER AND CONTROL

1. Introduction

In the interest of clarity, we list here the six main comparative methodologies used to study education administration.

1. The macro-cross-cultural approach, using typological headings to categorize systems. An early exponent was Mallinson (1957) who used the labels 'Centralized', 'Regionalized' and 'Localized'. Turner (1960) was concerned with how stratified societies promoted mobility through education and characterized them according to whether they were based on contest or sponsorship. Following on from here, Hopper (1971) asked four questions to elucidate the selective features of systems and produced a 'total classification' of countries in these terms. Davies (1970) added a further refinement by raising questions of his own specifically about the curriculum and the knowledge content which selection was based on. Young (1971) also identified knowledge as being the central problematic, and included a cross-cultural dimension to his analysis.

2. Studies explicitly using classical theories of power, such as those of Marx or Pareto or Weber (e.g. Bowles and Gintis 1976). These assume the theories to be cross-cultural, though most confine themselves to national case studies.

3. Studies using Functionalist theories (e.g. Banks 1968) to understand and explain the influences exercised by particularly powerful institutions and the interaction between them and other bodies within the system.

4. Historical, Political-Economy case studies. These try to unravel the genesis of particular policies and reasons why they were adopted by political parties or governments or educational administrators, and

how they set about implementing them (e.g. Cremin 1961; Katz 1971; Gumbert and Spring 1974).

5. Studies using theories or organization after, say, Etzioni (1971) or Silverman (1970) to depict individual institutions or general systems.

6. Micro studies: (a) studies of the way particular pressure groups act successfully upon a system or systems; (b) detailed field work investigations (often using participant observation techniques) into the consequences of internal and informal institutional mechanisms, such as decision making (Richardson 1973; CERI 1973), or counselling (Cicourel and Kitsuse 1963).

It does not follow that these approaches are incompatible, indeed much would be achieved if a synthesis of findings were available. The macro approaches are flawed because of the high level of generality in many of the claims made and the absence of specificity regarding time and place. However, they often provide penetrating flashes of insight. Local and micro studies are often informative and interesting, but because they are so confined, they can rarely be relied upon as having general validity. It could be, of course, that their message is to eschew determinism; that events are largely governed by piecemeal minute accidents — a respectable enough historiographical tradition.

In this chapter we attempt to provide a simplified description of the administration of education in five countries, pursuing an eclectic path through what is undoubtedly a methodological minefield. The discussion attempts to identify two things. First, the real loci of power in each country; second, the direct effects that the exercise of this power has upon the life and work of schools.

2. General patterns of administration

In attempting to make comparative sense of the administration of education, Mallinson (1957) drew attention to the fact that some systems are centralized, like the USSR and France, some are regionalized, like the GFR, and some are localized like the USA. In the centralized systems, it is the responsibility of the central government, through its particular educational agencies, to decide about and provide education. Some tasks may be delegated to regional or local authorities, though they tend to be very specifically implementory, with those variations from national norms which will be tolerated being carefully instanced. On the other hand, in the GFR and the USA it is regional authorities who are constitutionally required to take responsibility for education. In turn, however, the American State Legislatures, and State Boards of Education leave a good deal to the discretion of the local School District's Superintendent's Office. It follows that, in the regionally administered systems, any central or federal educational bodies which do exist have general surveillance duties and can only exert influence through persuasion. It is useful to summarize this depiction of things (see Figure 10) with those agencies which warrant Mallinson's three labels shown in capital letters.

AGENCIES COUNTRIES	CENTRAL	REGIONAL	LOCAL
USSR	(i) ALL SOVIET MINISTRY OF EDUCATION (ii) Ministry for Secondary Specialist & Higher Education (iii) Ministry of Education for the Republics	Ministries of Education in the 15 Union, and 22 autonomous republics	Education Committees of the City or District Soviets
FRANCE	FRENCH MINISTRY OF EDUCATION	25 Regional Academies, each with a *Rector*	95 *Département* offices
GFR	(i) GFR Ministry of Education (ii) Council of *Länder* Ministers of Education	12 LÄNDER MINISTRIES OF EDUCATION	Local administrative districts
USA	US Office of Health, Welfare and Education	(i) State Legislature (ii) 52 State Boards of Education	LOCAL SCHOOL DISTRICTS, EACH WITH SUPERINTEN-DENT

Figure 10

Mallinson then went on to argue that some types of administrative structures were more likely to generate and achieve change than others. From the evidence of recent history, however, no obvious or consistent correlation, let alone necessary causal relationship of this sort exists. Conversely put, a tendency to inertia is not, ipso facto, the prerogative of any one type of structure. A CERI study (1973), which set out to unravel the chronologies of a number of known cases of successfully accomplished change, produced one general finding. This was that change occurred when those with real power decided that it was necessary, and it was achieved because they had enough clout to enforce their wishes upon the tardy. (What were less clear were the reasons or motives which prompted them to decide to initiate change.) It follows, then, that power and control are of central importance in matters of administration. The agencies which were identified by Mallinson as critical in each country, are so because they have the power to act; they have control, for example, over finances and over what exactly people do in schools. They can use their power to generate change or, alternatively, to sustain the status quo.

It therefore becomes essential that the methods of exercising power and its sources are clearly delineated. There are two general dimensions to the provision of education in any State, namely the formulation of policy, and its implementation. So, all our countries have agencies external to their schools, responsible for, and with powers over, both these modes of administration. In the first sense, they govern the work done; in the second they sustain it. Two broad forms of governance are, in turn, fairly obvious, namely the legislation passed and the decrees, circulars and memoranda issued by the relevant bodies constitutionally mandated with such powers. There is usually another distinction worth making here; that between political and executive officials. Sustenance is provided in many ways, but always includes the provision of finance. This is not only restricted to raising revenue, for it also provides for categories of legitimate expenditure, and thus has potential control functions. It is important, therefore, to explain in greater detail those areas which administrators do control.

The first obvious area is the broad structure of pre-, compulsory, and post-school institutions, together with those institutions which will be tolerated beyond the State's purview. Control will invariably be exercised over the supply, education, certification, appointment, promotion and dismissal of teachers. The curriculum is also included, covering the list of subjects which must be taught, the syllabus content of each discrete subject, the textbooks to be used, even the methods of teaching to be adopted. Financial headings include teachers' salary scales, teacher-pupil ratios, building specifications and costs, special facilities or equipment, and the purchase and use of materials. Control over this whole range of matters is invested in administrative agencies in our foreign countries, whether central, regional or local.

The bases of power differ somewhat between the nations. In the USSR it rests on the fact that the Communist Party controls the whole State apparatus, the Ministry of Education included. In the other countries, the principle of democratic election, variously interpreted and organized, is applied. In theory at least, then, ultimate authority rests with the people (or with the Party because it is the people). Power is therefore limited by the extent to which educational policy is politically explosive and potentially lethal as a vote loser or catcher. Again, much depends on the status of educational agencies within the general national, regional or local context. A given Ministry of Education (and its Minister) may well be very junior to more prestigious and powerful economic Ministries.

Yet despite these reservations it must be reiterated that the powers exercised by administrators, at whichever level, do control what goes on in the schools of the USSR, the GFR, France and the USA. They do so in the following manner. Schools are directed in some detail as to what is taught; by whom; to whom; how; and when. This is not to say that debates about, even struggles over, power do not intermittently occur.

3. The USSR

It is extremely difficult to discover precisely how educational policy decisions are arrived at in the USSR, because they emerge from behind the closed doors of Party deliberations. Certainly there are very many professional journals designed to encourage an exchange of ideas, with articles on a wide variety of topics whose diverse authorship includes teachers. However, their general tone is that of disseminating new ideas from above, rather than reporting novel proposals from below. New ideas from the grass roots are sometimes permitted, but always on a limited, monitored, experimental basis. What is certain is that changes of policy and practice always involve very close liaison between the Ministry of Education and the Academy of Pedagogical Sciences, which has an overall research responsibility. Conversations with members of the staff of the Academy in 1972, 1973 and 1974 about three reforms then in process are worth recounting.[1]

First it was said that Kruschev's proposed changes in the facilities for gifted children had been halted because thousands of letters had been received from citizens and Party workers objecting to the overt élitism involved. It was claimed that popular political pressure had caused this policy to be stopped. Second, in the late 1960s the Ministry had commissioned the Academy to research the feasibility of reducing the time taken over the curriculum of primary level classes from four years to three. They did this by establishing a number of experimental classes in ordinary schools all over the Soviet Union, which attempted the task. After careful monitoring, the Academy's researchers reported positively, and this led to decrees requiring that the necessary adjustments be made in all schools. A third example was that of the reform of subject syllabus contents. It would appear that this time certain Academicians recognized the increasing inadequacy of the encyclopedist model of subject syllabus content. They were invited by the Ministry to select relevant teams of experts and convene them as national working parties — one for each subject area — each to produce new organizing principles and new syllabus contents. This phase was followed by the production of teaching materials and textbooks, which were tried out in controlled experiments. On being shown to be acceptable they were then issued to all schools.

On this evidence it would be wrong to see the Academy as merely the servant of the Ministry, and probably quite inappropriate to use some form of conflict model to describe the relationship between the two. What is clear, however, is that policy decisions over education are not left solely to the Ministry or the Academy; for in the end they are relatively junior partners who service more powerful political, economic and planning Ministries which, for example, lay down such things as the manpower needs contained in Five Year Plans (which the education sector is required to produce). Similarly they service pre-stated political and ideological ends, which they see no reason to question. Doubts remain, however, about the degree of success achieved in implementing reforms. It is significant that, despite the powers of inspectors and the compulsory nature of weekly in-service teacher education, senior educators and Academicians made constant reference to the difficulty they experienced in getting classroom teachers to change their traditional ways.

There is some evidence worth recounting about the relationship between Moscow and the Autonomous Republics. It is commonly claimed in the West that the major feature of this relationship is that of Russification — in short that the Russians attempt to systematically exploit the Republics economically, while at the same time imposing a standard culture upon them in which educational policy is an important element. The Russian case is that they positively encourage, even subsidize, cultural pluralism. Personal observations in Latvia would support the fact that a struggle along these lines does occur there. In line with general Soviet policy, the Latvian language is not only permitted in schools; it is the medium of instruction for all subjects, though their content is that as specified by Moscow for all schools. Russian is a compulsory language, but so that other foreign languages can also be taught, schooling is extended from 10 to 11 years. The Latvian Ministry of Education is responsible for producing all necessary textbooks and teaching materials, including those containing sections on local history and geography. However, all this material is under the close scrutiny of the central Ministry and has to be approved by Moscow. Running parallel to the Latvian language schools are Russian language ones, provided for the large numbers of Russian nationals now resident in Riga — another form, it might be thought, of Russian expansionism. Many of the claims made by expatriate Latvians resident in the West were seen to be greatly exaggerated. National costume, dancing, music and crafts were widely evident in the schools, not least at the pre-school level. On the other hand, Russified place and street names were common, and the Russian language television and radio media were all-pervasive. Similarly, in Latvia's rural areas, the curricula of schools do not reflect in any sense their special setting, and the collectivization of farming does erode a culture which was partly the consequence of the older village pattern of demography. Nevertheless, in conversations with the education committees of the Riga City Soviet, the tensions, even hostilities, between Latvian and Russian members were perfectly obvious and made public. So a power struggle does go on, though within, rather than against, the Communist Party, and apparently involving nationality and culture rather than ideology.

4.   The USA

The notion that the locus of educational power rests regionally or locally in the USA is constitutionally accurate, but in fact federal agencies have increasingly exercised much control. For decades the role of the Department of Health Welfare and Education was restricted to gathering and disseminating interesting or useful evidence about schooling, often from abroad. Although it did not press a consistent line, or have a general overall direction in mind, states adopted piecemeal many of its suggestions. However, as Fellman (1969) showed, the Supreme Court through its judgements on constitutionality has been both norm setter and enforcer.

The most notable case was that of Brown v. Board of Education 1954, which not only made segregated education illegal, but also required the establishment of desegregated schools, colleges and universities. The Federal Civil Rights Acts 1956, 1964 clarified the situation totally, though it took armed intervention to implement this policy in some Southern school districts. Thereafter federal legislation came thick and fast, augmented by the post-Sputnik argument that the nation's defence and welfare were at risk.

Huge federal budgets were allocated, to be spent on a variety of educational programs designed to protect these twin interests. The 1958 National Defense Education Act provided aid for education in science, mathematics, foreign languages, counselling and guidance, and educational technology. In 1963 the Vocational Education Act and the Higher Education Facilities Act made federal grants available for constructing vocational schools and improving facilities in all colleges, both public and private. In 1964, amendments to the National Defense Education Act extended aid to include English, reading, history and geography. In the same year, the Economic Opportunity Act's war on poverty made money available for remedial education and retraining. The 1965 Elementary and Secondary Education Act, and the Higher Education Act provided federal grants to school districts with low-income families, and to colleges, students and teachers. Thus, almost every aspect of American education was affected; for tight conditions were imposed on the recipients of these funds. Federal legislation had been passed prior to this period — for example the 1914 Smith-Lever Act provided federal funds for agricultural and home economics instruction; the 1943 Vocational Rehabilitation Act and the 1944 GI Bill gave federal aid to disabled war veterans; in 1946 the George-Barden Act increased the scale of appropriation in the 1914 legislation; and, in the same year, the National School Lunch Act gave funds for feeding public and nonpublic school children. But the scale and force of the activity of the 1960s was quite unprecedented, and it would not be an exaggeration to say that in this period the Federal State in America ran the educational ring.

Another way in which power has been, and still is, exercised in the USA is through the actions of determined pressure groups. In fact two such groups, the civil rights movement and the military, were between them successful in provoking the legislation catalogued above. Textbook companies and the philanthropic foundations of certain corporations (see Chapter 4) have had a considerable if less dramatic impact. Several national associations should also be remembered for their pressure group activity. For example, through its nationwide membership, annual conventions, subcommittees and publications (e.g. the 1932-42 Eight Year Study) the Progressive Education Association (1919-1955) had considerable success for several decades in making its ideas the conventional wisdoms, which were then implemented by School Superintendents. This is also true of the National Education Association, especially through its 1918 report, Cardinal Principles of Secondary Education. Similarly, the various teachers' associations are active in pressing the interests of their members, as does the National Association of

Parent Teacher Associations, the National Association for the Advancement of Coloured People, and even the Daughters of the American Revolution.

There can be little doubt that local PTA groups have always exercised considerable influence on schools. This is primarily because members of the State Boards of Education and most local District Superintendents are voted to office. Thus, they are particularly vulnerable to a local pressure group of this kind, for the power of the ballot box looms close. Finally it is clear that school teachers, including principals, are vulnerable to external demands. They are in constant receipt of directives concerning all aspects of their work at school, though this is not to say that they are always submissively compliant. Indeed many become adept at developing strategies to circumvent, if not to actually subvert the intentions of 'the system'. Within American schools, formal power systems exist, as exemplified by the bureaucratic structuring of decision making and communications. However, many informal processes are also at work, involving sub-groups of teachers who act collectively, so that what actually happens is rather different from what is planned by 'line and branch'.

Historically and currently, there has been and is a constant ebb and flow in the patterning of power in American education. However, in 1956 Mills argued convincingly that a small power élite has always succeeded in being in ultimate control. Later, Bowles and Gintis (1976) concurred, though they described this élite as corporate capitalism, while Gumbert and Spring (1974) demonstrated some of the ways the élite achieved control, notably by the iron grip of its ideology and its manipulation of federal and state governments. We shall return to these conclusions in Chapter 7.

5.   France and the GFR

Several excellent studies of the recent history and current administration of education in our European countries are readily available, (e.g. Hearnden 1974, 1976; Fraser 1971; Halls 1965, 1975). A brief recapitulation of certain main themes will suffice here. In France a major theme has been the way in which various post-war governments have tried to solve the Church-versus-State problem. Another has been far-reaching legislation producing extensive structural and curriculum changes. The reasons behind the latter process were both philosophical and economic. However, there has been and is a constant war of attrition conducted by Paris to get the letter and spirit of these laws actually implemented by classroom teachers, who continue to conduct surprisingly successful holding operations. The other very noticeable development has been the reforms in higher education, through the establishment of new universities and improvements in existing ones, wrought after the 1968 student revolt movement. It is entirely possible, however, that the reforms were ephemeral and that more traditional habits have by now been reverted to.

In direct contrast, comparatively few major changes have occurred in the GFR since the establishment of the constitution in 1949, which is best understood in terms of power being used to sustain the *status quo*, for there has not been an absence of reformist ideas. The Permanent Conference of *Länder* Ministers of Education, with a powerful secretariat and an impressive list of standing and temporary committees — the latter quite active in publishing plans and suggestions — has only managed to agree two nationally binding policies. The first concerned the adoption of common labels for the grading of children's work. The second established inter-*Länder* agreements designed to phase school summer holidays. A federal Ministry of Education was established in 1969 as an attempt by Chancellor Brandt to break this inertia; and an energetic and imaginative Secretary of State, Dr. Hildegard Hamm-Brucher, was appointed to it for the same reason.[2] The Ministry had some success in pressing all *Länder* to set up mechanisms which would give effect to the 1946 constitutional guarantee: that parents must have the rights of consultation and representation on *Länder* educational decision-making bodies. Again, in 1972 the Federal Constitutional Court delivered a judgement which supported the government's policy to make it compulsory for all *Länder* to introduce a common observation cycle for the fifth and sixth years of schooling, thus delaying selection. The Ministry also supported the moves towards common secondary schools (*Gesamtschulen*) begun in some areas like Hamburg. In general, however, it is not surprising that federal agencies, which were deliberately kept weak in 1949, have failed to manufacture change; for they do not have the power to do so. Those few power struggles which have occurred have been at the *Länder* level, because local districts and their schools are firmly under the control of its agencies. Some of the salient features of one struggle, as revealed in Beattie's brilliant study (1977) of events in Hessen 1967-1974, must be recounted.

Having achieved some restructuring of Hessian schools, the SPD, influenced by the theories of Saul Robinson, decided to set about the task of totally reorganizing their curriculum, especially that of the common secondary schools. Content and methods were to be brought up to date and the integration of subjects was to be sought. Between 1967 and 1972 a large number of working parties and committee meetings were convened, involving not only educational experts, politicians, and administrators but also teachers — a totally novel departure for the GFR. However, Beattie says (p. 20): 'Two sorts of decisions were in fact being made: (a) overall decisions about the pace, and (very generally) type of change, which were made essentially at the political level; (b) lower-level decisions about the content and detailed planning of the curriculum, which were left almost entirely in the hands of what might be described as an "educational establishment". In fact what we observe... is a familiar division of powers between the political and executive branches of government.' Parents were, at this stage, deliberately excluded, but their turn certainly came when the new Curriculum Guidelines were published in 1972. Two of the 19 texts which made up the Guidelines, those on German, and Social Studies, caused a furore. The other 17 went unremarked. By the spring of 1973, variously constituted interest groups — the Employers' Federation, Trades Unions, the Hessian Parents' Association — were involved in televised public teach-ins which 'were extremely outspoken, violent and disorderly' (Beattie 1977, p. 23), and which reverberated throughout the nation. The key to all this was that the CDU published its comments on the Guidelines under the title *Marx statt Rechtschreibung* (Marx before Spelling). Its anonymous author fastened onto two, and only two, facets of the Guidelines which could be guaranteed to be politically explosive. The Social Studies Guidelines recommended encouraging critical thought by children about some traditional German social arrangements such as the family and marriage. The German Guidelines, based explicitly on the work of Basil Bernstein, and seeking to overcome linguistic deprivation, sought to encourage children's self-expression in their local dialect forms rather than in *Hochsprache* (High German). These public outrages caused the Guidelines to be withdrawn and those for German and Social Studies were heavily modified before the whole package was eventually agreed and implemented, though not before causing both the retirement of the Minister of Education, Von Freideburg, (who returned to his chair of Sociology), and considerable SPD election losses.

Beattie provides a penetrating analysis of the implications of these events. But for present purposes several things significant for the educational scene in the GFR can be summarized as follows: (i) The continuing assumption that education as *Bildung* is an autonomous, neutral, relatively unchanging, non-political, cultural matter and the province of rather few privileged people; and the irony that the SPD, implicitly holding this view, were simultaneously attempting to implement mass education. (ii) The explicit use made of the work of two theorists of education, who had acquired international renown. (iii) The assumption that educational experts know best about education;

politicians may have the right to suggest its very general orientations; teachers may be consulted (and this was a novelty), and parents are presented with a *fait accompli* (upon which they commented in no uncertain manner). However, the fact is that in the GFR, schools are normally required to obey *Länder* ministerial decrees. (iv) Ruthless party political capital was made of the episode, and it is revealing that the response of parents about social issues and spelling was to support very distorted conservative arguments. The dichotomization of politics and education was temporarily in suspension.

Two questions of international relevance also emerge: (a) In educational debate, who is to decide? It does appear that teachers do need some protection from ill-informed and possibly malicious external pressure groups; community opinion cannot be guaranteed to be sympathetically tolerant and liberal. (b) When consensus does break down, the alternatives seem to be that force is invoked by those with power, or that compromises are negotiated, or that things stay as they are.

Before turning to England and Wales, let us summarize the way the discussion of the administration of education has so far been conducted. The scheme of the arguments put was as follows:

1. In all countries an administrative structure exists to provide, service and facilitate the activities of the State's schools.

2. It is possible to describe, even categorize or classify, the statics of the formal patterns of administrative institutions in our various countries and to highlight their similarities and differences. However, the dynamics of each structure — that is the way the various elements interact with or act upon each other, and the effects of internal informal mechanisms — always involve matters of power and control.

3. Power and control is exercised over both the specification and the achievement of goals or ends. Some aspects of both sides of this equation are overt and public, whilst others are covert and unofficial. Matters of politics and principle are inevitably involved, so that power conflicts tend to develop. Resultant struggles are, in turn, for, of, or over the use of power. An outline analysis for each country, showing what the various struggles have been and are about, how they have been locally defined and how they have variously ebbed and flowed, has been attempted. In particular the activities of central government agencies and pressure groups, and their use of such weapons as those of finance, legislation, decrees and the ballot box, have been identified.

4. The exercise of power, in each case, is fundamentally about control over schools, and specifically directed at what is taught, how, when, who by, and to whom. In these terms the administrative agencies in our foreign countries continue to direct and prescribe the everyday work of teachers and children.

What follows is a comparative discussion of England and Wales, with these issues in mind.

6.   England

There are several obvious parallels between the administrative structures so far discussed and those which exist in England. Central, regional and local agencies do exist, and if not constitutionally, then clearly by legislative process (e.g. the 1944 Education Act), their general powers, responsibilities and duties are specified. The main outline of how these institutions are organized is summarized in Figure 11.

As in other countries, our central and regional bodies have two general dimensions, one political and the other executive. Notionally there is some division of labour between them, in that the former is concerned with policy decisions and the latter is responsible for their implementation. However, the relationship is rarely as simple as this. While the political personnel do wield ultimate power, because of their elected status their tenure can be temporary. So, major initiatives and decisions are often taken by the more permanent, and in some ways more expert, executive side. Similar to other countries, the central education ministry operates within the context of the current priorities of the government of the day, and can thus be either the victim or beneficiary of the thrust of its general policies. This point applies in local terms, to the Education Committees of LEAs. As elsewhere, education always has a powerful political dimension and cannot any longer be seen as a neutral, technical matter.

Any attempt to describe the dynamics or workings of this structure would have to involve, as abroad, the identification of many pressure groups acting upon it at its various levels. Some of these, like the teacher unions and associations, the Association of Education Committees, the CBI, the TUC, the Confederation for the Advancement of State Education, or the Boards of Education of the various churches, are nationally organized and also have powerful local branches. Local Authority Education Committees are particularly vulnerable to action by pressure groups, because the percentage of rate income spent on schools is very high, so that education is always a

C **E** **N** **T** **R** **A** **L**	Department of Education and Science	

Secretary of State, Ministers of State, Under Secretaries of State	Permanent Secretary, Deputy Secretaries, Under Secretaries and other grades of Civil Servants	Senior Chief Inspector and HMI

R
E
G Local Education Authority
I
O
N
A
L

| Education Committee
and
its sub-committees | Chief Education Officer,
his deputy and other
administrative officials | Inspectors
and Advisors |

L
O
C Individual School — say Secondary
A
L

Board of Governors,   Head Teacher
constituted to
represent various
interests, including   Deputy, Pastoral   Deputy, Curriculum
the LEA
                         House or Year   Heads of Department
                         Tutors
                                                Assistant Teachers

Figure 11

potentially volatile issue. Parents can also exert pressure at this level very successfully. In an unpublished paper, Sallis (1972) has shown in some detail how a local action group in Richmond-upon-Thames succeeded in forcing this local authority to implement comprehensive schooling long before it might have been predicted in an authority which has always been a Conservative stronghold. (The real significance of this episode is revealed by the fact that a neighbouring Conservative authority, Kingston-upon-Thames, has still not gone comprehensive.) Undoubtedly the mass media also have a noticeable effect on how the structure operates, particularly when sustained campaigns are conducted by national or local newspapers. However, to get past the sub-editors of popular newspapers, education journalists must couch their stories in somewhat sensational and simplistic terms with obvious unfortunate consequences.

Despite these similarities with the situation elsewhere, it is usually argued that the English style of educational administration is still, comparatively speaking, unique. This is because, typologically, the relationship between the various bodies, and in turn their interaction with the schools, has to be classified as one of *partnership*, with no permanent or overriding locus of power. In this model, decisions, policies and practices are arrived at by tolerant mutual good will and through informed consensus. It is necessary to examine this version of things with some care, not merely because classifications and typologies should be empirically valid, but also because of the possible consequences of general acceptance of this sort of conventional wisdom.

It is not difficult to point up some illustrations of how the partnership model is an applicable one. An obvious case is the Schools Council. Initially, the intention of its founder, the then Minister of State for Education, Edward Boyle, was to give his ministry's Curriculum Study Group the remit to consider all curriculum and examination matters, to be a sort of national clearing house for educational ideas and to advise him, the LEAs and schools, accordingly. Criticism by the Authorities and the teacher associations about the centralist and monolithic features of such a body caused him to alter his ideas drastically. Thus Richmond's contemporary description (1971) of the Schools Council's actual constitution, composition and early activities bears out the idea of partnership. He shows that its decision-making apparatus contained a balanced representation from the main interested parties: the Ministry, the LEAs, and the teacher associations. Its role was cast as one of dissemination and persuasion, through its publishing activities. Its very independence made it incapable of requiring schools to adopt any of the many innovatory projects it instigated. Indeed it could be argued that ascribing such a task to any major body in England would violate the long-established concept of partnership.

Another particularly good example of the partnership principle is that of HMIs, who, technically, are appointed to the DES by the sovereign. This legal nicety has the intention behind it of ensuring that HMIs' reports are independent of ministerial or governmental pressure. Their role is para-doxical, for it includes garnering information for the DES, simultaneously inspecting and advising schools, and acting as pollinators of good classroom practice. They could be seen as the very agents of good will between consenting partners.

The statutory guidelines for the work of the Central Advisory Councils in England and Wales are another interesting instance. The Councils are required by law to advise ministers about educational theory and practice — as they see fit, and on any issue referred to them. Members are appointed for six years only, and one third are replaced annually. It is a requirement that some have to have had experience of the educational system, while others must represent informed lay opinion. One of the most recent Reports (1977) of one of the Councils, chaired by Taylor, promulgated the principle in its very title, *A New Partnership for Our Schools*, and its major recommendations were entirely based upon it. Further support for the partnership idea is provided by Kogan and Van der Eyken (1973, particularly p.29 ff.) who show that three Chief Education Officers at least, viewed their work in part as being mediatory partners between central government and local schools. These officers appear to have nothing in common with regional administrators elsewhere, for, as has been shown, their equivalents in the USSR and France are recipients and implementors of orders from above, and in the GFR and the USA they direct and closely supervise those below.

All the examples cited so far relate to the early 1970s or before. This suggests that while the idea of partnership might have been valid in the past, it may not be so now. One way of exploring this hunch is to look at the evolution of the policies of central governments in matters of education since 1945. What follows, therefore, is an attempt to sketch boldly the salient features of such policies, which we suggest fall into three quite distinct periods.

In the 1940s and early 1950s the main task of the Ministry of Education was the implementation of the requirements of the 1944 Education Act. An initial emergency period had to be negotiated, which involved attending to those school buildings ravaged by war, and, through the Emergency Training Scheme for Teachers, supplying schools with the extra staff they needed. The broad assumption was, after the Spens Report (1938) and the Norwood Report (1943), that while all children were to receive a secondary education, they would do so in a tripartite system. The Ministry actively and successfully opposed those LEAs like Middlesex and the LCC, who sought to introduce common or bilateral schools, and only tolerated them in very rural and sparsely populated areas (e.g. Anglesey, Pembrokeshire), where the costs of duplication would have been prohibitive. Education at this time was seen as one of several services provided, in the post-Beveridge (1943) welfare state, on grounds of human rights. As such, however important and proper the service, it involved cost to the Treasury. The Ministry of Education had relatively low status in Whitehall even when compared with other welfare ministries like Health or Housing. No Minister of Education up to 1954 (Ellen Wilkinson, George Tomlinson, both Labour; Frances Horsborough, Conservative) was a member of the Cabinet of the government in which he or she served. The role of the Ministry was restricted to that of surveillance, ensuring that LEAs complied to certain standards with regard to school provision. These included nationally binding regulations over salary scales for teachers, minimum pupil-teacher ratios, maximum and minimum annual holiday periods, and specifications about school buildings and their facilities. In these matters, and because it met approximately 60% of the costs of education, the Ministry could be seen as ensuring the broad principle of the equalization of national educational provision. The LEAs were its agents of enforcement, and the partnership between them has often been referred to as running a national system locally administered.

In the mid-1950s and 1960s things began to change, slowly at first but then with increasing speed, and with apparently far-reaching results. The cause was the confluence of two powerful but quite different arguments, one of utility and one of principle. Both can be found in Halsey et al. (1961). The first argument which gained general acceptance emerged from the writings of economists like Vaisey (ibid.). Put quite simply it was that education should be seen, not as a service, but as an investment and thus as capable of producing profit. The link with the economy was now regarded as being more than the production of scientific and technical manpower as suggested in the 1956 White Paper on Technical Education. The 1962 NEDC White Paper implied that education's contribution was far more general and wide ranging than this. The then Minister of Education, David Eccles, was a crucial figure in this process, for he accepted, sponsored and promoted these ideas. It is also significant that, as a relatively senior figure in his party, he was appointed to Education, to supervise new policy directions.

At about the same time, sociological criticisms of secondary schools emerged. The 'late developer' phenomenon (Pedley 1963), the inaccuracy of the 11+ examination as an instrument of selection (Vernon 1960), the disadvantages suffered by children from working-class backgrounds (Jackson & Marsden 1962; Douglas 1964), wide variations in educational opportunities (Glass 1959), were all highlighted. Thus arguments of principle were raised, for these features were seen as unfair, unjust and inappropriate in a meritocracy. But it is essential to recognize that principle and utility arguments cohered. It was not only a matter of injustice: inefficiency, through the wastage of talent which could be put to better use for the benefit of the economy, was also involved. This new consensus about education — shared, as Kogan (1971) showed, by both the Labour and the Conservative ministers in the critial period 1962 to 1967 (Edward Boyle and Anthony Crosland) — had one overwhelming consequence. This was that the work of the central government's education agency changed considerably, from that of surveillance to that of giving direction. This involved the Ministry in taking far more initiatives and being much more interventionist. It follows that its status and relative power increased as well.

The most obvious example of this process is the dramatic increase in national spending on education: for example, on improving teachers' salaries and extending their period of training; on school buildings and facilities; and in particular on the expansion of higher education urged and legitimized by the Robbins Report (1963). Another example is the drive towards comprehensive secondary schools, instigated by DES Circular 1066, 1966 and continuing in spite of the brakes temporarily applied by Circular 1070, 1970. Benn and Simon (1972) argued that legislative direction should have been given in the initial stages of this process, yet it cannot be denied that at least the institutional form of secondary education in this country was drastically changed by the DES.

The climate of ideas changed yet again in the early 1970s, signalled by James Callaghan's invitation to enter the Great Education Debate and inaugurating a third distinct period. By this time doubts were being raised about the truth of the 'education as investment' dictum, not only by those academics who had failed to find a correlation between educational spending and economic growth, but also by such interested parties as the CBI. The suggestion was that the products of the system, whether from schools or higher education, were either inadequately or inappropriately equipped for business and industry. Blame was variously apportioned, though fault was particularly found with progressive primary school methods, which were heavily attacked through the publicity given by the media to the arguments put by authors of *The Black Papers* (Cox and Dyson 1969a, b) to such incidents as the Tyndale Affair (ILEA 1976), and to the findings of the Bennett 'Report', as it was called (1976).

This mood was directly reflected in the policies of the Conservative government elected in 1979, under the premiership of Margaret Thatcher, for it contributed directly to her party's success. In general terms, the Prime Minister rejected the traditional liberal ideology shared by most middle-ground governments, of whichever party, in the post-war period. She has sought to divest the State of many of its traditional powers, and to induce the free play of market forces in all aspects of life, not merely in the economy. Ironically her government has had to be exceptionally active, intrusive and directional in the dismantling process. Currently, educational policy contains several interconnected strands.

First there is the reduction in spending across all levels and phases resulting in reduced services and facilities and the threat of teacher redundancies. Such a financial climate (whether induced by world recession or monetarism) enables the government to force its policies on LEAs, schools and higher education. As a result the vigorous actions of the DES, aimed at achieving particular ends, tend to succeed. These include: (a) an insistence upon higher standards in basic skills in primary and secondary schools (of necessity at the expense of other types of school work) though the testing activities of its Assessment of Performance Unit; (b) the effective production of a specified secondary school curriculum based on the ideas contained in its own publications (DES 1977, 1980, 1981), to be achieved by the establishment of a common 16+ examination involving nationally examined courses; (c) the withdrawal of DES funds for the Schools Council, so as to prepare the way for an alternative body, less broadly based, but with powers to require these things of schools.

The 1980 Education Act is a further obvious part of the general strategy. It requires all LEAs to provide parents with extensive information about their secondary schools, including full details of the public examination results of each school. The Act provides that, within the limits of administrative possibility, parents must be given the right to choose to which secondary school they send their children. This is offered as the principle of freedom of choice in legislative form, releasing parents from the restraints of State planning and the social engineering of the liberal era. On the other hand, it might be seen as a shrewd political move by the government, aimed at harnessing the opinions of articulate, yet often conservative, even self-interested, middle-class parents to its cause — that of bringing pressure to bear upon schools. If these market forces cause some schools within an Authority to become inordinately popular, the rest will inevitably be forced to follow the approaches and practices of the few, and the result will be conformity or similarity.

Each of these measures then, it might be suggested, is evidence from the education sector of the end of the partnership tradition, with its qualities of tolerance and variety. Central government is now dictating policy and using a variety of tactics to achieve compliance. This suggests that we are moving closer to the pattern in other countries, and that a new model is needed to characterize the administration of English education. However, the implications are in fact more complex than this.

Running through what has been said so far about England, a consistent pattern can be discerned concerning: (i) the way in which the shifts in the conventional wisdoms held by the makers of educational policy have been generated; (ii) how these policy makers have attempted to implement such ideas, and thus change the practices of schools. This pattern, and the major linkages within it, can be put diagramatically (see Figure 12). Some examples of some of the processes involved in Figure 12 are appropriate. We have already seen how two different sets of arguments, published in the 1960s, brought about the comprehensive reorganization decision. Another case is provided by Gordon and White (1979). They show in precise detail (pp. 69-88) how the idealist philosophy of T.H. Green directly affected those responsible for designing and implementing the 1902 Education Act and therefore shaped the character of the new State-aided Secondary schools established in this period. The impact which psychologists and IQ testing had on the way in which secondary schools were structured in the years following the 1944 Education Act is more familiar. Here, however, psychology received sponsorship because it did not challenge certain conventional views that social stratification was inevitable. Bell-shaped Man was perfectly congruent with Platonic Man, which, despite Crossman's *Plato Today* (1937), was still the norm. They did provide a most welcome new criterion for ascribing children to different points in the national pyramid - merit. They also gave comforting answers to technical questions about people, and how to distinguish one from another. It is unlikely that the processes are always as neat as these instances suggest, for the centre-to-periphery model of influence which could be constructed from them does insufficient justice to the interactive nature of the relationships in Figure 12. Ideas of seminal importance can be taken up because they confirm the conventional wisdoms of the milieu or they can be used as critical inspirations for challenging and changing these wisdoms. More empirical studies are needed to show exactly why certain ideas were so successfully received, and acted on.

The partnership idea, involving cooperation and good will, does seem to characterize the relationships between several elements within the system shown in Figure 12, at least up to 1979. However, in one highly significant respect there was never, at any time, a real partnership. This is because teachers remained autonomous, so that the day-to-day realities of the educational process remained under their control. Governments did manage to persuade LEAs to change the structure of their secondary schools; finance was provided in large amounts; innovations were promulgated assiduously. But at

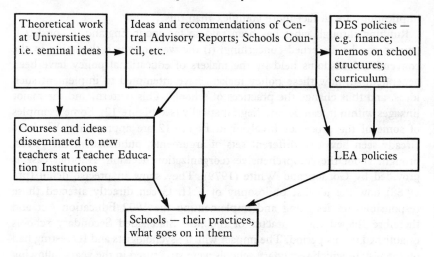

Figure 12³

all times, teachers had to be persuaded, influenced or cajoled. So they were partners in name only, for they were able to operate on their own terms, accepting, rejecting, but more usually seriously modifying ideas as they chose or determined. Stenhouse's Humanities Curriculum Project (1970) was a clear victim of this process, for many teachers used the materials in such a way as to totally distort what they had been developed to achieve. To avoid similar misuse, teachers wishing to use a later course, MACOS, were required to do a period of training before being allowed to purchase it. Nevertheless, Dorling (1981) showed that in the case of SCISP the process of adaptation and its consequences continue.

Two further illustrations of the partiality of partnership must suffice. First, in the mid-1970s employers and the press asked that the education system give an account of itself. It was charged that many school leavers were deficient in such basic skills as numeracy and literacy, and that undergraduates were taught subjects inappropriate and irrelevant to the needs of industry. As such the system had not come up with the goods. However, in the halcyon expansionist era, when huge amounts of capital were invested, no one had been able to specify what 'goods' education was to come up with. Investment had been made into unspecified stock, and used to turn out unstated products. Second, the general institutional form that comprehensive secondary schools were to adopt was delineated,⁴ but precisely what comprehensive *education* was to be was left vague and unspecified. Thus teachers had the power to define it as they saw fit, and what actually emerged was often the consequence of a series of local accidents. Some schools, which gained show-piece stature, were in fact nothing more than tripartism on one campus; others were radically reoriented. It therefore remains impossible to give anything but the vaguest account of exactly what even the general aims and achievements of comprehensive schools are, and if they are in any senses different from their predecessors.

The validity of this claim regarding teacher autonomy, already argued at some length in Chapter 3, is shown conclusively by Glatter (ed. 1977) in the Proceedings of the 5th Annual Conference of the British Education Administration Societies. Contributors from France and the GFR particularly, but also from Scandinavia, show that, comparatively speaking, teachers in England control and have power over the really crucial decisions. English contributors describe some of the constraints put upon schools by way of finance, architecture, staffing, and so on. But compared to teachers elsewhere, the limits or boundaries thus established are very broad indeed. They are required by the administrative system to do very little, and yet retain control over the fundamental decisions as to what to teach, how, when, to whom and where.

It is not surprising, therefore, that current demands for teacher accountability are being pressed with increasing urgency. From a comparative perspective such a development is both proper and justified. Over recent years teachers, and particularly their trade union or professional association spokespeople, have seemed publicly vociferous only in matters of status, salary, and conditions of employment. This may have been a response to an increasingly abrasive political climate and the overly coercive stance and style of the present government, and so in line with the responses of many other occupational groups similarly threatened. But teachers do have to give an account of themselves — initially to tax and ratepayers, their fellow citizens, who after all pay the bills. It may be that this paymaster metaphor is inappropriate, but it makes the point that schools do not exist solely to benefit teachers. This accountability issue will not recede in the event of a new government, of whatever political complexion, being elected. All parties seem agreed that, whatever economic climate their policies manage to produce, the 1980s are to be years of nil growth in the educational sector. It had its day in the 1960s and early 1970s, and the lessons of the uncontrolled spending of that period have been widely learned.

The external controls exercised in other countries do contain serious dangers, not least that teachers can become the victims of ill-informed philistinism or even malevolent political dealing. But children and their parents are also at risk. This makes it even more imperative that teachers at all levels take the initiative in explaining themselves more adequately; for their silence encourages the suspicion that they have much to hide. Teachers should start by identifying precisely what they are about, and to whom they consider themselves accountable. If they don't then others will; if they can't then others, quite rightly, must.

7. Summary and conclusions

We began by showing the ways in which the administration of education is similar in each of our five countries. We identified those agencies which wield power and exercise control. We looked at some examples of policy formulation and implementation in the Soviet Union, and how the American federal government and a variety of pressure groups have affected policy decisions and schooling practices in the USA. We summarized one detailed case study from the GFR and drew attention to its implications. I argued that what goes on in schools in each of these countries, and in France, is firmly controlled by administrative agencies external to them.

Because of this, England's system of educational administration has been seen as a unique partnership between its various elements. We then gave several examples of this idea, but showed how 'partnership' has been eroded by the present government's policies and recent actions by the DES. We surveyed the evolution of government educational policy since the Second World War and I argued that, because of the autonomy of teachers in England, no real partnership existed in this period. I concluded that current pressures to make teachers accountable are not only understandable, but, comparatively speaking, both proper and justified.

However, in this chapter we have also shown that the accountability issue is a complex one. We have demonstrated several good educational reasons why teachers should be protected from certain types of pressure. For these reasons, Chapter 7 considers what is said about the purposes and functions of education in all our five countries. But first, Chapter 6 discusses the fundamental principle of equality and how it is variously understood and applied in education.

Notes

1. Comparative Education Society of Europe study tours 1972, 1973, 1974.

2. It is worth noting that almost all suggestions and policies for change, whether at national or *Länder* level, have emanated from the SPD party with lukewarm support from the FDP.

3. The arrows on the diagram do not necessarily imply that the flow of ideas is a one way process. As the examples cited indicate, there is interaction involved.

4. DES Circular 10/66, 1966, in which six alternative and acceptable models of secondary comprehensive systems of schools were suggested.

CHAPTER 6

EQUALITY AND EDUCATION

1. Introduction: the equality principle

For Aristotle, the equality principle was quite fundamental, for justice was necessarily dependent upon its proper formulation. His formula was that equals must be treated the same and unequals treated differently. Conversely, injustice occurs when equals are treated unequally and unequals treated equally. Many societies, including those under discussion here, have knowingly accepted these pithy premises and have organized themselves according to them. Other societies who cannot have known of them, can be understood in their terms.[1] Implicit in these equations, however, is that there is some 'good' which a society can, will, or must dispense to its members. Distributive justice involves the apportionment of these goods equally to equals, unequally to unequals. However, the 'good' has to be established and equals have to be distinguished from unequals. Consequently three profoundly difficult problems are encountered. First, the provision of adequate definitions of what counts as 'the good'; second, justifications for the propriety of the criteria used to differentiate as between people; third, the identification of who, or what, is to do the distributing. It follows that various societies have, and do, set about these analytical steps in many different ways. A few examples seem appropriate.

The criterion of birth governed the ascriptions 'freeman' and 'slave' in ancient Greece; holiness of birth controlled the more complex Asiatic caste system; kinship and blood, sometimes augmented by age, were used in African, North American and Anglo-Saxon tribalism. In European feudalism, while birth was the major consideration, exceptions to it were found to be necessary. So, for example, kings could sometimes be deposed and serfs freed. Specificity and significance of function within, and on behalf of, the general structure were supplementary reasons for particular ranks. European colonialism distinguished by nationality. In oriental mandarism, merit was paramount.

In each of these cases, the crucial criteria were always justified. Things were said to be as they were on such propositional grounds as 'by God', and thus by faith or belief; or 'by Nature', and thus by example; or even 'by Science'. So the good, whether it be wealth, health, freedom, or the law, could be disproportionately distributed between people thus categorized. It follows that all these societies were heavily stratified, with people occupying clearly delineated positions of hierarchized status or rank, which in turn provided highly differentiated access to such crucial things as power, freedom and wealth. Again, the intentions behind such stratifications have varied. In some the design had the common good of all in mind, with differentials of responsibility or duty in direct proportion to those of power. Many societies thus founded and formed (for other examples see Beteille 1970) remained viable and stable for centuries, for they rested on very powerful, almost immutable legitimizing rationales, which few could, or wanted to challenge.

Historical, anthropological and sociological theories of social change abound, so that it would be a hopeless task to try and review them, and an impertinence to attempt to synthesize them. For example, in the history of England alone, no agreed explanation exists for the demise of feudalism, the political upheavals of the seventeenth century, or the onset of the Industrial Revolution. Yet undeniably the spheres of economics, politics, technology and ideas were, in each case, inextricably connected. One thing that certainly happened before and during periods of change was that existing paradigms used to order society were successfully removed, because new ideas were developed which denied the validity of the existing criteria used to categorize people. This was done by rejecting the existing justificatory grounds and replacing them with new ones. For example, novel intra-Christian theological claims emerged in the seventeenth century. What God actually said, was quite differently reported by Nonconformists, and this had far reaching social consequences. Similar events have occurred in the histories of each of our other countries. Included within the confluence of causes which precipitated the revolutions of 1789 and 1917 was a network of new ideas. French Rationality and Russian Bolshevism both rejected what they called the theological and naturalistic fallacies which had justified Catholic Monarchy and Orthodox Tzardom. The alternative societies which emerged were reconstructed on totally new foundations. The post-1783 order of society in America was founded upon a 'self-evident' and thus totally *a priori* claim about the Nature of Man — so long as he was white and with Woman not necessarily included. In 1870, nation and Emperor replaced city or princely states in Germany.

What Aristotle produced then, was not in fact a formula, but a conundrum, which has subsequently been worked and reworked in many different ways because it has not as yet been amenable to total, objective, timeless solution. However, versions of the equality principle are used to justify the way in which a particular society is stratified. Contemporary approaches to equality tend to reject, officially at least, both birth and colour as proper criteria for distinguishing between people, for they are deemed both arbitrary and irrelevant. Further, the 'State' is now designed to negotiate the processes of distributing the 'good'. Nevertheless each of our countries is heavily stratified and, some argue, inevitably so. With regard to the distribution of status, power and wealth between its citizens, each country represents some pyramidic variant. However, the general claim is that justice is being better served today than before because stratification is based on merit. This is why, in all our countries, education becomes quite crucial, for it is used to both confer and discover merit. Thus education has become the interconnecting catalyst between the equality principle on the one hand, and social stratification on the other. What must now be shown is what counts as merit in our various countries, and what versions of equality and the State operate within each of them.

For reasons of subtlety rather than pedantry, it must also be said that the relationship between education and equality is put in one or several of the following ways: equality *and* education; education *for* equality; educational equality; equality *in* education; equality *of* education; equality of educational opportunity. So far as the good to be distributed is concerned, Chapter 3 is a review of the various analyses and interpretations put upon its content, as indicated by the curricula of schools. Chapter 7 focuses upon it in terms of purposes and functions. The following sections in this chapter highlight some of the relationships identified above.

2.   Similarities and generalities: equality of education

There is no doubt that in each of our countries equality of education is sought, and several similarities exist between them about how they proceed to achieve it. Thus, because in each of them education is regarded as a 'good', then its provision should be the same in several respects. So, for example, as was shown in Chapter 2, education is compulsory for all up to a particular age, in schools which are structurally common. Several methods of measuring the details of this provision are also agreed internationally. Financial indices are generally used to demonstrate that annual per capita spending is constant. This is put arithmetically in data relating to pupil-teacher ratios; teachers' salaries; the quality of school buildings; and the budgets allocated for the equipment and materials used in them. The training and certification of teachers is standardized; every effort is made to ensure that teachers are distributed equitably throughout the system, as measured by the length of their experience and the levels of their qualifications. Checks of qualitative inequalities, such as the quantification of teacher turn-over rates, are widely adopted. Here then, through the use of agreed units of measurement, all countries try to make sure that certain initial minimum inputs are equalized. They would all want to remedy any obvious anomalies.[2]

Many methods of categorizing and defining the recipients of these common inputs are also very similar. So children become listed under similar headings — according to which administrative area they live in; or by the geographical region or sub-zone (rural, suburban, urban, inner-city, 'twilight') which they inhabit. Other headings, such as race, ethnicity, gender, nationality, religion, sub-culture, language, or social class, are also widely adopted and accepted as valid. In all countries some types of children are picked out for special or extra attention because they are different. These include the physically or mentally impaired, those whose behaviour is disruptive, and those who are particularly gifted. The criterion, chronological age, is also entirely common; for as children get older they are always treated more and more differentially, and at specific cut-off points some get no further inputs of education, while others, like university students, get continued and especially generous treatment. There are then, in all these things, shades of the Aristotelian equation, but beyond such beginnings lie many differences. Again some examples seem appropriate.

The use of words like 'ability', 'aptitude', 'achievement', 'interests', 'needs', and 'wants' occurs in all our countries. But this does not mean that they are understood or used in identical ways. While it is true that the word 'ability' is usually used as a criterion of difference, and children are thus categorized and then treated accordingly, definitions of ability and types and scales of treatment vary considerably. Again, in some countries one or other of these terms is given pre-eminence, so that achievement, say, becomes more important than aptitude. Further, the fact that some groups of children claim to share similar interests or have identical wants may be discounted as irrelevant. On the other hand, if *individuality* is stressed and sought, then categories of any sort may become less necessary, even redundant. Cultural difference is another interesting instance, for it can be construed either as an unfortunate deficit or a welcomed diversity. Special treatment may mean compensations to eradicate it, or supports to sustain it. Social class is yet another case. It is used variously — as an occupational category; as a way of describing differentials of wealth; to indicate discretenesses of culture, values and feelings of identity; as a method of analysing the dynamics of social structures by showing how people function within them; as a depiction of peoples' articulation with the economic system in capitalism. Each approach has very different implications for both equality and education. Serious differences exist over those who are physically or mentally impaired. Sometimes the latter is understood solely in terms of the former, and may be inclusive or exclusive of the emotional and social domains. Children who are blind, deaf or who have Downs' syndrome are recognized everywhere; but this is not necessarily so for the maladjusted, the autistic, or the dyslexic; and even if they are recognized, they are explained and treated very differently. Again, to call all, or any, of these children handicapped or retarded or subnormal or deficient or as having special needs has diverse connotations of cause, esteem and consequence.

It is for these reasons, then, that we must consider the relationship between equality and education in each of our countries, emphasizing as usual differences rather than similarities. It is also important to stress that, in each country, the equality principle has a history, and the key points in each of them have to be plotted.

3. The USSR

Discussion of equality in the USSR must begin by stressing certain quite fundamental contextual features. First, there is the question of the prevailing conditions in Russian society prior to 1917. The Bolsheviks always claimed that, irrespective of the ravages of civil war, the country was, even by the European standards of the time, fundamentally backward in all respects. Further, quite gross, even obscene inequalities in the most basic of human needs, such as shelter and food, were rife. This, they have continued to argue, was their inheritance, and the scale of the problem which they set out to solve. What they meant by equality, how they set about achieving it, and the measures of success which they have used, must be understood in these terms. So, for example, the initial goals set were relatively limited, though none the less vital, namely the elimination of poverty, starvation and illiteracy.

Definitions of the good to be distributed have subsequently become more complex, but they have nevertheless had to take account of certain further factors, particularly those of size and diversity. The Soviet Union stretches across approximately one sixth of the world's land mass, with an estimated population of about 250 million people. Although 70% of the inhabitants live in Europe, over 100 separate languages are officially recognized, and perhaps over 1,000, if dialects are included, are commonly used. Because the USSR is transcontinental the expressions of religious, cultural and national variety are enormous. Significantly, in Marxism, nationality is seen as an expression of the falsenesses of both identity and consciousness. Our starting point for a discussion of Soviet equality must, therefore, be that of the categories in use there.

The overarching conceptual category which has always been used in the Soviet Union is that of social class, used, obviously, in a Marxist sense. Communism involves its total eradication and socialism is a stage in this process. The concept 'class' is not used to classify people or their children within the USSR — all people are workers, with occupational titles — for in theory they no longer relate to each other or with the State in class terms. However, it continues to be used as the major tool in analyses of other societies, particularly capitalist ones. It is because of the pre-eminence of social class that Soviet educational theory has not and does not consider race or colour, nationality or gender as relevant distinguishing categories. Obviously the wants, even the needs of individuals are entirely subordinate to those of society, and although it is admitted that differences between individuals do exist, these are not seen as important or significant. Instead the stress is put on those human qualities which all people share — particularly cooperativeness, not competitiveness; selflessness, not selfishness. Neither, as was shown in Chapter 2, are children grouped in terms of ability or aptitude, because both these notions are entirely subsidiary to that of achievement. As was shown in Chapter 3, intelligence is rejected, both as a method of defining and identifying ability, for it is seen as a pseudo-scientific invention used as a means of justifying social stratification in capitalist societies, once the criterion of birth had become uncomfortable. Thus it is on the basis of proven achievement that some children are selected for special treatment, and giftedness understood. The other groups who get special attention are those who have some physical and physiologically measurable defect; they are educationally subnormal or defective in these, and only these, terms. Soviet rejection of psychoanalytical and Western developmental psychology means that terms like maladjustment have no credence. All remaining children, and it must be stressed that these are the overwhelming majority, are seen as totally equal recipients, who must therefore be treated absolutely identically, with no good reasons existing for doubting that they will all benefit from the good. On top of this common provision, their special individual interests are encouraged to flourish in their Pioneer activities.

However certain exceptions are made regarding matters of religion and culture. The arguments about why religious differences should not be given special treatment, and why cultural differences should, are cameos of the Soviet equality principle in practice. Each therefore needs to be explained.

Marxism denies the validity of any theologically premised arguments about social arrangements, and uses scientific materialist alternatives. But it goes further, for, when religion is an opiate, it becomes a defrauding agent of false consciousness and a means of oppression. The relationship between the Orthodox Church and Tzardom is cited as a particularly good example. Rasputin was an extreme case of the typical; not an extraordinary exception. Thus the USSR has always been an atheistic society, whose constitution debars, as does that of the USA, any established Church. This explains why no special State provision is made for the education of religious minorities. However, the constitution also guarantees, again like that of America, freedom of religious conscience and practice; which would seem to make any examples of the persecution of religious groups, of which there have been very many, quite indefensible. The defence which is put is that such action is perfectly proper when conducted against any group who see some power outside of, or other than, the Soviet State as their ultimate authority. So, the regime says, it is Zionism, not Jews; Ultramontanism, not Roman Catholics; World Free Church Council members, not Baptists, who are discriminated against, and legitimately so.

The approach to cultural diversity is quite different, for here expressions of historical and traditional regional cultures — music, costume, dance, and craft forms — are positively subsidized and sustained. The language policy adopted in education since the inception of the Republic is particularly important here. Those languages which, in 1917, had not developed a written alphabet or script, were provided with them. The mother tongue is, whenever possible, used as the medium of instruction. It is not so used only when it is insufficiently developed grammatically, syntactically or in terms of its vocabulary, and is therefore an inadequate vehicle for mastering the curriculum. However, all children must be taught Russian, for without it they are excluded from many riches, both cultural and economic, and thus have only partial access to the good. On the face of it, this sounds like a powerful, even exportable, model of education and ethnicity, where minorities are not denigrated, but sustained, and given full access to the main streams of society, with a multi rather than mono-model of culture as well as language. However, there are inherent difficulties. Most of the examples given above are cultural manifestations of a past and often rural way of life. The spread of new means and methods of production, and thus new patterns of living, make them increasingly archaic. If they are not organic expressions of contemporary culture, then their sustenance at best fulfils limited archivistic uses. Conversely, any values or loyalties which they evoke which are dysfunctional to socialism are not tolerated.

The founders of England's Sunday Schools set out to give children access to the Bible. The fact is, however, that many preferred instead to read, at first silently and privately and then publicly and aloud to those still illiterate, the works of Paine, Owen and Cobbett. Similarly the newly literate in the USSR became victim or beneficiary according to what they read; or more pertinently, what they were allowed to read. It is one thing to be taught in the mother tongue, but taught what? The mother-tongue teaching we have described could be nothing more than a psychologically well-founded and apt insurance against diversity, through the tolerance of inessentials. There is some injustice in this cynical cultural imperialist interpretation of Soviet approaches, however, for, like some versions of the condition of the Third World, it is a romanticization which omits from memory the privations of ill health and the shackles of overwhelming poverty which typified many prior cultures. What must also be restated is that the good in the Soviet Union is defined as that knowledge and those attributes necessary for the emergence of Communism. Chapter 4 describes these knowledge components, attitudes, values and behaviours. These have to be acquired in identical amounts by all children, at least to the age of 15. Differentials of provision after this stage are tolerated only when these things have been learned and because of the specialist and various manpower needs of society. However, social stratification is a consequence of this system. Some forms of inequality become indefensible, and no attempt is made to defend them. The relatively poorer facilities in rural schools as compared with urban areas, or in some distant Asiatic region of the USSR as compared to Western republics, are a constant source of embarrassment. Every effort has been put into remedying them (Noah 1967). In addition, school knowledge is supplemented and not contradicted, because the media, the supply of books, even cultural and recreational facilities are all carefully controlled by the Party. But alternatives are not tolerated. This, then, is an expression of what equality *of* education means in Soviet terms.

We must now consider the ways in which certain inequalities in Soviet society are officially explained and justified. One argument used is that while enormous progress has been made since 1917, Socialism is still in an evolutionary state. The Patriotic War 1941-1945 slowed the pace down, as did some unfortunate digressions, such as the period of the Cult of Personality. Perfection has not yet been achieved, but will be. In this, then, we have a conception of education *for* equality. Meanwhile, however, the distribution of status, power and wealth is inequitable, so that, while all people are equal, some, manifestly, are more equal than others. This is because, the argument is, of the inevitable divisions of labour and specialisms in a complex society. So far as wealth is concerned, although all contribute to the common good, are held in equal esteem, and are not denigrated or thought less of because of their station in the structure of things, some make disproportionate contributions and so merit greater rewards. Status is founded on merit, and this is measured by the degree to which individuals have mastered socialist knowledge in its various forms. Failures, guilty of 'social parasitism', are pilloried and punished. Meanwhile, power is granted only to those of the highest merit, namely those recruited by the Communist Party to enter its ranks. This total and comprehensive control is temporarily essential, for the Party members are the suitably endowed guardians who supervise the period of socialism. But this power involves heavy duties and responsibilities, because in Soviet theory it is exercised selflessly to the benefits of all, and will eventually be self-relinquished.

An alternative interpretation to this one is deferred until Chapter 7. Meanwhile one comment about those Western Marxists who criticize capitalism and its educational system is necessary here. The critiques they sometimes offer set the theory (i.e. some ideal version of a society which they construct from first principles) against the practice of capitalism — warts and all. In fairness, what *might be* or *ought to be*, should not be compared with *what is*. Similarly, of course, what is, in a society founded on Marx's ideas, may be a total contradiction of his principles, so that it is also wrong to define Marxism as that which goes on in such a society.

4. The USA

The search for equality in any society, whatever form it takes, cannot be pursued in isolation, for there are other often totally conflicting principles at play, notably (as the Utilitarians showed) that of freedom. This ethical dilemma is well recognized in the USSR, but there individual freedom and freedom of choice are quite consciously made totally subservient to equality, both of treatment and in treatment, and education becomes, with few exceptions, exactly the same for every child. In the USA, the central theme of the relationship between these two principles is reversed, with equality being construed in terms of individual freedom. Not surprisingly therefore, a very different profile of the equality principle exists. So, what follows in this section is a discussion of the main features of three revealing American case studies, namely the treatment of the 'Negro', the idea of individuality in progressive education, and the ideas which infused New Frontierism in the 1960s and early 1970s.

(a)   Black Americans and equality

Black people in America have commonly been referred to as Negroes, and the equality principle with respect to them has evolved through three quite distinct legal phases — slavery; segregation; integration. The principle of human freedom was not extended to everyone in 1783, and the slave category was retained until 1861. In colonial America, any education which black people had was *for* slavery, with plantation owners teaching those skills appropriate to the various graded levels of work required, from field hand right up to household service. Franklin and Jefferson disagreed about what blacks should be taught, but they both stressed the centrality of vocational and practical learning. Christian missions did succeed in making some inroads into overwhelming illiteracy. Cash (1941) documents how the Southern version of paternalistic slavery became romanticized. Those few blacks who escaped to the North were technically free, and in Massachusetts a state law of 1835 integrated them into the school system. Most other areas, however (e.g. Connecticut, Maine, Rhode Island) were guided by the Supreme Court's ruling, Roberts v. Boston 1849, that segregated schools were acceptable. With the removal of slavery in 1861, the segregation approach was generally adopted and it became legally formalized by the famous 'separate but equal' dictum of the Court in its 1896 Plessy v. Ferguson ruling. However, Yerkes' First World War findings about the distribution of intelligence amongst military recruits was construed by many as scientific proof of their opinion that the black man was not only different but inherently genetically inferior (Spring 1972). This idea was heavily reinforced by the childlike, jovial, innocent, simpleton image of black people given in the media, and especially in motion pictures. A particular mode of segregation, namely treating inferiors less well, was justified, and generally practised. The challenge to this formulation came from several quarters. One contributor was Cox (1948) who saw the black condition as one of caste rather than class or race. The widespread illiteracy and poverty of Second World War black conscripts reduced complacency; and discomfort increased greatly when Myrdal (1944), commissioned as an outsider to investigate black America, reported his findings. Two Supreme Court rulings in 1950 on access by black students to all-white graduate law schools (Sweatt v. Texas; McLaren v. Oklahoma) gave warning that the fundamental premise which had governed white-black relationships for nearly 100 years was becoming unacceptable. In 1954, in the Brown v. Board of Education judgement, the Court inverted the 1896 principle and ruled that 'separate means unequal' and that such inferiority was unconstitutional.[3] This principle was central to the Civil Rights Act 1966, in which discrimination was made illegal because it involved treating various racial or gender or religious groups differently for no proper reason.

This was how the official white approach to the equality of black people evolved. The response of black people to this process is also highly significant. During the Reconstruction period, Booker T. Washington and William E.B. du Bois were the two major black leaders of educational thought, but they held quite dissimilar views. The former effectively founded the famous black university, the Tuskegee Institute in Alabama, and his main preoccupation was with promoting the economic advancement of his people, which he saw as a prelude to political and civil rights. To this end, in 1900 he organized the National Negro Business League from Boston, and it followed that he promoted a largely vocational, technical and commercial model of education. Initially, du Bois supported these ideas, but during his teaching career at Atlanta University, first in the 1890s and again in the 1930s, he developed the thesis that Washington's 'economic ladder' argument led black people up a cultural and power *cul-de-sac* and thus into continued subservience. To counter this he advocated a classically liberal education, and pressed for a model of black higher education of academic excellence. He supported such trends at Fiske, Atlanta, and Howard Universities. In 1909 he helped establish the National Association for the Advancement of Coloured People, and was joint editor of its journal *Crisis*. His lectures and publications urged negroes to reject segregation and demand equal political rights. By 1919 his ideas had become even more radical, for in that year he organized a Pan-African Congress in Paris, after which he rejected the possibility that black people would ever be granted real equality in a white system, and so developed the idea of a selfsufficient, closed negro group. His *Black Reconstruction* published in 1935, was an overtly Marxist analysis of the *post bellum* South; he won the Lenin Peace Prize in 1959.

These contrasting evolutionary and integrationist versus revolutionary separatist arguments continued to resonate through subsequent Black attitudes, though du Bois' stance was adopted by a minority. One rather grandiose and obviously non-Marxist version was that developed by Marcus

M. Garvey, which flowered briefly between 1919 and 1923. In 1914 he founded the Universal Negro Improvement Association, whose journal *Negro World* had a circulation of perhaps as many as 2 million at one stage. His separation involved the establishment of negro-controlled and owned business enterprises — hence his Negro Factories Corporation of 1920, and the Black Star Shipping Line, which were to finance the counter-migration of black people back to Africa (a process which did begin and gave rise to the Republic of Liberia). A much later expression of separatism was the Black Power movement of the 1960s. Here the Black Moslems sought pride and alternative purposes through the theological teachings of Elijah Mohammed.[4] Other charismatic leaders, such as Malcolm X (1964), Carmichael (1967) and Cleaver (1969), denounced, amongst other things, the continued psychological enslavement of their people and for a time saw separatism as the only solution.

The ultimate fate of these and other attempts at radical alternatives, either to the white definition of 'the good' or to the white version of the equality principle, were identical: total collapse. It is also significant that almost all the leaders of such movements came to similar ends. Du Bois and Garvey were both hounded out of America, the former ending his days in Ghana, the latter in London. When Paul Robeson, a resounding success by conventional standards, rejected them and took to Communism, he was branded traitor and ruthlessly punished. Malcolm X died violently at the hands of an unidentified assassin; his contemporaries were also silenced, though in different ways. So, control over the shifts of logic and conclusion remained white; black alternatives were not permitted, though in fairness few espoused them. Some, through being outstanding entertainers, sportsmen or academics, scaled the white pinnacles to the heights of wealth and national hero status, and were used to show that, irrespective of origins, merit was rewarded. When Booker T. Washington died in 1914, a national monument was erected to his memory at his birthplace in Franklin County, Virginia.

(b)   Individualism and equality

The American version of equality can only be properly understood in terms of a long-standing tradition of individual freedom. The idea of America as the land of the free is doubly founded: first, constitutionally — 'We take it as a self-evident truth, that all men are born equal and free.' — and second by seeing its history as that of freedom-seeking migrants, fleeing from European oppression, whose descendents thereafter strove to conquer one literal or metaphorical frontier after another. Whatever else, the American State had to maintain and maximize its people's freedom — hence the minimal model of State.

It had also to ensure that those status and wealth hierarchies which might develop from the healthy competition between individuals were justly populated by those who deserved to be there because of their own efforts. Inequality among equals was justified by achievement. Around the turn of the nineteenth century, Dewey thought it necessary to rework and revitalize these long-held principles. He saw all around him, on his move to Chicago from Vermont in 1894, evidence that urbanization and industrialization were threatening the values which had impregnated the small rural settlements which were the typical American demographic and thus societal units. He conceptualized those values as Democracy, and gave Education the most fundamental role in sustaining it. He was also unhappy with the nineteenth-century version of freedom which stressed the maximization of *wants*, for which he therefore substituted *needs*. However, these needs were still identified as those which individuals had. From this basis there emerged an educational precept which was characteristic of, and unique to, the pragmatic school of philosophy, namely child-centredness. But it also gave philosophical backing to an instrumental version of knowledge, so permitting individuals to learn that which they found useful. (It was, incidentally, on this point that Boyd H. Bode parted company with his erstwhile colleagues in 1938.) What must be stressed is that the three crucial societal, individual and knowledge dimensions were refashioned and then widely disseminated. In this sophisticated formulation, education guaranteed both democracy and freedom. But more important for the purposes of this discussion, the equality and education relationship was constructed thus: first, treating all individuals differently — according to their needs; secondly, facilitating individuals in their quest for self-determined goals; thirdly, ensuring, in these terms, equality of educational opportunity; and finally, therefore, furnishing afresh for each succeeding generation the chance of socio-economic mobility, with inherited advantage minimized. Competitiveness, which had always been seen as the energy of American social dynamism, was retained, but was given better ethical foundations, as was the social stratification which it inevitably produced.

So far then, consideration has been given to how definitions of the category 'negro' have changed, and why individualism became the crucial element in the American version of equality. We must now look at why the equality issue was such an urgent matter in the 1960s, and how it was handled.

(c)   'New frontiers' and equality

The equality issue resurfaced in America in the 1950s and 1960s, because external pressures from the USSR and internal critics (e.g. Conant 1961) suggested that certain things had gone seriously awry with American society in general and with education in particular. The issues were set out dramatically by President Kennedy in his famous but shrewd phrase 'new frontiers to conquer', which, because of the familiarity of the metaphor, guaranteed him a widespread supportive response. The problems were subsequently debated and energetically assaulted, so that the years of the Kennedy-Johnson presidencies became known as those of New Liberalism. The developments which occurred in this era are familiar and well documented, but their main features must be briefly recounted. In essence, the *problem* was seen in terms of the Judiciary's ruling regarding negro segregation — that they were being treated differently from others for no good reason, which was therefore improper, unfair and unjust. The central *principle* therefore became discrimination, which by extended application came to apply to other groups such as the poor, women, and religious minorities. The *task* was defined as the eradication of the inequalities thus defined. The *agent* of rectification was to be the Federal Government. Several clearly identifiable strands can be seen in the policy solutions which followed.

The spate of federal legislation — upwards of 25 Acts between 1958 and 1966 — contained two common elements, those of principle and finance. People improperly treated were identified (e.g. the Civil Rights Acts); money was made available to help them (e.g. the National Defence Education Act, the Economic Opportunities Act). To maximize its impact, aid was integrated rather than piecemeal; the housing, education, health and employment services were cohesively planned. To ensure efficiency and for reasons of cost-benefit and economies of scale, many of the authorities who administered the aid were reformed through consolidation into larger units.

Educational policy was entirely consistent with these general trends. Regional interstate agreements were arrived at; more local city plans were made (e.g. the Atlanta Model Cities Program). The US Office of Education was energized and expanded, to perform its federal tasks effectively. It was mandated by the Civil Rights Act 1964, to conduct an Education Survey of Equality of Educational Opportunity. Its Report, published in 1966, became the central nub of subsequent thought and action. The investigations undertaken were extraordinarily exhaustive. First, educational *inputs* were meticulously measured and grouped, and correlations were produced between these and finely indexed categories of recipients. Intangibles, such as school 'morale' were included, as well as more obvious things such as facilities, teachers and curricula. The aim here was to discover the extent to which educational provision was equal. Second, the more novel step was taken of describing educational results, given equalization of input. These *outputs* were arrived at by the quantification of children's attainment, according to national intelligence, reading and achievement tests, success at the high school graduation level, entry into higher education and to particularly prestigious institutions within that sector. In addition, comparative rates of absenteeism, delinquency, and high school drop outs were compiled. A third step followed, namely the labelling of the underachievers thus discovered, as deprived, not merely economically, but linguistically, culturally, maternally, emotionally and socially, and again measures of these forms of deprivation were also discovered. The fourth consequential stage was the advocacy of compensations for such children. Policy solutions went beyond the mere eradication of inequalities of input, for they were designed to discriminate positively on behalf of some children. At the time, this was a novel extension of the equality principle, which is why it gained international recognition and renown and was widely imitated.

The assault launched on the inequality frontier which followed (see Little and Smith 1971) was enthusiastic and diverse. In 1967 alone, 350 million dollars was spent on 9 million children in more than 3,000 communities. Programs — Headstart, Follow Through, Teaching Force, Upward Bound, College Bound, Higher Horizons — were launched. Critical age periods — pre-school, early adolescence, 19-21 — and skills — motor, reading, language, learning — were identified. New types of schools — middle, model, free, storefront — were opened. Projects — for physical health, environmental, intellectual and familial enrichment — proliferated. Some were in-school; others were community or parent based. Classrooms became 'open', 'natural', 'spontaneous', 'self-directed' or 'structured'.

This expenditure of federal energy and money was carefully monitored and one consistent finding which seemed to emerge was that, with only rare exceptions, the performance of those children identified as in need of help because they were underachievers did not, even after massive investment, improve at all. Indeed, some seemed even to regress. The responses to federal activity in general, and explanations given for this phenomenon in particular, are of considerable interest and significance. The reactions which came were in one or other of the following general forms:

1.   There were declarations that all forms of federal interference in education were infringements of State rights and therefore

unconstitutional. The equality model was not challenged, but an attempt was made to confuse the issues by raising the irrelevant but effective banner of freedom.

2. Affluent families were able to exercise other freedoms and either moved house to an all-white neighbourhood, or removed their children from de-segregated schools and placed them in the private sector. Thus they circumvented the threat equality posed to the advantages they had built up.

3. There was the opinion that New Liberalism and federal intervention had not been needed in the first place; a proper appraisal of the evidence showing that the alleged inequalities were grossly distorted (Mosteller and Moynihan 1971). Social engineering was not only manipulative, but quite unnecessary.

4. The genetic explanation of disparate interracial intellectual performance was resurrected (e.g. Jensen 1974). This was augmented by the resurgence of the 'common sense' view that nothing could be done for the poor, because they were so through faults and inadequacies of their own.

5. There were charges of fallibilities of measurement in the data — first for technical reasons such as computational inaccuracies, or the misleading uses made of averages and norms, or the inappropriateness of some of the tests for some of the testers; second, because no account had been taken of the unquantifiable gains made. Thus, the whole monitoring exercise was invalid. Both inputs and outputs had been defined exclusively in terms of what could be measured; the uncountable had never counted.

6. It was claimed that results were being expected far too quickly. Inbuilt generational disadvantages could not be eradicated rapidly; persistent application of the policies would eventually bear fruit.

7. It was argued that education was an insignificant variable in providing equality and the improvement of life chances. It was other, broader and general societal arrangements which should be altered. For example, incomes should be equitably redistributed and schools should be made pleasant places which teachers and children enjoyed attending (Jencks et al. 1972).

8. The fundamental error had been to define children as deprived, because such a pathological deficit view denigrated them, their families and their culture and denied them their identity. Their

actions were not those of incompetence but were systematic acts of non-compliance and a rejection of something they found deeply offensive. They were exceptionally perceptive, not inordinately stupid; different but not deficient (Baratz and Baratz 1972; Labov 1972). Thus compensatory education, by seeing the individual as the problem, was essentially conservative and never questioned the validity of existing social arrangements (Morton and Watson 1971).

9. For many, New Liberalism sought increased conformity and a halt to diversity. Under the guise of equality of educational opportunity, the values of capitalism were being more efficiently imposed; and as such it was repugnant to a wide assortment of American opinion. Those holding to the classical liberal tradition, sought to return to individuals and families the freedom and liberty over education which was threatened by large companies and federal agencies. Others saw it as crushing alternative radical ideas because they were potentially dangerous to the *status quo*. Thus, free schools and education vouchers were supported for totally different and contradictory reasons, including those of the extremes of the political spectrum.

Most of these reactions were predictable, for the truth is, as was demonstrated by Coleman in a brilliant article (1968), that the terms of reference given to the Commissioner of Education for producing his report, the approach which therefore had to be adopted in gleaning the evidence, and the ways in which the findings were subsequently discussed, were all based on entirely traditional grounds. The report was to investigate *only* equality of educational opportunity; its remit was conceptually barren so far as the principle of equality was concerned. The exclusive concern was with providing a staggered race (i.e. a fair start). While some objected to this — for they saw that their medals were at risk — Jencks and Labov were exceptional in being among the very few who actually challenged the American race metaphor of equality. The former sought to redefine it, and came close to doing so in socialist terms (Jencks et al. 1972); the latter rejected it and advocated totally alternative activities (Labov 1972). Not surprisingly their ideas, like those of some predecessors who had made similar attempts, got nowhere. The improprieties which New Liberalism had suspected, however manifest and serious, and however caused, were thought of only as short-term imbalances. The government's licence to act was a temporary one, intended at best to reestablish traditional values and freedoms, and at worst to assert their capitalist counterparts. Novel equality alternatives were at no time contemplated.

We do not mean to suggest by the preceding argument that the American profile of equality is by definition inadequate. *Given its premises,* it is perfectly coherent. We have shown how official attempts were made to include those initially excluded, and to reestablish, periodically, its consistency; and how various groups and individuals have unsuccessfully challenged the validity of its ground rules.

5.   France and the GFR

Both the USSR and the USA were founded on fresh and bold, though strikingly different premises about equality. But by their rejection of traditional versions of the equality principle they became important influences upon the subsequent evolution of European ideas. Equality in each of our European countries has been greatly influenced by their common inheritance of the medieval category of birth. In each of them this criterion has become increasingly unacceptable, though it has lingered stubbornly in all of them. Marxism has been an important intellectual influence in this process, so that social class has been in the forefront of European discussions of the equality principle. However, these discussions have often been more preoccupied with explaining inequalities than with the positive pursuit of equality, though an attempt has been made in Europe to substitute merit for birth as a way of justifying inequality. While this line of argument is held to in both the USA and the USSR, we have seen that what counts as merit and achievement is very different in each of these countries.

Broadly speaking, merit in Europe has been defined and recognized in terms of the acquisition of knowledge. Given the analysis of the European approach to knowledge provided in Chapter 1, and the discussion of the purposes and functions of education in Chapter 7, the comments which follow upon France and the GFR can afford to be extremely brief. In somewhat idealistic terms, it could be said that merit in France and Germany is understood by the degrees of mastery of *culture générale* or *Bildung*. Individuals are assessed by neutral, unbiased, though competitive examinations, and each has the opportunity to acquire and demonstrate merit. Categories of any kind, whether of origin or region, by gender or race, are totally irrelevant — all that counts is performance. Differentials of treatment as children get older are justified because the evidently superior qualities of some have been demonstrated. Those less well endowed are treated equitably by being treated differently — separate but equal, though with parity of esteem. The persistent and continued underachievement of children from working-class backgrounds is often seen as an unfortunate feudal hangover, but is not regarded as the result of their not having been given a chance. In any event, for society to flourish, some people have to perform its more mundane tasks. Efficiency and survival, as well as justice, are served when the able work at the difficult matters of import. Serious objections to the claim that children are treated unfairly are muted by powerful feelings of national pride and identity, typified in de Gaulle's 'La France', or sufficiency in economic standards as in the embourgeoisment of the German working classes. A tolerably coherent, consistent and convincing version of the European equality principle can be produced, though alternative constructions are provided in Chapter 7. What follows is an investigation of the equality principle in England. The argument is that here, yet again, we are anomalous and idiosyncratic.

6. England and Wales

The dominant concern in the recent history of educational ideas in England has been that of social class. Much scholarly energy has gone into the study of all senses of the term. The discrete systems of culture, language and values between classes have been investigated; the distribution of wealth and power between occupational groups has been identified; class has been used as an analytical device to explain the statics and workings of societal structures. This activity has been entirely justified, for English society can only be understood through a proper appreciation of the place that social class has within it. Just one example is sufficient to demonstrate this. Without doubt, the Industrial Revolution generated England's class structure: a new working class with, according to Thompson (1963), a deep sense of its own separate identity; an entrepreneurial class with a bourgeoisie to service it. Throughout this turmoil, meanwhile, the old landed élite developed clever defensive tactics. When threatened by the *nouveaux riches*, they developed subtle techniques of exclusion and ostracization, such as rituals of behaviour, modes of costume and speech, novel esoteric accomplishments, private clubs and societies, most of which defied imitation. But they were shrewd enough to sponsor some of the outstanding wealth and talent into their ranks. This mechanism had two advantageous consequences for them. Aspiring groups, given this hope, were persuaded to join rather than challenge the élite, whose continued vitality, in turn, was guaranteed by the controlled infusion of vigour. In this way, the landed were a class not an interest group. They were more than just remarkably resilient to change: they actually harnessed it to their own advantage and thus retained power. It is appropriate, therefore, to discuss the evolution of the way in which the equality-education relationship has been understood here with this perspective in mind.

During the nineteenth century there were, according to Coleman (1968), 'striking' similarities between the educational treatments of the various English social classes and those provided in the Southern American caste system. At this time no attempt was made to provide equality of educational opportunity; indeed quite the reverse, for differential opportunities according to stations in life were the avowed intention. The 1870 Education Act was a case in point. It was intended to do no more than meet the developing needs of a changing economy by providing employers with a work force endowed with certain necessary new skills, and to 'educate' the newly enfranchized to cast their votes wisely, to ensure that their masters remained so. It was a case of 'separate and unequal'; education reinforced rather than reduced inequalities. Victorians, comforted in their notions of class by the 'rich man in his castle' type of Anglican theology, found nothing odd in this. The debate continues about whether the subsequent history of English education is one of sustaining this stance (Simon 1960, 1965, 1974) or of gradually dismantling it.

However, a distinct shift does seem to be recognizable, in the years immediately prior to 1914 and the inter-war period, to one of 'separate but equal'. This was the general tone of the 1902 and 1918 Education Acts, and was clearly the approach used by the Board of Education throughout this time. The regulations for schools 1904, 1905, so important to the early development of the grant-aided grammar schools, all stressed very heavily the quite separate character of secondary and elementary schools, and the latter were expressly prohibited from teaching the curriculum of the former. But in fairness there is no hint in the memoranda or circulars in the period 1902-1922 that the grammar schools were expected to be the exclusive preserve of the middle classes. (Indeed between 1911 and 1920 the Board's Inspectors in Middlesex were constantly vigilant about that authority's tendency to favour the 'snobbish villa dwellers of Enfield at the expense of the labour element of Tottenham'.)[5] Again, bursaries were provided to aid needy working-class scholars, even if in niggardly quantities and miserable amounts, which suggests that the assumption was that they would be few in number. Certainly the general feeling that very few could be expected to benefit from an academic education was fully supported by the official Reports of the 1930s. The very best construction, and perhaps a reasonable one, which can be put upon this highly élitist version of equality is the proper unequal treatment of unequals.

There is no evidence to suggest that this official assumption was ever seriously challenged — certainly not by the main contributors to the orthodox socialist thought of the time. The writings of such important intellectuals as the Webbs, the Coles and other Fabians at the beginning of the twentieth century all assumed differentials of treatment. Tawney's tract *Equality* (1923), so vital to the Labour Party's approach to education for three subsequent decades, did likewise. The TUC conference debates and resolutions in the 1930s often referred to secondary education for all, but the talk here too was of bilateral secondary schools. It is for these and other reasons that Finn, Grant and Johnson conclude (1977) that the Labour Party did not ever get beyond the position of being 'an educational *provider* for the popular classes, not an educational agency *of* and *within* them'. So, the tripartite policies developed by LEAs in the years after 1944, and fully supported by the Ministry of Education (see Chapter 5), were not simply because of the ideas of Norwood, Spens, McNair et al. Alternatives were not considered, because none had been forthcoming. Most Labour-held LEAs (not least those in Wales) saw grammar schools as the salvation of working-class children, offering them a ladder of escape from the privations of their class. (In Welsh the word *ysgol* is both school and ladder.)

Throughout this period, equality involved giving those previously denied the opportunity the chance to be upwardly mobile to positions of wealth and status. But there was still the assumption that they would be rather few in number and that social stratification was inevitable, either for reasons of principle (societies were inevitably so) or of realism (because those in power would tolerate nothing else, the best had to be made of a bad job). Yet it did represent a marked shift away from the birth criterion and towards that of merit, which was more just and had the added benefit of improving efficiency. This was particularly noticeable in the matter of the new concept, 'intelligence', which was warmly welcomed because it was seen as a way of discovering those with intellectual potential, and thus merit, irrespective of their social origins. (This was Burt's avowed purpose, however dubious his consequent procedures may have become.) It was on this basis that the tripartite system of education was developed, which retained the separatist tradition of equality, but with children of different abilities being differently treated. As was shown in Chapter 5, the Ministry of Education at this time saw its main task as that of equalizing educational provision, in such things as per capita spending, teacher supply, and so on, between the different types of schools and throughout the country.

In the late 1950s and onwards, some critics of the Ministry charged that they had not been vigorous enough in their pursuit of this process, for many examples of inequities of provision, by region and social class, were demonstrated. The same is true of the Plowden Report's approach to equality. However, by analysing the difficulties of some groups of primary school children in the exact terms of the US Office of Education Report (1966), and through its compensatory recommendations, it introduced to England the new dimension of positive discrimination which resulted in the establishment of Educational Priority Areas. However, all the inequalities which persisted were in principle amenable to rectification without disturbing the 'separate but equal' idea. This was not the case, however, in Olive Banks' charge (1955), which was that parity of prestige and esteem between the different types of secondary schools had not been achieved, and, much more significantly, neither was it ever attainable if separation was retained. This point gave particularly powerful credence to the common comprehensive school idea, through primarily as a way of delaying selection and reducing the stigma laid upon the majority not so favoured at 11. In those common schools established solely for those reasons, with the limited intention of giving all children a chance at a 'grammar school' education, the separatist equality principle again remained intact.

So far, several close and interesting parallels have been drawn between the USA and England. However, the contemporary English version of the equality principle cannot be understood exclusively in these terms, for there is another very strong tradition here, namely that of treating children on the basis of their individuality. This idea was imported directly from America, as Holmes' evidence (1965) of the cultural borrowing carried out by a number of official Reports shows. The other crucial link was the trans-Atlantic connection in the Progressive education movement. Child-centredness was a central tenet of the Froebel movement, which was highly influential in the education of primary school teachers. Thus generations of teachers were trained to seek out the interests and the individual needs of children, to respect them as unique persons and to develop teaching methods and learning contents accordingly. This they have done with great sensitivity, sympathy and humanity, changing radically the tone and ethos of primary schools. In a sense, this idea was also enshrined in the 1944 Education Act, which required that children be educated according to their age, aptitude and abilities, and this has been an important influence in secondary schools ever since. All these ideas provided a very different set of reasons for treating children differently.

These further similarities between England and America are, however, misleading; for the situation here is in all respects different from that anywhere else. To support this claim, we must delineate the four parameters of the current English version of the equality principle.

1. **Our nineteenth and early twentieth-century inheritance** — still intact. The separate treatment of separate broad categories of children — at first by social class, later by ability; initially 'separate and unequal', later 'separate but equal'. Both justified as the unequal treatment of unequals.

2. **The American influence** — an overlay upon the above. The treatment of children as individuals, according to their uniquely personal needs and interests, not merely to make teaching more effective, but as the means by which the actual content of learning is chosen and designed. A new form of justifying treating children differently.

3. **The European tradition** — about what counts as knowledge. Here (see Chapter 4) the worthwhile, the 'good', is identified in terms of various subjects, or forms of knowledge, which are heavily hierarchized. Merit is defined and rewarded in these terms.

4. **The élite by merit proposition** — put in one of two ways: (a) the élite should be constituted exclusively by merit; (b) some children of merit should be sponsored to join the existing élite.

It is obvious that these components are irreconcilable in logic, though a consistent equality profile could be constructed by reducing one or other element to a subsidiary position. When an issue is discussed in England in terms of equality, it is certainly conducted in these terms; but never consistently. Sometimes it is the child's individuality, at others his or her social class, at yet others the nature of knowledge which is used as the overriding premise. Not surprisingly, therefore, when it comes to the stage of distributive justice, total confusion reigns. Now this may be no bad thing, so long as it works, for justice is not necessarily best served by reason. We must now look at some specific examples.

Comprehensive schools were established for several reasons, but one of the central arguments used was that of equality of educational opportunity. Children would be treated more justly when they all attended the same type of school, whose status and material resources could be made identical. Mixed-ability teaching groups for the younger age ranges replaced streaming (tripartism in miniature) for the same reason. Here the differences between children were disregarded, because only through identical treatment could parity of regard be achieved. Efforts were also made to ensure that teachers were equitably distributed to each group according to their seniority, qualifications and experience. However, the logic of these steps towards identical provision, and a rejection therefore of the separatist tradition, is not extended to what children are taught, which varies from school to school, even within given schools. Chapter 4 showed that even in years 1-3 the fact that identical subject labels appear on a school's timetable does not mean identical subject syllabuses, whilst the options offered to children in their last two years contain no system either. All children are not given equal access to the high-status knowledge areas. Neither is it a case of deferring selection or differentiation until the evidence about children's capacities or abilities has been carefully gathered. The options offered by most schools are extensive, but the ways in which children and their parents take them up is often arbitrary and random. Many are unaware of the implications of the choices they make. The explanation given for this situation is couched in the other form of the equality argument, namely that options and differentials in the curriculum exist so as to meet individual needs and interests. Now it is just possible that this represents a brilliantly subtle solution to the 'European tradition' and the 'American influence' dimensions of equality. But what is more likely is that it represents a compromise in which the advantages of both are lost. Irrespective of logic, to hold to both versions of equality simultaneously is dishonest, for it misleads children and has serious consequences for them. Either hierarchies of knowledge must be eradicated, or children's interests must be made supplementaries and developed in some other way. Meanwhile, to underestimate the crucial significance to equality of opportunity, and consequent life-chances, afforded by the merit earned through acquiring high-status knowledge, is to reinforce the advantage of some and the disadvantages of others which comprehensive schools, in part at least, set out to remove.

Some current approaches to what children from working-class, or ethnic minority backgrounds should be taught must now be considered. Some teachers maintain that the content of many traditional school syllabuses, the behaviour and attitudes of many of their colleagues, even the ethos and value systems of schools, have marginalized and denigrated black and working-class people. These factors are seen, as in the Rampton (interim) Report (DES 1981), as contributing to their underachievement. So on grounds of equality, and to counter the deficit model applied to such children by the Plowden Report, they are taught the content of their own culture, and their own heritage — hence black or working-class history, literature, etc. They are encouraged to express themselves in their own linguistic and musical registers, and to take pride in them. This is entirely proper, laudable and valid, if used as a starting point, which recognizes where children are, which treats who they are with integrity, and which admits the validity of what they stand for. But only so long as the path to other vistas is thereby opened. If it stops at any point short of this, it is a disastrous transformation which inverts equality into inequality. This is because it debars children from any alternative understandings, any other cultural forms, which if not superior are at least different, and enriching. It can, through the romanticization of their culture and its values, leave children uncritical of some features of their world (e.g. the sexism and racism of some popular music), so that they remain exploited by worshipping those false heroes foisted upon them by unscrupulous leaders of fashion. It was just these dangers that du Bois recognized, and warned black Americans about. Similarly, there are the seeds here of a latter day version of our nineteenth-century separatist inheritance; a Victorian-style education for a station in life; a permanent consignment to inferiority and powerlessness.

Similar unsatisfactory confusions exist in the way in which many other issues are currently discussed — for example, children with special needs; the provision of pre-school places; the generosity with which students in higher education are treated when compared with their peers; the special problems of the 16-19 age group. But serious consideration must be given to one other possible explanation for what has been described so far. In short, that far from being confused, these appoaches to the equality issue are in fact radical, even revolutionary alternatives. What could be happening is that through the systematic encouragement of individual interests, and different values and beliefs, as expressed in cultural alternatives, the European version of knowledge becomes redundant and social stratification becomes unnecessary. Such a novel reworking has many attractions, but what must now be shown is that, at the moment, it is unrealistic and premature. This can be shown through reconsidering the case of the independent sector of education in England.

Let us *assume* first of all that the official version of the equality principle, and its relationship to education in England is as follows: (i) the existence of social stratification is inevitable, but for reasons of justice and efficiency it should be properly constituted, with the educational system designed to play a crucial role in ensuring this; (ii) all hierarchies, including that of the élite, should be constructed by merit, and this is best defined and measured in terms of people's performance in acquiring knowledge, broadly understood in traditional European terms, and irrespective of their separate origins; (iii) the American influence is seen as a sympathetic, humane, and pedagogically astute way of aiding all sorts of different children to acquire knowledge; (iv) eventually children will have to be differently treated and discretely ascribed, but the proprieties of ethics and utility suggest that the longer these things are delayed, the better. It may well be that such a profile is agreeable to most people, and that many believe that it is the one currently operated here. What can now be shown, however, is that it certainly does not apply, because of the independent sector.

Independent schools in this country have, whatever else, two characteristics. They are a classic example of our nineteenth-century inheritance, for they run parallel to the maintained sector, and they are separate from it. Their clientele is overwhelmingly composed of boys whose parents have the wealth to pay the fees they charge. It is true that these pupils have to demonstrate a basic academic attainment, by passing the Common Entrance examination, and for some public schools a great deal more. It is significant, however, that the examination is not common at all, for by including classical and modern languages in its content, any child who has proceeded through the maintained primary school system is effectively excluded from attempting it. Such children who do achieve entry through local scholarships or the Government's assisted places scheme, do so in such insignificant numbers that they can be safely disregarded. The equality argument is not usually used to defend independent schools, for in truth, how could it? It is still possible to justify the separate treatment of some children on certain grounds, but no longer simply on those of wealth. So an alternative principle, involving freedom of choice, is resorted to, namely that the freedom of some parents to choose a different education which they think appropriate for their children must not be withheld. The objection that most people do not have such a freedom, for want of money, could actually be met quite easily by extending the principle already used for 'voluntary' schools (i.e. where State funding is provided to sustain schools organized on religious ideals) to include all parents who wish to send their children to schools independent from the State. It is significant that this idea is not accepted.

So far then, parallelism; and this might be acceptable, or could be made so. But there remains the second characteristic of the independent sector, namely its separatism. It is so because it provides the majority of entrants to our most prestigious universities. The exact scale of this situation is best understood thus: 55% of the combined student numbers of the universities of Oxford and

Cambridge are recruited from the public schools, whose total population represents 5% of all pupils attending secondary schools. Now, as Sampson has consistently shown (1962, 1965, 1971, 1982), all our power élite groups (the military, the judiciary, the administrative, the political, etc.) are overwhelmingly composed of Oxbridge products. What we have here, then, is the nineteenth century's version of the equality principle in pristine form, with the élite being recruited from a closed, private system of schools. There is no application of the equality of educational opportunity idea, with upward and downward mobility on grounds of merit alone. In all the other countries discussed above, the educational system, sometimes through consciously planned and designated institutions within it, caters for the generation of an élite. Again, abroad, upper and middle-class parents with extra financial resources, and knowledge of the system, do chisel out unfair advantages for their children; but not to this extent. Only in England is such a degree of inconsistency tolerated; even fraud perpetrated.

7.   Summary and conclusions

None of our foreign countries hold to the same version of the equality principle, and each contains degrees of anomaly. But in each of them an open, accessible version of the equality and education relationship exists. Because of this, citizens know where they stand; critics can demonstrate inequalities, and highlight injustices, thus logically understood, and require their rectification, though the promulgation of alternative versions of equality is made quite difficult.

In England, no such consistency exists, for several versions, both of equality and its relationship to education, are held to simultaneously. Further, in argument, shifts are often made from one to another. This tactic is of considerable convenience to those with some reasons for falsifying through confusing. Whilst equality involves the principle of justice, advantages of utility also accrue. The many personal injustices which result from our confusions are compounded by general social and economic inefficiency. The first task of rectification in England is to make public what actual ground rules are used, to get them generally recognized. Then to require that obvious inconsistencies of application are removed. It is only then that some variant can be developed, making real alternatives feasible. To pursue alternatives, however valid or well intentioned, too prematurely, is to risk contributing to the confusions of pluralism which are used to sustain the *status quo*. Further, to misinform children about what the current realities actually are, and not to grant them opportunities within those terms, is to reinforce their disadvantages and consign them to permanent powerlessness.

Notes

1.   Societies in many parts of the world, such as the tribal ones mentioned in the next paragraph, cannot have known Aristotle's ideas. But they can still be analysed in his terms.

2.   Invaluable empirical data along these lines for the mid-1970s is available in *Education, Inequality and Life Chances* (OECD 1975).

3.   For details on all these cases see Fellman (1969).

4.   His allegory of Yacob, which explains the origins and spiritual development of black (good) and white (evil) people is certainly quaint and obviously spurious, but no more so in these respects than that of Cain and Abel, used for identical ends, though with reversed conclusions, by the Dutch Reform Church in South Africa.

5.   Public Record Office, catalogue ED.53 No. 106 SC 3076. Internal Board of Education memo (23 April 1968) from HMI Edwards to the Secretary to the Board, over a dispute with Middlesex County Council about its policies regarding free places in grammar schools.

CHAPTER 7

THE PURPOSES AND FUNCTIONS
OF EDUCATION

1.   Introduction: general patterns of argument

Whether implicitly or explicitly, schools exist for some ultimate purposes and fulfil certain clear functions. It is therefore imperative that an effort be made to discuss these, which must include rehearsing those arguments which are used to justify the original establishment and continued existence of schools. The history of educational ideas constitutes a library of diverse definitions of and statements about education, which is being constantly augmented by contemporary contributions from all sorts of sources. It is possible, however, to organize this plethora of ideas into two broad categories of argument without doing too much violence to their subtleties and complexities.

First there are arguments about what *education* is about. Here attempts are made to answer such questions as what it has to be, must be, should be, can be; why it is needed and who is to receive it. Typically here the discourse is philosophical, though not exclusively so. It is often infused with optimism and is often concerned to demonstrate the intrinsic worth of educative processes. Education and schooling are not always used synonymously, though what counts as the former is used to justify or criticize the latter.

The starting point of the second pattern of argument is not that of abstraction or prescription, but rather of utilitarian and functional answers to questions about *schooling*; what it actually is; what it does. Here education becomes defined, justified and criticized in terms of actualities and realities. Such accounts are largely, though again not exclusively, sociological and often flavoured by scepticism, even cynicism.

It is unfortunate that these schools of thought have been seen as necessarily contradictory. In fact they both have obvious strengths and weaknesses. For example, when those adherents to the second approach seek out alternatives to what they find, they have to resort to non-empirically founded political, and thus neo-philosophical premises. It is often claimed or assumed that the analyses of education which result from both these approaches are applicable to all countries and certainly to those under discussion in this volume. A comparative perspective therefore needs to discover those ways in which the arguments are complementary and the extent to which they are culture proof. We must now consider certain further details of both patterns of argument.

Many statements about the purpose of education see it as a basic human right, because many benefits acccrue to those who receive it. Education is seen as something which civilizes and enlightens, by heightening aware-nesses, broadening horizons, widening understandings, sharpening perceptions, intensifying sensitivities. Through it people grow and are fulfilled; are made happier and wise. It makes them free from ignorance and superstition — and allows them to make proper and richer sense of their experiences. Above all it confers power; enabling recipients to have control over their own destinies by making them autonomous, knowing choice makers. However, it is not only individuals who benefit. New, even ideal societies emerge when composed of people thus ennobled. Education is seen as the crucial mechanism in this process of the perfectibility of people in general, for it ensures that the knowledge successfully accumulated by succeeding generations is not lost (as it nearly was in the Dark Ages). Through education, knowledge is diligently preserved, used, improved and handed on, so that progress, to the benefit of all, is ultimately inevitable. When put in even more inspirational and radical terms, education is seen as the main weapon in people's fight against tyranny and oppression, and so an agent of revolution.

Seminal thinkers in all our countries have construed and justified education in these broad general terms. Dewey and Marx certainly did so, though they held very different views of people and society and the way the former relate to the latter. So, when attempts are made to particularize these generalities, major and irreconcilable differences between thinkers and countries emerge. Diverse opinions exist about what needs to be learned to become educated. If it is thought that only some people have the capacity for education, then differentials in educability legitimize hierarchies of humanity.

The nub of the second pattern of argument is that schools perform four basic functions in society. First, they are the major agencies used by society to transmit the knowledge, traditions, values and norms necessary for its con-tinuation. Here education is a stabilizing force designed, in one version of things, to guard against the ephemeral, and in another, to sustain the *status quo*. Second it is argued that all contemporary societies are stratified on grounds, and for reasons of merit, variously defined. Education functions as the main agent of socio-economic selection. Children are ascribed to particular niches in social-status hierarchies, according to their success in acquiring specified educational credentials. An extension of this idea is the claim that the existing élites define what counts as education — knowledge, culture, behaviour — and then, to ensure their self-replication, provide differential access to it for various groups or categories of children according to groundless criteria of their own invention. A third economic function follows from this. Here education acts as the principal selective device in the division of labour. It also serves the manpower needs of the country, teaching future workers that knowledge and those skills and attitudes needed in their designated work places. Without this, the economy would flounder, to everyone's detriment. It also fulfils a useful subsidiary child-minding function, by freeing some adults, particularly women, for the labour force. Implicit in all of this is a fourth political function. Certain exclusive educational institutions exist which select, train and produce the political, administrative, judicial and military leaders which any society must have. Here a limited amount of innovatory, even original, thought is encouraged as a guarantee against stagnation and its resultant perils. Meanwhile the schools attended by the remaining majority inculcate the particular political views held by the society and necessary for its continuation. Alternatively put, children are controlled, even coerced by the existing dominant ideology.

Both patterns of argument contain several salutary reminders. For example, that education is sometimes potentially ennobling, but that schools are undeniably socially and ideologically contexted. What might be, even what can be, is not necessarily what is. We must now investigate which features of these general arguments apply to, or fit, our five countries. The comparative argument is that various profiles of educational purpose and function exist, reflecting some but not all of the tenets or claims outlined above. These profiles differ according to specific national or regional ideologies which are in turn closely related to varying Epistemological Styles. As such they are temporary but locally satisfactory solutions to what is otherwise an insoluble puzzle, namely, how to square a triangle made up of the conflicting needs, wants, desires, interests, etc. of (1) individuals (2) society — and all this in relation to (3) varying definitions of worthwhile, useful knowledge.

2.   The USSR

Two tenets attributed to Lenin have been consistently held in the USSR regarding the purposes of education. First: 'Education is first and last a political matter. Anyone who says otherwise is either a hypocrite or a liar.' Second: 'Without teaching there is no knowledge and without knowledge there is no communism.' Those changes of emphasis about what knowledge needs to be taught *en route* to communism (compare Krupskaya and Lunacharsky with Stalin and Kruschev) are seen as unfortunate deviationary errors. The official Soviet version of their political system is that since 1917, their society has been, and continues to be, in the process of change from socialism to communism. Due to their Tzarist inheritance, because of the many reactionary forces in their society and the false consciousness thus induced in the minds of the masses, it is necessary for the State to control all aspects of life so as to guarantee this evolution. The Communist Party is temporarily vested with total power over the State's apparatus but carries the profound responsibility of the proper supervision of this process. At the onset of communism, both Party and State will wither away, for by then the people will need neither. Meanwhile, they work on behalf of and with the people to this end. The purposes of education and the functions of schools are defined and designed as logical and unambiguous consequences of this political context. Communism arrives because of education; schools function to fashion and form children and so guarantee it. This general enterprise, launched on behalf of all, is too important and urgent to tolerate individual dissidence. A glorious goal justifies rough, even ruthless means, to avoid the risks of digression or sabotage.

So, following this official line of argument, the Soviet profile of purposes and functions, put in a series of interconnecting propositions, would be as follows. There is nothing more important than education; it is the central radical revolutionary force which overthrows the tyranny of ignorance and produces enlightenment. From it a new order of society dawns, by the way it induces in people a totally new sense of what they are. As such it achieves human perfectibility. In the socialist interregnum, the drive to equip all children thus is already proceeding. The teaching and learning carried out in schools is designed in these terms. However, socio-economic stratification and differentiation is temporarily inevitable, but with the good of all in mind. Schooling functions, therefore, to select those most fitted for those various niches which exist even in socialism. However, it does so justly and properly — for example those it selects for Party membership are exceptional masters of knowledge who demonstrate those further qualities of selflessness and a devotion to the duty they owe to the people. Economic growth is of paramount importance to the achievement of communism, so schools must act as agents in the division of labour. State planning ensures that they produce the manpower needs of the economy. However, all people, whatever their station or occupation, are equally regarded, for they are mutually interdependent and they all contribute vitally to the ultimate good. All these propositions are unified and systematized in that unique Soviet concept called Polytechnical Education.

The danger is that what has been said above will be read by some as a parody. That was certainly not the intention. Rather it was to present as genuinely as possible the way in which senior Soviet educationalists treat matters of purpose and function in their country. They also argue that education inevitably serves political goals in all countries, and schools are always used as agents in achieving them. The only differences which exist are those of variations in ends and of means. What is more, they maintain that whilst the USSR openly and proudly proclaims its intentions, others proceed covertly and secretly. So, denials of the political nature of education are conspiratorially construed.

Critiques of Soviet education can take several forms. First it can be argued that in certain fundamental respects it is antithetical to both the spirit and the letter of Marxism. Here the charge could be made that communism cannot possibly result from a vanguard party model of socialism. It can only emerge when the masses have the right to express opinions, and learn from the ongoing process of making decisions. An exclusive Party by its very nature is divisive. It patronizes, even denigrates others. It will inevitably, therefore, serve its own interests and be self-replicating. Schooling becomes a mechanism to serve its ends. Partial Party notions of education are systematically forced upon children, and because no real alternatives are countenanced, they should be recognized as the propaganda of indoctrination and profoundly anti-Marxist. Similarly, the Soviet economic system, involving urban concentrations of capital intensive industrial units, sharp divisions of labour, wide salary and status differentials, and where the inheritance of wealth is tolerated, has been called State capitalism. This is because it is similar in most respects to Western corporate capitalism, because its identical structures cause workers to become employees, albeit of the State, rather than the company, but alienated nevertheless. Schools are not able to do anything other than service this process.

A second and familiar criticism, this time from a non-Marxist perspective, usually argues that Marxism produces totalitarianism, with the USSR as a case in point. It is depicted as a country where Marxist rhetoric was used to precipitate a revolution, after which a narrow, politically recruited élite took over power from one based on monarchy and aristocracy. Education is seen as something designed by the new élite to indoctrinate citizens into conformity and acquiescence. Schools are used as one of many agencies in a concerted propaganda exercise. This line of argument, although pervasive in the West, must be viewed with suspicion. Its starting premise lacks any logic; it makes no attempt to dismantle the basic tenets of Marxism; it does not countenance the possible validity, for them at least, of Soviet versions of things; it usually emanates from sources themselves intent on propaganda.

Soviet replies to both these critiques rest on what they consider to be two undeniable facts. First, the evidence they can produce, using 1917 as a base line, of the progress which has been achieved, largely through their system of education, as measured by such indices as the removal of illiteracy, starvation and poverty, and their scientific and technological advances, including space exploration. No other country, they claim, can match this record. Second, the success and popularity of their version of Marxist Society, not only within the USSR, but as indicated by its adoption in other countries all over the world. This international impact, they suggest, could not have been achieved by subversion and coercion; it required willing commitment. Their ultimate argument is simply, 'Wait and see'.

This discussion of the purposes and functions of Soviet education has raised three themes which will need exploration in our other countries.

1. Whether official versions of educational purpose are used to legitimize a particular political doctrine.

2. What a given doctrine is set up to achieve.

3. What significance should be attached to those inconsistencies which may be identifiable between officially stated purposes and the practical actualities of schooling.

3. The USA

In Chapters 3 and 4, we showed how and why the provision and practice of education is very similar, if not totally identical, throughout the USA. Chapter 6 described the genesis and development of the widespread cult of individualism, and how John Dewey's school of Pragmatic Philosophy restated and refined this tradition. A national school system exists, designed according to a coherent propositional system with specific purposes in mind. To recap briefly, it is claimed that this system of education is a guarantor of democracy. It serves the needs and interests of a free people. Knowledge is worth while according to whether it is useful to individuals in the achievement of self-determined ends. Eccentricities of thought are therefore tolerated. Schools provide the opportunity for socio-economic mobility for anyone, irrespective of origin. Vigorous but fair competition is stressed. Social stratification is just, for it is the product of rewarding merit by achievement.

The other facet of American thought which must be considered is the American school of Functionalist Sociology (e.g. Parsons 1951), for it was a powerful subsequent influence upon these ideas. The benign analyses it offered suggested that education performed, quite adequately and properly, certain functions useful to society, yet without infringing sacrosanct principles, such as individual freedom. These functions included the selection and training of manpower, the promotion of social mobility and the provision of social coherence. Each of these claims was given empirical validity through the complex mathematical and statistical measures which Functionalists devised. Those cases where the system appeared momentarily out of balance (for example the regional inequalities of educational opportunity which were discovered) were called dysfunctional because they caused inefficiency and instability within it. Functionalists recommended that, as central ringmaster, the Federal Government should intervene to rectify things, offering to it, as ready remedies, those tinkering and tuning techniques which they had developed. Their metaphors were equilibrium and symbiosis. Functionalists, then, worked within a *status-quo* framework, seeing no reason to question it, and therefore sustaining it.

It follows from what has been said so far that America has always held a noninterventionist model of State, whose agencies were granted minimal and carefully regulated powers, without which the rights of individuals might be infringed. It is worth recounting briefly three recent crises in American society, as illustrations of these ideas. In the 1950s and 1960s the American Federal Government was temporarily licensed to act energetically only because the general defence and welfare of the nation was at risk. First it was necessary to purge American society in general, and education in particular, of those threatening alien ideologies identified by McCarthyism. Second, so as to counter another Soviet challenge, there came the nationally funded space programme which also had implications for what schools taught (see Chapter 3). Third, through judicial, legislative and budgetary measures, compensations were to be offered to those children, some poor, some black, many both, who had been found to be educationally and socially disadvantaged (see Chapter 6). Having achieved these tasks of rectification, and aided by the crises of confidence in an over active Federal Government induced by the Vietnam war, and in the Presidency itself by the Watergate hearings, the State withdrew to its former unobtrusiveness. This process was supervised by a new president, Jimmy Carter, and by his successor, both of whom were elected because it was thought they could do so.

So far, an account has been given of the most widely held version of the purposes and functions of American education. Radical critics (see 147 and Chapter 6) do not deny that this is how things were put, and have come to be accepted. What they say is that it is a pervasive, cover-up ideology, used to achieve general compliance and to foil any attempts made at an accurate appreciation of reality. One way of illustrating this (and already hinted at in Chapters 3 and 6) is the following depiction of American education.

Whilst Dewey was right in thinking that democracy was under threat at the turn of the nineteenth century, what he failed to realize was that the real enemies were his contemporaries, the Robber Barons. Through their industrial entrepreneurship, what these few individuals and their families did was to amass such enormous wealth that they were able to gain overwhelming control over American society (Mills 1956, chapter 6). Metamorphosed over time into a new form, that of the national or international corporation, they managed to subvert the political system by colonizing its decision-making institutions with their own hired personnel. The people were persuaded that what was good for the company was good for them, and this was substituted for truly democratic interests (op.cit., chapter 12). Korea, Vietnam, even space, were invaded in turn, each in the name of freedom but in fact for reasons of profit (op.cit., chapter 8). Liberal, progressive education was similarly hegemonized (Gumbert and Spring 1974, chapter 2). The socio-economic mobility it claimed to promote was in fact a myth, for those who managed to achieve it were increasingly rare exceptions (Bowles and Gintis 1976, chapter 4). Designed to emancipate, it in fact taught conformity and acquiescence. Education came to serve the purposes, and to function to the benefit, of corporate capitalism. New Frontier Liberalism in general and compensatory education in particular were cases in point. They were cunning political strategies in two senses. They implied that capitalism cared. But they also encouraged the moral that failures were essentially no good people, for whom nothing could be done, as was shown when succour was given them. They were no more than a soothing cosmetic balm upon certain embarrassing facial features of capitalism, though none the less effective for so being.

What we have in the USA, then, as in the USSR, are two quite different and contradictory versions of education. In both cases incongruities exist between the realities of schooling, and thus their implicit purposes and functions, and the official or widely held view of what ends education serves. What may be occurring in both countries is that a false educational ideology is successfully perpetrated for particular political ends.

4. France and the GFR

In Europe the starting point for any understanding of the nature of education has been the premise that those people who acquire knowledge are bettered. This idea was initially put by classical Greek philosophy and was then variously reworked by Medieval theology, Renaissance culture, and during the eighteenth-century Age of Enlightenment. It is recognizable in the nineteenth-century model of the liberally educated gentleman. The pursuit of knowledge made people in turn wise, holy, culturally accomplished, rational, enlightened or civilized. Knowledge made them intellectually, spiritually, aesthetically, emotionally, and thus personally noble. The forms which this necessary knowledge took changed over time, but in each succeeding redefinition it remained unworldly, objective, neutral and noninstrumental. Whilst societies of people endowed with this knowledge would inevitably be better ones, education was not conducted with this end in mind. Indeed Plato's initial argument that only some men were capable of mastering it (reinforced by the fact that for centuries only the ecclesiastical, aristocratic, masculine few attempted to do so) was consistently accepted. A subsidiary consequence, however, was that education, thus understood, justified élitism. This was because only those it ushered into a state of grace were endowed with the ability to govern justly, in the interests of all. The majority had stations in life which befitted them. It is clear that this educational tradition is a very powerful contemporary influence in each of our European countries.

In France, education is still seen very much in terms of the acquisition by those few with the capacity to do so, of that body of superior knowledge conceived of in the term *culture générale*. Undoubtedly, serious attempts have been made in recent years to reform education in at least three major ways. Their impact and success should not be in any sense minimized. But in each instance they were conducted in essentially traditional terms. First came the drive to democratize education (Fraser 1971). What this meant, however, was giving all children, rather than some, access to it; providing everyone with a chance at it. It did not involve using the concept 'democracy' to redefine education or to change those who controlled it. School structures were changed to delay selection; not to abolish it. Children's attainments are still measured by competitive examinations with the percentage of those destined to pass pre-determined. Second came extensive changes in what schools taught, involving not only the up-dating of existing syllabuses, but also the introduction of new subjects. The new common curriculum for 11-14 year olds included both these features, whilst at the 14-18 level, new scientific, technological and commercial *baccalauréats* emerged. However, what was involved here was the adjusting, modernizing or refashioning of *culture générale*; not its rejection or replacement. Thirdly, France strove to revitalise its economy through complex national plans. Some of these had serious 'manpower needs' implications for the educational sector, which was to play its part by producing the correct number of suitably trained entrants for particular occupational categories. But this was not a direct threat to education as *culture générale*. The additional utilitarian knowledge which society needed was added to that which was already taught, often in specialist institutions such as the commercial *lycées* or new universities, expressly designed with these limited purposes in mind. None of these policies changed the fundamental French ground rules which argue the ethical propriety and utilitarian efficiency of social stratification by merit. They were meant, rather, to apply the ground rules more profitably. They were put into effect by powerful central departments of State, established in history to guarantee that temporary injustices or inadequacies are eradicated. They were merely new waves in the same ocean.

French critics of education do so on several counts. Socialists deny the basis of a meritocratic model of society with its heavily competitive and individualistic overtones. Others maintain that the official version of French meritocracy, in which education acts neutrally to repopulate its various levels from scratch with each succeeding generation, is mere rhetoric. They charge that little social class mobility occurs in France. They argue that the evidence shows that working-class children continue to grossly underachieve; crucial institutions at the tertiary level of education remain closed to them and, what is more, always will. This is because of the way the upper classes constantly manage the intellectual colonization of *culture générale*, through defining it in their own terms and in their own interests (Bourdieu 1971). The existing élite replicates itself by controlling what knowledge counts, and what counts as knowledge.

Traditionally the Germanic and Gallic approaches to questions of educational purpose have been very similar. *Bildung*, like *culture générale*, was a concept of education where neutral, objective truths were learned by the few, for their own sake and irrespective of society. Education's virtue and strength was that it was unpolluted by social concerns or political machinations. Indeed, as in a Glass Bead Game model of the German university, easily extrapolated from Hesse (1943) and subscribed to by Thomas Mann, it was something best conducted outside society. However, since 1945, policy trends in education in the German Federal Republic have been different from those in France. This is partly because economic pressures have not made it so necessary for the GFR to radically reassess or reinterpret the relationship between education and society. When such efforts have been made, for other reasons, they have been thwarted. Educational innovation has been rather limited. We must consider further some explanations of this situation.

In the new republic of 1946, legal efforts were made to ensure that the control and content of education was nonpolitical. The express purpose here was to ensure that education was never again to be subverted by a specific political doctrine. Consequently, entirely traditional and pre-1933 notions of purpose, function and practice were reverted to. The CDU, who held political power for a long period after 1946, had no ideological reason to challenge this situation, and so ostensible and formidable support grew for an educational *status quo*. The SPD's position, when it came to power in 1966, was rather different. It did present arguments in favour of making the control of education more democratic, and introduced policies to promote equality of opportunity and social harmonization (see Chapter 5 above). However, due to the powerlessness of the federal government's educational agencies, those changes it managed to achieve remained marginal. In any case, the SPD never doubted the basic traditions, for it thought that all decisions about substantial educational issues should be left to qualified technicists, made expert by having been educated.

Undoubtedly the relative performances of the GDR and the GFR have been central to the East versus West propaganda battle. The main measures of comparative success have been those of economic growth and individual freedom. Every effort was made by the Western Alliance to ensure that the GFR's economy boomed, at first by direct subsidy, and later by advantageous international fiscal arrangements. It never became necessary, as was the case in France, to adapt the functions of schooling for economic reasons — the long-standing tradition of compulsory vocational training for the non-academic majority already served such ends extremely well. Similarly, no international political reasons existed to cause serious alterations in education, indeed some reforming measures were baulked by being described as policies designed to make the GFR more like the GDR.

Nevertheless, the schools in the GFR do perform social functions, such as the selection and preparation of children for various occupational levels. This applies to the *Gymnasia* as well as to the other secondary schools, for the *Abitur* is the route to the professions and the power élite. Today then, it could be argued that education does appear to fulfil these functions perfectly adequately, at least by internal national criteria, and in these terms also, to satisfactory standards.

Since the 1950s, internal critics have launched many attacks upon various aspects of German society. Through the medium of literature (e.g. Grass), and particularly that of the cinema (e.g. Fassbinder), such things as hypocrisy, complacency and the vulgarities wrought by economic growth have been attacked, sometimes ferociously. However, the conventional idea that the great strength of education lies in its neutrality, objectivity and separateness from politics has gone relatively unchallenged. It is essential, therefore, to focus upon the political dimension in education in the GFR and to attempt some reinterpretation of it.

An alternative construction which could be put upon German education is that it is, and always has been *Politische Volksverdummung* — the political stupification of the people. This thesis *was* put by Taylor (1945), who argued that it was a nineteenth-century inheritance. He saw the political history of the first two decades of the post-1870 Empire as a series of calculated manoeuvres by Bismarck aimed at ensuring that power lay with the *Junkers*. His success in achieving this end had the obvious consequence of excluding most people from the exercise of power. It also precluded them from gaining experience in any aspects of the processes of politics. The highly convenient view of education's separateness was encouraged. It became entrenched because, given the boredom and sterility of the political world, the educated turned elsewhere for intellectual gratification. Many facets of society benefitted greatly from the erudition and the literary and artistic energies of university graduates. Industry in particular was transformed by their scientific researches. But control over the use of the resultant vitality and wealth, so severally generated, stayed with the few. The majority were in no position to doubt the direction in which they were led. When Bismarck eventually ran out of tricks, his successors, with the encouragement of the industrialists, the connivance of the military and the support of blind patriotism, were able to usher in the initial glories of 1914 but the ultimate Armageddon of 1918.

A similar theme runs through the history of the Weimar Republic, and the reasons for its failure. The economy was crippled, initially by the terms of the post-war settlement, then by increasing recession and eventually by the chronic inflation in the world economic climate of the 1920s. The country was run by idealists who had little expertise in mundane matters of organizing a political system. National Socialism became a general panacea, for it promised both economic revitalization and a restoration of national pride. Power was originally granted to Fascism through due democratic processes, exercised however by a gullible electorate. Germany had only had ten years or so to learn to know better.

In the years immediately after 1945, there were two major rival arguments both concerning the division of the old Germany into the two states which had resulted from the Soviet and Western occupations. First came the thrust for reunification on long-standing grounds of nationality. At this stage the Germans in the East were seen as victims of Russian oppression and were not real communists at all. However, this idea became submerged by a second more dominant consideration relating to the capitalist versus communist power game, in which both sets of strategists saw both states as important pieces. Their own always had to be defended and made shining examples of their alternative systems, but they could also be used for attacking purposes. To this end, it was imperative that the GDR be recast as a threat, and that its people be recognized in the GFR as enemies. So a new capitalist model of *Grossdeutsch* was successfully perpetrated in which the search was to be for the economic rather than the geographical hinterland.

In these developments, the traditional version of education was highly convenient. Yet past tragedies could have been avoided had education's political dimension been differently construed. Important contemporary political consequences, and dividends, could arise if education became, even in part, the dispassionate study of society. But, by excluding it, schools play their part in the ideological struggle with the GDR and confirm the claim that the GFR is its overall superior. The brutal response to the student protest movement of the 1960s, and the bitter hostility which has greeted their successors is explainable in these terms. In a highly charged propaganda war, when the successful and privileged offer radical criticism it is inevitably seen as treason.

5.   Summary

Before we discuss the purposes and functions of education in England, it is important that we summarize what has been argued so far in this chapter.

Statements of educational purpose and function are dependent on what constructions are initially put on the terms society, knowledge and people. These three determinants can contain contradictory elements when discussed as separate abstractions. (What society needs may not be what individuals want.) To solve this problem, each of our foreign countries grants one determinant overriding importance — society in Soviet Marxist-Leninism, the individual in American Pragmatism, knowledge in European classicism. So three very different contemporary profiles of educational purpose and function exist. Each profile contains or subsumes several other complex concepts, principles or theories — for example, equality, freedom, justice, authority, the State. Most of these defy permanent and absolute definition, for each is based on premises which are not amenable to objective verification. All three profiles are therefore differing educational ideologies — used in the nonpejorative sense. They may be the result of honest and thoughtful attempts to resolve profound and contentious questions. Nevertheless, they are also political in character, again in the best sense. In each of our countries, each educational profile is widely subscribed to, does promote social cohesion, and has considerable potential resilience.

Criticisms of these educational ideologies are constructed in one of three ways. First, that whilst they represent an acceptable rationale for what should be, even what once was, they are currently applied partially or inconsistently. Certain temporary imbalances need rectification. Here the critiques are within the terms of the existing ideological system. Second, the official or widely held ideology is shown to be internally incongruous and to bear little relationship to the reality of what education actually does. It is therefore construed as a spurious invention, used by those in power to legitimize what they do and to delude and control the majority. Third, the fundamental premises of a given ideology, and therefore its consequent superstructure, are challenged. Alternative grounds and rules are advocated.

Our discussion has shown that in each educational ideology, education is seen as something which produces laudable consequences, and results in progress. Its central principles include the development of understanding and critical awareness in people, who achieve personal emancipation and autonomy through its processes. Education is of benefit to people and therefore causes crucial changes in society. It is sometimes seen as revolutionary in character because by changing people, a radically new and better society is produced. Alternatively, change can be of an evolutionary nature, which education simultaneously generates and facilitates. The connection between education and society can also be seen as one of *status quo*. Here education meets the needs of a society already properly organized. Schools can be thought of as institutions designed by the State to further any one of these educational ambitions.

However, we have also seen that schools often limit their activities to skill training, and pursue limited instrumental purposes. Not only are they socially controlled; they are means of social control using modes of operation like persuasion, manipulation, even coercion. Because of this they can function to sustain the *status quo*, in an improperly founded society. The terms schooling and education are not therefore necessarily synonymous, though there are no obvious reasons why they cannot become so. Everything depends upon what purposes they exist to further and who controls what goes on in them. Schools are potentially arenas of struggle between the forces of enlightenment on the one hand, and those of repression on the other. The autonomy of teachers in England becomes quite crucial in this context, for on the face of it, they can use their room for manoeuvre to either of these ends.

The concluding discussion of education in England is conducted with these considerations in mind. An attempt is also made to draw together some of the issues and arguments raised in previous chapters and to draw certain general conclusions about English education.

6. England

Each previous chapter has made explicit the comparative implications for England of the various issues discussed. A large number of idiosyncrasies in education in England have been highlighted. This does not mean that our principles, processes or practices are necessarily unwarranted or untenable. It does suggest that they need to be reconsidered, reexamined and reassessed. In each case, some attempt has been made to indicate the main arguments involved. It has been shown that educational structures, school and classroom life, the curriculum, and matters of principle, such as power and control and equality, are more confused in England than anywhere else. We must now consider this consistent theme, namely confusion, for it bears directly upon matters of purpose and function.

One way of explaining this aspect of the English educational scene is to see it as one of amiable muddle, in which inconsistencies are tolerable because they represent an important aspect of the English quality of life, in which common sense is cherished and tidy formalism, both in argument and of system, is deemed unimportant. Certain resultant inefficiencies have to be tolerated and are a price worth paying.

A second version has to be taken much more seriously, and has many champions. Here the idea is that our modes of operating are expressions of the central tenets of English liberalism, whose socio-economic and political evolution represents a quite unique English achievement. What has been identified in previous chapters could be seen as a series of examples of the tolerant pluralism of our brand of liberalism, where qualities like generosity, flexibility and the mutual respect for persons have produced a balance between the public good and the interests of individuals. Thus ambiguity is not only a merit, it is an absolute necessity.

In liberalism the purposes and functions of education in England would be represented as an indefinite but infinitely subtle compromise between conflicting theories about knowledge, society and people, which is unamenable to neat propositional specification, so that any attempt to do so would be a contradiction of its essential spirit. English liberals might claim that their adherence to the European tradition regarding knowledge, rather than the needs of the economy, ensures that truth and children are best served. They might also claim that they pay serious attention to children's individuality, with due credit being given here to the American influence, except that it is made suitably sensitive and humane by local interpretation. These are the explanations which might therefore be given for such things as the absence of vocational education (with its narrow, utilitarian, training connotation) and the suspicion with which such subjects as 'social studies' or 'citizenship' are looked at in schools here. The autonomy of our teachers could be similarly defended, for they need wide discretionary limits to exercise their professional expertise in making constant sensitive judgements. Their freedom is seen as inhibiting the invidious political pressures which might otherwise be exerted on education. Indeed liberalism classes education as being both above politics and nonpolitical.

In discussing each of our other countries, we offered a more critical alternative to the official, or widely held, version of purpose and function in education. Such a juxtaposition of opinion is certainly possible in England. This third interpretation must be taken equally seriously, and its main lines of argument are as follows:

1. English liberalism can be recognized through the limits it puts upon the way in which issues are discussed. Strict parameters exist in this respect, and debates are only tolerated within their confines. Those who stray outside them, by their eccentricities of thought or behaviour, find that although they are treated benignly, they get nowhere, are excluded and so go unheard.

2. Liberalism has very clever techniques of exclusion because it adopts methods consistent with its own rhetoric. For example, tightly knit arguments are deflected into obscurity by being dubbed overstatements; certain modes of expressing ideas are not censored, but defused by being labelled as embarrassing antics.

3. On the other hand, liberal ideas appear to be balanced, sane and impartial, but these surface qualities are used to cover up deeper realities.

4.   The ideology is widely, systematically and successfully perpetrated by many agencies, but particularly by the mass media. It is not always easy to recognize that media news coverage is selective and that the comments contained in it are partial, for the distortions involved are clever and subtly handled. For example, the way that knowledge and wisdom come to be defined, by a multiplicity of popular quiz programmes, as the recall of facts, the more obscure the better, is not widely understood. The cosiness, brevity and superficiality of most radio and television discussion programmes is another prime case. A taste of the constraints of liberalism can be savoured in one of the most popular and long lasting of these, namely 'Any Questions?', whose bland conventions both of presentation and content epitomize what debate becomes when conducted in its terms. Again, the daily string of radio's current affairs programmes do not necessarily edit out radical ideas, for some are aired; but they come to be discounted by the techniques of jocularity and dismissiveness used by presenters. Managerial misjudgement, error, even incompetence, must inevitably occur in British industry, yet these are never publicly documented or illustrated. So strikes, and the events leading up to them, tend to be reported in such a way as to suggest that they are always caused by trades' unions.

5.   Whilst overtly espousing an evolutionary theory of social change, all that liberalism achieves are certain superficial surface alterations, so it is an essentially *status quo* ideology. Woolliness and confusion of argument become essential and cleverly operated digressionary tactics, for through them the obfuscation of reality is achieved. A profusion of inconclusive arguments is encouraged to ensure that nothing changes fundamentally.

We must now demonstrate how a comparative perspective lends support to this acidic and radical interpretation of the purposes and functions of education in England. We must begin by reconsidering some of the central contradictions in our situation. First, it cannot be denied that certain tough, resilient and crystalline epistemological ground rules have been laid down in England. Yet these are not applied consistently. So, if we hold that there are high-status subjects and believe in equality, why is it that these subjects are not required learning for all? Why has White's plea (1973), that a common curriculum for the years of compulsory schooling be consensually constructed, gone unheeded? Why do DES documents a little along these lines (1980, 1981) remain valueless by being so unspecific? If we dislike Soviet or French, even American or German models for being too prescriptive, why not follow the Danish Ministry of Education's *advisory* curriculum. Its guidelines spell out what details of subject content and methods of teaching are needed if certain educational principles are to be fostered. It encourages local, flexible interpretation of these ideas, so ensuring that corporate national needs and individual interests are served. Perhaps the trouble is that this would provide English parents with too many good questions to raise at the childrens' schools, requiring adequate answers from Local Authorities about what goes on in them. This is why liberal replies come couched in terms of alternative but digressionary principles — freedom of choice and individual differences.

Second, the liberal defence of the independent sector of education needs reconsideration. As we saw in Chapter 6, the argument is that the freedom of some parents to choose what education they want for their children, or how they spend their money, must not be withheld. The anomaly that most parents do not have any choice whatever is not countered logically by an extension of the voluntary aided principle. Instead, convoluted propositions are produced regarding what happens when a resolution has to be found between two principles in collision. In this case most people's equality must be denied so as to retain a few people's freedom of choice. The form of social stratification is then condoned by finding convenience in the meritocratic argument and often through the use of suitably emotive analogies. Liberals argue that doctors, say, have serious responsibilities to execute, which only some people have the ability to succeed at. They deserve the rewards which they earn, not least because their selfless service saves lives. But liberals deny the validity of an extension of their metaphor into the area of preventative medicine. They rebut the evidence that far more good accrues to society from the many more lives saved by public health workers, or by garbage collectors and workers in water and sewage plants, by saying that anyone can perform these tasks. Only a few have the mental potential to master the complex skills and complete the rigorous training needed for cerebral surgery.

This is the kind of smoke screen in which the real conspirators hide, with their plot cunningly concealed. Rich parents do not spend their money on a public school education for their sons for nothing; it is not even a calculated investment risk. Such schools exist and flourish because they are known to guarantee the self-perpetuation of the establishment. In this context, the depiction of French education or the schools of the GFR as dual systems becomes a smug impertinence. In both countries, the name of the game and its curriculum requirements are available by publication. For Schleswig-Holstein write to:

> Schmidy and Klannig (Publisher).
> Ringstrasse 19,
> Kiel 2300
> GFR.

At this point, the liberal ideology becomes pernicious. Through it, nice looking reformist causes can be tolerated, even sponsored; for they are essentially digressionary, though useful in expending the frustrations and energies of their champions in irrelevant directions, and on immaterial courses. Teachers in State schools are allowed their autonomy to go their well intentioned way and extend their instructional role into others (e.g. facilitator, child mentor, even community worker) because their perfumed pedagogy at least ensures that children are contained better, or entertained more. Many sound and valid developments, such as progressive child-centred primary school methods, comprehensive secondary schools, mixed-ability learning groups, new courses and examinations to test them, multi-cultural education, learning activities premised on the validity of working-class culture and its language, non-sexist curricula, and many others of similar ilk, can be comprehended in these terms.

There is the added advantage in some of these of the mystification of the educational process. When classroom activities are poorly executed — which they are often permitted to be — point and purpose can be made of their openness and their disorganization and lack of definition only by those few children who bring prior structures and work habits from their homes to make sense of, and gain something from, the situation. Thus are bright, sharp children from all sorts of backgrounds pointed towards, led up, or left to drift along paths which are cul-de-sacs in terms of social mobility, status, wealth, and more important, power. Herein lies the charge of the crypto-élitism of liberalism; for, whilst at best being amused by engaging in new school activities conducted in a humane context, children — black and white alike — are multi-defrauded. What they learn denies them a meal ticket; they learn to be tolerant of each other and cooperate together when life in the adult world remains intolerant and competitive. They are not provided with those cognitive and affective understandings which traditional disciplines at their best provide — for why else were they invented and are they pursued? By being asked to choose before they know how, children acquire few conceptual tools to enable them to be autonomous choice-makers and largely remain the flotsam and jetsam of the repressive mechanisms of social forces. Just a few recognize that all of this is happening — no wonder they vent their frustrations through such aggressive behaviour and then settle for that little which they realize is their destiny (Willis 1977).

The liberal preoccupation with individual differences is also treacherous, for the criteria for identifying these have not changed. Man (and Woman) in England, and the society they inhabit, remain Platonic. The masses are still conceived of in these terms, even if new structures and novel pedagogies of form, content and style have become necessary, for stark repression has had to give way to gentling. By such strategies the disunity and naive acquiescence of the majority is fostered, to ensure that even if the élite lose the occasional skirmish, requiring tactical retreat, battles are not, and the war remains won. To this end, plausible but essentially distorted depictions of the purposes and functions of our educational system are perpetrated. But most people must as far as possible be kept ignorant about the educational system, so that those who know its terminology, and how it actually works, can continue to use it to their best advantage.

English Marxists have succeeded in producing penetrating analyses along these lines. The fact that they have failed to achieve much popular agreement is an indication of the power of liberalism, and the success of its tactics of confusion. But this has also been partly their own fault; for whilst their conspiracy theories have been most persuasive about what is being plotted, they have rarely succeeded in accurately identifying the plotters. Nor have they *shown* that calculated, premeditated, malevolent intentions are involved. Marxist broadsides have struck at such a variety of targets that they have only managed to generate hostility, particularly amongst the middling classes, who have understandably been offended by the inexactitudes in such castigation. Most people hold firmly to the liberal ideology because they have been persuaded by the tiny few above them, who make up the real power élite, that it is in their interests to do so. Change is only likely when people can be persuaded otherwise, and convinced that they too are being manipulated.

Much would be achieved by requiring that our existing ground rules be made public, be properly understood by all, and that they be applied logically. (It may be that this initial step will become a necessity shortly for reasons of utility — to aid the economy and diminish social unrest by reducing the high levels of inefficiency and disfunction which the present situation generates.) For radical change to be achieved, new ground rules will have to be produced and widely accepted. No one could pretend that this second step will be easy, for it involves an attack upon the justificatory and legitimizing bases for the existing distribution of power. The hope is that this book will facilitate each of these two ambitions, for the latter is only feasible when the former has been accomplished.

CHAPTER 8

CONCLUSION

An educational allegory

Education in the Soviet Union is a continuous mass-marathon event, which everyone has to enter and where everyone is expected to finish. Some cooperation is necessary between the participants, especially on behalf of laggards, but the course is heavily signposted, marshalled and stewarded, making initiative unnecessary and slogging, individual persistence a primary requirement. Those who finish early are considerably rewarded for their stamina and lack of waywardness in following the route, and for not questioning where exactly it leads. Runners achieve fitness through their participation, and decisions about what alternative events are to be organized in the future await the arrival of all at the finishing post. In America, education is a middle distance, staggered, track event for individuals, which is assiduously prepared for, but with continuous exhaustive and eliminatory heats. Gold, silver and bronze medals of great value are awarded, though they tend to be won by runners of a consistently similar colour, gender and build. In France and the GFR, jumping is involved, though it would appear that some sorts of competitors have, seemingly, more attempts, and so eventually go further or higher than others. In all these countries, everyone knows what the event is and how to train for it, though, because it is not encouraged, no one seems to consider suggesting doing something different. They would not be allowed to do so even if they did.

In England, athletes are camped at two different kinds of stadia. One is secret, private and guarded from intruders. Payment is required to enter and thus rather few competitors attend. Rumour alone informs others about what exactly goes on at these centres, though it is known that those who go seem very pleased to do so, for they attend for weeks on end, and are provided with sleeping and eating as well as training facilities. At the other stadia attendance, although compulsory, is on a short daily basis. Here there are large numbers of athletes, but they spend much time milling about, paying brief and desultory attention to one type of equipment or one training programme after another. No consistency exists between training regimes, and in some the participants are quite inventive about what they organize. Their coaches, who tolerate all this with smiling equanimity, appear to be totally unsupervised. Closer examination, however, reveals that a few athletes seem to be training as decathletes, endeavouring to cover any eventuality, and with the help of their parents continue to do so daily after their dismissal.

Just prior to the finals, the announcement is made that the name of the game to be played, and one which, it transpires, has been assiduously prepared for at the special centres, is polo. At this stage most competitors resignedly give up, but a few, usually the decathletes, go off and buy ponies and other accoutrements, merely to be told that they can only play if they belong to a polo club. Some make approaches to a club of their acquaintance, though most are told that, due to over-subscription from the friends and families of existing members, membership is closed. However, by some unexplainable quirk of chance, a few do get accepted, though rumour has it that they spend many hard years riding as hired professionals for sponsors who, although vigorous enough, are too old, too heavy, even too superior to actually play themselves. Some riders, after years of successful combat, can be invited to act as referees, may become nonvoting coopted committee members, even the official coaches to club teams. A tiny few, often in their dotage, are admitted to full club membership, and this elevation in status leads to a change of name and title as well. Each of these honours is publicly and proudly announced and, strange to tell, they are applauded and acclaimed by everyone.

GLOSSARY

Abitur (G.F.R.) Award granted on successful completion of an academic course of study, usually at a *Gymnasium*, which qualifies holders to enter higher education.

A.C.A.C.E. (England) Advisory Council for Adult and Continuing Education.

Agrégé (France) Award granted to those who pass a very selective competitive examination, which qualifies them to teach in any *lycée*, though they usually only take senior classes and are required to teach 15 hours per week.

Baccalauréat (France) Award granted on successful completion of a long, three year second cycle course of secondary education, usually at a *lycée*. All courses have a common core of subjects but the specialized study of optional subjects is also involved, e.g. classics, modern languages, sciences, technical or commercial subjects.

B.E.C. (England) Business Education Council.

Bildungsrat (G.F.R.) Education Council.

Brevet des collèges (France) Award granted on successful completion of the first cycle of secondary education.

Brevet de technicien (France) Award granted on successful completion of a three year second cycle technician's course of secondary education, usually at a 'vocational education' *lycée*.

Brevet d'études professionelles (France) Award granted on successful completion of a two year second cycle course of Secondary education, indicating competence in a particular vocational field.

Bund-Land Kommission (G.F.R.) Combined national-regional government commission.

C.A.P.E.S. (France) Secondary school teacher's certificate, including five years of theoretical and practical study, and the passing of a competitive examination. Holders are required to teach 15 hours per week.

C.A.S.E. (England) Campaign for the Advancement of State Education.

C.B.I. (England) Confederation of British Industry.

C.D.U. (G.F.R.) Christian Democratic Union.

C.E.E. (England) Certificate of Extended Education.

Censeur (France) Non-teaching member of a school's staff, responsible for discipline.

C.E.R.I. Centre for Educational Research and Innovation.

Certificat d'aptitude professionelle (France) Award granted on successful completion of a two year second cycle course of secondary education, indicating competence in particular vocational skills.

C.E.G. Collèges d'enseignement général (France) First cycle, common Secondary schools for children aged 11—15.

C.N.N.A. (England) Council for National Academic Awards.

Concours (France) Competitive examinations which qualify successful candidates for entry into the *grandes écoles*.

Conseillers d'education (France) Assistants to *censeur*, usually responsible for 100 children each.

Conseil de responsables (France) Representative body of students in a secondary school, which is consulted about various aspects of school policy by the school's authorities.

C.S.E. (England) Certificate of Secondary Education.

Département (France) Regional administrative area.

D.E.S. (England) Department of Education and Science.

École normale (France) Institution which prepares intending primary school teachers. The *baccalauréat* is an entry requirement.

École normale supérieure (France) Ultra selective institution of higher education, originally designed to provide secondary and university teachers, but now used to prepare students for the highest offices in the country.

École Nationale d'Administration (France) Ultra selective institution of higher education designed to prepare students for the highest posts in government administration.

École Polytechnique (France) Ultra selective institution of higher education, designed to produce outstanding engineers, scientists, administrators and businessmen.

E.E.C. European Economic Community.

Filières (France) System of grouping children for teaching purposes according to their academic achievements.

F.P.D. (G.F.R.) Free Democratic Party.

Gastarbeiter (G.F.R.) 'Guest worker' — recruited from abroad, especially from southern Europe, notably Turkey.

G.C.E. (England) General Certificate of Education. O.L. Ordinary Level. A.L. Advanced Level.

G.D.R. German Democratic Republic.

G.F.R. German Federal Republic.

Gesamtschule (G.F.R.) Common or comprehensive secondary school.

Grandes Écoles (France) Highly selective institutes of higher education which offer various courses of professional preparation in engineering, technology, business, sciences, public administration etc.

Gymnasium (G.F.R.) Selective secondary school.

Grundschule (G.F.R.) Primary school.

Hauptschule (G.F.R.) 'Main' secondary school for those not successful in gaining entry to a selective secondary school.

H.M.I. (England) Her Majesty's Inspector (of schools).

I.L.E.A. (England) Inner London Education Authority.

Instituteur (France) Primary school teacher. Preparation includes a two year course at an *école normale*, the passing of an examination and a probationary year. They are required to teach 27 hours per week.

I.Q. Intelligence Quotient.

Ivy League. (U.S.A.) Term used to refer to the five most prestigious and influential universities in America, each of which was established prior to the many outstanding state universities, and has independent funds. Harvard, Princeton, Stanford and Yale are always included.

Land (G.F.R.) A regional governmental and administrative unit. Plural *Länder*.

L.C.C. (England) London County Council.

L.E.A. (England) Local Education Authority.

License (France) University first degree, involving three years of study.

'Link' (U.S.S.R.) A group of four children in the Octobrist or Pioneer youth movement.

Lycée (France) Selective second cycle secondary school, preparing children for a *baccalauréat* award.

M.A.C.O.S. (U.S.A.) Man A Course of Study.

Maîtrise (France) University degree, involving four years of study.

Maîtres d'internat (France) Members of the disciplinary staff of a school.

'Octobrist' (U.S.S.R.) First stage in the Soviet youth movement for children up to the age of 10.

O.E.C.D. Organization for Educational and Cultural Development.

P.E. Physical Education.

P.E.A. (U.S.A.) Progressive Education Association.

Pedagogical Institute (U.S.S.R.) Institute of higher education which prepares students for teaching involving four years of study for the Primary level and five years for specialist Secondary teaching. (All 'Institutes' in the U.S.S.R. have the same status as universities, but specialize in one field of study, e.g. Institute of Agronomy, of Agriculture, of Technology etc.)

Pedagogical School (U.S.S.R.) Now being phased out. Previously used to train pre-school and Primary level teachers, and were extensions of the school system rather than part of higher education.

Pädagogische Hochschule (G.F.R.) Teacher training institution, mainly for Primary teachers.

'Pioneer' (U.S.S.R.) Second stage in the Soviet youth movement, for children aged 10—15.

Professeur Agrégé (France) Teacher who has passed the *agrégé*

P.T.A. (U.S.A.) Parent-Teacher Association.

Quarter (U.S.A.) Half a Semester.

Realschule (G.F.R.) Selective secondary school, offering courses which can lead to higher education and certainly to skilled employment in business, commerce and industry. Less prestigious than the *Gymnasium.*

Redoublement (France) Repeat a year, due to unsatisfactory progress.

S.C.I.S.P. (England) Schools Council Integrated Science Project.

Semester (U.S.A.) Half the school year.

S.M.P. (England) Secondary Mathematics Project.

S.P.D. (G.F.R.) Socialdemocratic Party of Germany.

T.E.C. (England) Technical Education Council.

T.U.C. (England) Trade Union Congress.

T.U.W.E.H.S.R.E. (U.S.S.R.) Trade Union of Workers in Education Higher Schools and Research Establishments.

U.N.E.S.C.O. United Nations Educational Scientific and Cultural Organization.

Y.C.L. (U.S.S.R.) Young Communist League, previously known as the Komsomol. Third stage in the Soviet youth movement for the 15—27 age range. Entry is selective and of those young adults eligible for membership, about a third are admitted.

BIBLIOGRAPHY

Archer, M.S. (1979) *Social Origins of Educational Systems*. London, Beverly Hills: Sage Publications.

Ariès, P. (1962) *Centuries of Childhood*. London: Jonathan Cape.

Armytage, W.H.G. (1967) *The American Influence on English Education*. London: Routledge and Kegan Paul.

Armytage, W.H.G. (1968) *The French Influence on English Education*. London: Routledge and Kegan Paul.

Armytage, W.H.G. (1969a) *The German Influence on English Education*. London: Routledge and Kegan Paul.

Armytage, W.H.G. (1969b) *The Russian Influence on English Education*. London: Routledge and Kegan Paul.

Arnold, M. (1868) *Schools and Universities on the Continent,* London: Macmillan.

Arnold, M. (1874) *Higher Schools and Universities in Germany,* London: Macmillan.

Banks, O. (1955) *Parity and Prestige in English Secondary Education*. London: Routledge and Kegan Paul.

Banks, O. (1968) *The Sociology of Education*. Norwich: Batsford.

Baratz, S.S. and Baratz, J.C. (1972) Early Childhood Intervention; the Social Science Base of Institutionalized Racism, *in* Cashdan (ed.) (1972).

Barnes, D., Britton, J. and Rosen, H. (eds.) (1969) *Language the Learner and the School*. London: Penguin Books.

Beattie, N. (1977) Public Participation in Curriculum Change: A West German Example. *Compare* Vol.7, No.1.

Bell, R. and Grant, N. (1974) *A Mythology of British Education*. St Albans: Panther.

Benn, C. and Simon, B. (1972) *Halfway There*, 2 ed. Harmondsworth: Penguin Books.

Bennett, N. (1976) *Teaching Styles and Progress*. London: Open Books.

Bereday, G.Z.F. (1964) *Comparative Method in Education*. New York: Holt, Rinehart and Winston.

Bereday, G.Z.F. and Lawerys, J.A. (eds.) (1958) *Year Book of Education: The Secondary School Curriculum.* London: Evans.

Bereiter, C. and Engleman, S. (1966) *Teaching Disadvantaged Children in the Pre School.* Englewood Cliffs: Prentice Hall.

Bernbaum, G. (1976) The Role of the Headmaster. SSRC Report, unpublished. British Library No. 026005. See Peters (ed.)

Bernstein, B. (1971) On the Classification and Framing of Educational Knowledge. 47–69 *in* Young (ed.)

Bernstein, B. (1973, 1974, 1976) *Class Codes and Control.* Vol.2 (1973), Vol.1, 2 ed. (1974), Vol.3 (1976). London: Routledge and Kegan Paul.

Bestor, A.E. (1953) *Educational Wastelands.* Urbana: University of Illinois Press.

Beteille, A. (ed.) (1970) *Social Inequality.* Harmondsworth: Penguin Books.

Blenkin, G. (1980) The Influence of Initial Styles of Curriculum Development, *in* Kelly (ed.) (1980).

Blenkin, G. and Kelly, A.V. (1982) *The Primary Curriculum.* London: Harper and Row.

Bloom, B.S. (ed.) (1956) *A Taxonomy of Educational Objectives,* 2 Vols. London: Longman.

Bourdieu, P. (1971) Systems of Education and Systems of Thought, *in* Young (ed.) (1971).

Bowles, S. and Gintis, H. (1976) *Schooling in Capitalist America.* New York: Basic Books.

Boyle, E., Crosland, A. and Kogan, M. (1971) *The Politics of Education.* Harmondsworth: Penguin Books.

Brake, M. (1980) *The Sociology of Youth Culture and Youth Subcultures.* London: Routledge and Kegan Paul.

Brearley, M. and Hitchfield, E. (1966) *A Teacher's Guide to Reading Piaget.* London: Routledge and Kegan Paul.

Bronfenbrenner, U. (1972) *Two Worlds of Childhood: USSR and USA.* New York: Simon and Schuster.

Bruner, J.S. (1960) *The Process of Education.* New York: Vintage Books.

Bruner, J.S. (1966) *Towards a Theory of Instruction.* New York: Norton & Co.

Cameron, J. and Dodd, W.A. (1970) *Society, Schools and Progress in Tanzania.* Oxford: Pergamon.

Capelle, J. (1967) *Tomorrow's Education: The French Experience.* London: Pergamon.

Carmichael, S. and Hamilton, C.V. (1967) *Black Power.* New York: Random House.

Cash, W.J. (1941) *The Mind of the South.* New York: A.A. Knopf.

Cashdan, A. (ed.) (1972) *Language in Education.* London: Routledge and Kegan Paul in association with the Open University.

Cicourel, A. and Kitsuse, J. (1963) *The Educational Decision Makers.* Indianapolis: Bobbs-Merrill.

Cleaver, E. (1969) *Soul on Ice.* London: Jonathan Cape.

Coleman, J. (1968) The Concept of Equality of Educational Opportunity. *Harvard Educational Review* Vol.38, No.1, Winter.

Conant, J.B. (1959) *The American High School Today.* New York: McGraw.

Conant, J.B. (1961) *Slums and Suburbs.* New York: McGraw-Hill.

Conant, J.B. (1967) The Comprehensive High School: A Second Report for Interested Citizens. New York: McGraw-Hill.

Cox, C.B. and Dyson, A.E. (eds.) (1969a) *Fight for Education: A Black Paper.* Manchester: Critical Quarterly Society.

Cox, C.B. and Dyson, A.D. (eds.) (1969b) *Black Paper Two: The Crisis in Education.* Manchester: Critical Quarterly Society.

Cox, C.B. and Boyson, R. (eds.) (1975) *Black Paper.* London: Dent.

Cox, C.B. and Boyson, R. (eds.) (1977) *Black Paper.* London: Temple Smith.

Cox. O.C. (1948) *Class, Caste and Race: a study in social dynamics.* New York: Doubleday.

Cremin, L.A. (1961) *The Transformation of the School: Progressives in American Education 1876—1957.* New York: Knopf.

Crossman, R.S. (1937) *Plato Today.* London: Allen and Unwin.

Dacey, J.S. (1979) *Adolescents Today.* Santa Monica: Goodyear Publishing Company Inc.

Dance, E.A. (1970) *The Place of History in Secondary Teaching: A Comparative Study.* London: Harrap for CCCCE.

Davies, B. (ed.) (1982) *The Education and Training of Physics Teachers Worldwide: A Survey.* London: John Murray.

Davies, I. (1970) The Management of Knowledge: A Critique of the Use of Typologies in Educational Sociology. *Sociology* 4, 1, January.

Dearden, R.F. (1968) *The Philosophy of Primary Education.* London: Routledge and Kegan Paul.

Dearden, R.F. (1976) *Problems in Primary Education.* London: Routledge and Kegan Paul.

Dewey, J. (1899) *The School and Society.* Chicago: University of Chicago Press.

Dewey, J. (1916) *Democracy and Education.* New York: Macmillan.

Dewey, J. (1922) *How We Think.* New York: Holt.

Dewey, J. (1938) *Experience and Education.* New York: Collier-Macmillan.

Douglas, J.W.B. (1964) *The Home and the School.* London: MacGibbon and Kee.

Downey, M.E. (1977) *Interpersonal Judgements in Education.* London: Harper and Row.

Eckstein, M.A. and Noah, A.J. (eds.) (1969) *Scientific Investigations in Comparative Education.* London: Collier-Macmillan.

Erikson, E.H. (1950) *Childhood and Society.* New York: Norton & Co.

Etzioni, A. (1971) *A Comparative Analysis of Complex Organizations.* New York: Free Press of Glencoe.

Fellman, D. (1969) *The Supreme Court and Education.* 2 ed. New York: Teachers' College Press.

Finn, D., Grant, N. and Johnson, R. (1977) Social Democracy, Education and the Crisis. *Working Papers in Cultural Studies* 10: *On Ideology*. Centre for Contemporary Studies, University of Birmingham.

Floud, J. and Halsey, A.H. (1957) Social Class, Intelligence Tests and Selection for Secondary Schools. *British Journal of Sociology* VIII.

Fraser, W.R. (1971) *Reforms and Restraints in Modern French Education*. London: Routledge and Kegan Paul.

Freidenburg, E. (1959) *The Vanishing Adolescent*. New York: Dell.

Freidenburg, E. (1963) *Coming of Age in America*. New York: Vintage.

Friere, P. (1970) *Pedagogy of the Oppressed*. New York: Herder & Herder.

Glass, D.V. (1959) Education and Social Change in Modern England, *in* Halsey et al. (eds.) (1961)

Glatter, R. (ed.) (1977) *Proceedings of the 5th Annual Conference of the British Administration Societies. The Control of the Curriculum: Issues and Trends in Britain and Europe*. London: University of London Institute of Education.

Goodman, P. (1956) *Growing Up Absurd*. New York: Vintage.

Goodman, P. (1962) *Compulsory Miseducation*. New York: Vintage.

Gordon, P. and White, J. (1979) *Philosophers as Educational Reformers: The Influence of Idealism on British Thought and Practice*. London: Routledge and Kegan Paul.

Grace, G.R. (1972) *Role Conflict and the Teacher*. London: Routledge and Kegan Paul.

Grace, G.R. (1978) *Teachers' Ideology and Control: A Study in Urban Education*. London: Routledge and Kegan Paul.

Grant, N. (1979) *Soviet Education*. 4 ed. Harmondsworth: Penguin Books.

Gumbert, E.B. and Spring, J.H. (1974) *Superschool and Superstate: American Education in the Twentieth Century 1918-1970*. New York: Wiley.

Hall, S. and Jefferson, T. (eds.) (1976) *Resistance Through Rituals: Youth Subcultures in Post-War Britain*. London: Hutchinson in association with the Centre for Contemporary Culture Studies, University of Birmingham.

Halls, W.D. (1965) *Society, Schools and Progress in France*. London: Pergamon.

Halls, W.D. (1970) *Foreign Languages and Education in Western Europe*. London: Harrap.

Halls, W.D. (1975) *Education, Culture and Politics in Modern France*. London: Pergamon.

Halsey, A.H., Floud, J. and Anderson, C.A. (eds.) (1961) *Education, Economy and Society*. New York, London: Free Press, Collier-Macmillan.

Hans, N. (1949) *Comparative Education*. London: Routledge and Kegan Paul.

Hargreaves, D. (1967) *Social Relations in a Secondary School*. London: Routledge and Kegan Paul.

Havighurst, R.J. (1966) *Education in Metropolitan Areas*. Boston: Allyn and Bacon.

Hearnden, A. (1974) *Education in the Two Germanies*. Oxford: Blackwell.

Hearnden, A. (1976) *Education, Culture and Politics in West Germany*. Oxford: Pergamon.

Henry, J. (1972) *On Education*. New York: Vintage.

Herndon, J. (1965) *The Way it 'Spozed to Be*. New York: Simon and Schuster.

Hesse, H. (1943) *The Glass Bead Game*. (1970, English edition) London: Jonathan Cape.

Hextall, I.J. (1976) Marking Work, *in* Whitty and Young (eds.) (1976).

Higginson, J.H. (1961) The Centenary of an English Pioneer in Comparative Education. Sir Michael Sadler (1861—1943). *International Review of Education* **7**, 3, 286—298.

Holmes, B. (1965) *Problems in Education: A Comparative Approach*. London: Routledge and Kegan Paul.

Holmes, B and Ryba, R. (eds.) (1973) *Proceeding of the Comparative Education Society in Europe. Recurrent Education — Concepts and Policies for Lifelong Education*. (Sixth General Meeting of the Society. Frascati 1973) Bury: CESE.

Holmes, B. (1981) *Comparative Education, Some Considerations of Method*. London: Allen and Unwin.

Holt, J. (1964) *How Children Fail*. New York: Pitman Publishing Co.

Holt, J. (1967) *How Children Learn*. New York: Pitman Publishing Co.

Holt, J. (1970) *The Underachieving School*. London. Pitman Publishing Co.

Hopper, E. (ed.) (1971) *Readings in the Theory of Education Systems*. London: Hutchinson University Library.

Hoste, R. and Bloomfield, B. (1975) Continuous Assessment in CSE: Opinion and Practice. *Schools Council Bulletin* 31. London: Evans/Methuen Educational.

Husén, T. (1967) *International Study of Achievement in Mathematics: A Comparison of Twelve Countries*. New York: Wiley.

Husén, T. (1979) *The School in Question: A Comparative Study of the School and its Future in Western Societies*. London: OUP.

Ideas, Nos. 1-15 (1967-70) (ed. Smith, L.) London: Curriculum Laboratory, University of London, Goldsmiths' College.

Illich, I.D. (1970) *Celebration of Awareness; A Call for Institutional Revolution*. New York: Doubleday & Co. Inc.

Illich, I.D. (1971) *De-schooling Society*. London: Calder.

Jackson, B. and Marsden, D. (1962) *Education and the Working Class*. London: Routledge and Kegan Paul.

Jencks, C., Acland, H., Bane, M.J., Gintis, H., Heyns, B. and Michaelson, S. (1972) *Inequality: A Reassessment of the Effect of Family and Schooling in America*. New York: Basic Books.

Jensen, A. (1974) Finding Facts or Generating Myths. *The Times Higher Education Supplement* 27.9.1974.

Jones, P.E. (1971) *Comparative Education: Purpose and Method*. St Lucia: University of Queensland Press.

Judges, A.V. (ed.) (1957) *Education and the Philosophic Mind*. London: Harrap.

Kandel, I.L. (1933) *Studies in Comparative Education*. London: Harrap.

Kandel, I.L. (1954) *The New Era in Education: A Comparative Study.* London: Harrap.

Katz, M.B. (1971) *Class, Beaurocracy and Schools.* New York: Praeger.

Keddie, N. (1971) Classroom Knowledge, *in* Young (ed.) (1971).

Kelly, A.V. (ed.) (1980) *Curriculum Context.* London: Harper and Row.

Keppel, F. (1966) *The Necessary Revolution in American Education.* New York: Harper and Row.

King, E.J. (1962) *World Perspectives on Education.* London: Methuen.

King, E.J. et al. (1974) *Post-Compulsory Education I — A New Analysis in Western Europe.* London: Sage Publications.

King, E.J. et al. (1975) *Post-Compulsory Education II — The Way Ahead.* London: Sage Publications.

King, E.J. (1979) *Other Schools and Ours: Comparative Studies for Today* 5 ed. London: Holt, Rinehart and Winston.

Koerner, J.D. (1963) *The Miseducation of American Teachers.* Boston: Houghton Mifflin.

Kogan, M. (1971) *The Politics of Education.* Harmondsworth: Penguin Books.

Kogan, M. and Van der Eyken, W. (1973) *County Hall.* Harmondsworth: Penguin Education.

Kozol, J. (1967) *Death at an Early Age.* New York: Houghton Mifflin.

Labov, W. (1972) *Language in the Inner City: Studies in the Black English Vernacular.* Philadelphia: University of Pennsylvania Press.

Lauwerys, J.A. (joint ed. annually 1948-1970) *World Year Books of Education.* London, New York: Evans Bros. in association with the University of London Institute of Education and Teachers' College, Colombia University.

Lauwerys, J.A. (1957) Scientific Humanism, *in* Judges (ed.) (1957).

Lauwerys, J.L. (1959) The Philosophical Approach to Comparative Education. *International Review of Education* **5, 3,** 281-98.

Lawrence, J. (1977) *Disruptive Behaviour in a Secondary School.* London: University of London Goldsmiths' College, Educational Studies Monograph No. 1.

Lawrence, J. (1980) *Exploring Techniques for Coping with Disruptive Behaviour in Schools.* London: University of London Goldsmiths' College, Educational Studies Monograph No. 2.

Lawrence, J., Steed, D.M. and Young, P. (1981) *Dialogue on Disruptive Behaviour: A Study of a Secondary School.* South Croydon: PJD Press.

Layton, D. (1973) *Science for the People.* London: Allen and Unwin.

Lewis, D.G. (1974) *Assessment in Education.* London: Unibooks.

Liebermann, M. (1956) *Education as a Profession.* New York: Prentice Hall.

Lister, I. (1974) *Deschooling.* Cambridge: Cambridge University Press.

Little, A. and Smith, G. (1971) *Strategies of Compensation: A Review of Educational Projects for the Disadvantaged in the United States.* Paris: OECD.

Little, A., Willey, R. and Gundara, J. (1982) *Adult Education and the Black Community.* Leicester: CACACE.

Macintosh, H.G. and Hudson, B. (1974) *Assessment Techniques, an Introduction.* London: Methuen.

Mahony, P. (1982) Silence is a Woman's Glory: The Sexist Content of Education. *Women's Studies International Forum* Vol. **5**, No. **5**, 463–473.

Malcolm X with Haley, A. (1964) *The Autobiography of Malcolm X.* New York: Gnome Press.

Mallinson, V. (1957) *An Introduction to the Study of Comparative Education.* London: Heinemann.

Markuschevitch, A. (1969) The Problems of the Content of School Education in the USSR, *in Proceedings of the Comparative Education Society in Europe, Curriculum Development at the Secondary Level.* (Fourth General Meeting of the Society, Prague 1969). Bury: CESE.

Mead, M. (1930) *Growing up in New Guinea,* (1963 edn.). Harmondsworth: Penguin Books.

Merchant, E.C. (ed.) (1967) *Geography Teaching and the Revision of Geography Textbooks and Atlases: Report of Four Council of Europe Conferences.* Strasbourg: CCCCE.

Mills, Wright C. (1956) *The Power Elite,* London, Oxford, New York: OUP.

Montgomery, R.J. (1965) *Examinations.* London: Longman.

Montgomery, R.J. (1978) *A New Examination of Examinations.* London: Routledge and Kegan Paul.

Morton, D.C. and Watson, D.R. (1971) Compensatory Education and Contemporary Liberalism in the United States: A Sociological View. *International Review of Education* 17, 3.

Mosteller, F. and Moynihan, D.P. (1971) *On Equality of Educational Opportunity.* New York: Random House.

Musgrave, P.W. (1965) *The Sociology of Education.* London: Methuen.

Musgrove, F. and Taylor, P.H. (1969) *Society and the Teacher's Role.* London: Routledge and Kegan Paul.

Myrdal, G. (1944) *An American Dilemma: The Negro Problem and American Democracy.* New York: Harper and Row.

Nicholas, E.J. (1980) A Comparative View of Curriculum Development *in* Kelly ed. 1980.

Noah, H.J. (1967) Economics of Education in the Soviet Union. *Problems of Communism* XVI, July-August.

Nuttall, D. and Willmot, A.S. (1972) *British Examinations: Techniques of Analysis.* Slough: NFER.

Parsons, T. (1951) *The Social System.* New York: Free Press.

Pedley, R. (1956) *Comprehensive Education: A New Approach.* London: Gollancz.

Pedley, R. (1963) *The Comprehensive School.* Harmondsworth: Penguin Books.

Peters, R.S. (1966) *Ethics and Education.* London: Allen and Unwin.

Peters, R.S. (ed.) (1969) *Perspectives on Plowden.* London: Routledge and Kegan Paul.

Peters, R.S. (ed.) (1976) *The Role of the Head.* London: Routledge and Kegan Paul.

Peterson, A.D.C. (1972) *The International Baccalaureate: An Experiment in International Education.* London: Harrap.

Poujol, J. (1980) The Lower Secondary School in France: A Note on the Haby Reforms. *Compare* Vol.10, No. 2.

Price, R.F. (1977) *Marx and Education in Russia and China.* London: Croom Helm.

Pring, R. (1976) *Knowledge and Schooling.* London: Open Books.

Pudwell, C. (1980) Examinations and the School Curriculum, *in* Kelly (ed.) (1980).

Reimer, E. (1971) *School is Dead: Alternatives in Education.* New York: Doubleday & Co. Inc.

Richardson, E. (1973) *The Teacher, the School and the Task of Management.* London: Heinemann.

Richmond, W.K. (1971) *The School Curriculum.* London: Methuen.

Rist, R.C. (1970) Student Social Class and Teacher Expectation. *Harvard Education Review.* **40, 3,** 411-451.

Rosenthal, R. and Jacobson, L. (1968) *Pygmalion in the Classroom.* New York: Holt Rinehart and Winston.

Rumpf, H. (1981) Leben wird nur vorgetäuscht. *Die Zeit* No.33, 7 August; No.34, 14 August.

Ryba, R. (1980) The Context of Curricular Change in Europe at the Lower Secondary Level. *Compare* Vol.10, No.2.

Sampson, A. (1962) *Anatomy of Britain.* London: Hodder & Stoughton.

Sampson, A. (1965) *Anatomy of Britain Today.* London: Hodder & Stoughton.

Sampson, A. (1971) *The New Anatomy of Britain.* London: Hodder & Stoughton.

Sampson, A. (1982) *Changing Anatomy of Britain.* London: Hodder & Stoughton.

Sewell, B. (1982) *Use of Mathematics By Adults in Daily Life.* Leicester: CACACE.

Silberman, C.E. (1973) *The Open Classroom Reader.* New York: Vintage.

Silverman, D. (1970) *The Theory of Organizations.* London: Heinemann.

Simon, B. (1960) *Studies in the History of English Education 1780-1870.* London: Lawrence and Wishart.

Simon, B. (1965) *Education and the Labour Movement 1870-1920.* London: Lawrence and Wishart.

Simon, B. (1974) *The Politics of Educational Reform 1920-40.* London: Lawrence and Wishart.

Skinner, B.F. (1959) *Cumulative Record.* New York: Appleton—Century—Crofts.

Skinner, B.F. (1968) *The Technology of Teaching.* New York: Appleton—Century—Crofts.

Spender, D. and Sarah, E. (eds.) (1980) *Learning to Lose: Sexism and Education.* London: Women's Free Press.

Spring, J.H. (1972) Psychologists and the War: The Memory of Intelligence in the Alpha & Beta Tests. *History of Education Quarterly* 3, Spring.

Stenhouse, L. (1975) *Curriculum Research and Development*. London: Heinemann.

Tawney, R.H. (1923. 4 ed 1931) *Equality*. London: Allen and Unwin.

Taylor, A.J.P. (1945) *The Course of German History*. London: Hamish Hamilton.

Thompson, E.P. (1963) *The Making of the English Working Class*. London: Gollancz.

Tight, M. (1982) *Part-time Degree and Study in the United Kingdom: the Report of an Enquiry*. Leicester: ACACE.

Trace, A.S. (1971) *What Ivan Knows that Johnny Doesn't*. New York: Random House.

Tropp, A. (1957) *The School Teachers: The Growth of the Teaching Profession in England and Wales from 1800 to the Present Day*. London: Heinemann.

Turner, R. (1960) Modes of Social Ascent Through Education: Sponsored and Contest Mobility. *American Sociological Review* 25, 5.

Tyler, R.W. (1949) *Basic Principles of Curriculum and Instruction*. Chicago: University of Chicago Press.

Ulich, R. (1967) *The Education of Nations*. Cambridge Mass: Harvard University Press.

Vernon, P.E. (1960) *Intelligence and Attainment Tests*. London: University of London Press.

Waller, W. (1932) *The Sociology of Teaching*. New York: Wiley.

White, J.P. (1973) *Towards a Compulsory Curriculum*. London: Routledge and Kegan Paul.

Whitty, G. and Young, M. (eds.) (1976) *Explorations in the Politics of School Knowledge*. Driffield: Nafferton Books.

Williams, R. (1961) *The Long Revolution*. London: Chatto and Windus.

Willis, P. (1977) *Learning to Labour: How Working Class Kids Get Working Class Jobs*. Farnborough: Saxon House.

Wilms, H. (1977) *Arbeitsbogen* 9, 1-11. Bonn: Inter Nationes.

Wiseman, S. (ed.) (1961) *Examinations and Education*. Manchester: Manchester University Press.

Wyatt, T.S. (1975) The GCE Examining Boards and Curriculum Development, *in* Schools Council (1975).

Young, M.F.D. (ed.) (1971) *Knowledge and Control*. London: Collier-Macmillan.

Young, M.F.D. (1972) On the Politics of Educational Knowledge. *Economy and Society* 1 (2), 194-215. Reprinted in Bell, R. (ed.) (1973) *Education in Great Britain and Ireland*. OU Set Book. London: Routledge and Kegan Paul.

Official Publications

Board of Education (1926) *Report of the Consultative Committee on the Education of the Adolescent* (Hadow Report on Secondary Education). London: HMSO.

Board of Education (1938) *Report of the Consultative Committee on Secondary Education with Special Reference to Grammar Schools and Technical High Schools*. (Spens Report). London: HMSO.

Board of Education (1943) *Report on the Secondary Schools' Examinations Council: Curriculum and Examinations in Secondary Schools* (The Norwood Report). London: HMSO.

Central Advisory Council for Adult and Continuing Education (1982a) *Adults, Mathematical Ability and Performance.* Leicester: CACACE.

Central Advisory Council for Adult and Continuing Education (1982b) *Adults — Their Educational Experience and Needs.* Leicester: CACACE.

Central Advisory Council for Adult and Continuing Education (1982c) *Continuing Education: From Policies to Practice.* Leicester: CACACE.

Central Advisory Council for Adult and Continuing Education (1982d) *Basic Science Education for Adults.* Leicester: CACACE.

Centre for Educational Research and Innovation (1972), *The Nature of the Curriculum for the Eighties and Onwards.* Strasbourg: OECD.

Centre for Educational Research and Innovation (1973) *Case Studies of Educational Innovation. Vol. I At the Central Level;* Vol. II *At the Regional Level;* Vol. III *At the School Level;* Vol. IV *Strategies For Innovation in Education, Summary and Conclusions.* Paris: OECD.

Ministry of Education (1959) *15 to 18. A Report of the Central Advisory Council for Education, (England)* (Crowther Report). London: HMSO

Department of Education and Science (1963) *United Kingdom Committee on Higher Education 1961-1963* (Robbins Report). London: HMSO.

Department of Education and Science (1967) *Children and their Primary Schools. A Report of the Central Advisory Council, (England)* (Plowden Report). London: HMSO.

Department of Education and Science (1975) *Committee to Inquire into the Teaching in Schools of Reading and Other Uses of English. A Language for Life* (Bullock Report) London: HMSO.

Department of Education and Science and the Welsh Office (1977) *Education in Schools: A Consultative Document* (Green Paper), 6869. London: HMSO.

Department of Education and Science (1977) *A New Partnership for Our Schools* (The Taylor Report). London: HMSO.

Department of Education and Science (1978a) *Curriculum 11-16.* London: DES.

Department of Education and Science (1978b) *Primary Education in England: A Survey by HM Inspectors of Schools.* London: HMSO.

Department of Education and Science (1979a) *Educational Statistics.* London: HMSO.

Department of Education and Science (1979b) Further Education Curriculum and Development Unit, *A Basis for Choice: A Report of a Study Group on Post 16 Pre-Employment Courses* (Mansell Report). Stanmore: DES.

Department of Education and Science and the Welsh Office (1980) *A Framework for the School Curriculum.* London: HMSO.

Department of Education and Science and the Welsh Office (1981) *The School Curriculum.* London: HMSO.

Department of Education and Science (1981) *Report of the Committee of Inquiry into the Education of Children from Ethnic Minorities: West Indian Children in Our Schools* (Rampton Report). London: HMSO

OECD (1975) *Education, Inequality and Life Chances.* Brussels: OECD.

Inner London Education Authority (1976) *Report of the Public Enquiry into Teaching Organization and Management of William Tyndale Junior and Infants' School* (The Auld Report). London: ILEA.

Schools Council, (1960) *Secondary School Examinations other than the GCE* (The Beloe Report). London: HMSO.

Schools Council (1966) *Examining at 16+: the Report of the Joint GCE/CSE Committee.* London: HMSO.

Schools Council (1967) *Society and the Young School Leaver.* Working Paper No.11. London: HMSO.

Schools Council (1970) *The Humanities Curriculum Project: An Introduction.* London: Heinemann.

Schools Council (1971) *Choosing a Curriculum for the Young School Leaver.* Working Paper 33. London: Evans/Methuen Educational.

Schools Council (1974) *Comparability of Standards Between Subjects.* Examinations Bulletin 29. London: Evans/Methuen Educational.

Schools Council (1975) *The Whole Curriculum 13-16.* Working Paper 53. London: Evans/Methuen Educational.

Schools Council (1975) *Examinations at 16+: Proposals for the Future.* Examinations Bulletin 23. London: Evans/Methuen Educational.

Schools Council (1978) *Examinations at 18+: The N & F Studies.* Working Paper 60. London: Evans/Methuen Educational.

UNESCO (1968) *Recommendation Concerning the Status of Teachers.* Paris: UNESCO.

US Office of Education (1966) *Equality of Educational Opportunity* (The Coleman Report) Washington D.C.: US Government Printers.

USSR (1979) *Today and Tomorrow. Education.* Moscow: Novosti Press Agency Publishing House.

INDEX OF NAMES

INDEX OF SUBJECTS